AI and Business Rule Engine Excel Power Users

Excel Power Users

Capture and scale your business knowledge into the cloud - with Microsoft 365, Decision Models, and AI tools from IBM and Red Hat

Paul Browne

BIRMINGHAM—MUMBAI

AI and Business Rule Engines for Excel Power Users

Group Product Manager: Alok Dhuri
Publishing Product Manager: Harshal Gundetty
Senior Editor: Nithya Sadanandan
Technical Editor: Jubit Pincy
Copy Editor: Safis Editing
Project Manager: Prajakta Naik
Proofreader: Safis Editing
Indexer: Pratik Shirodkar
Production Designer: Arunkumar Govinda Bhat
Developer Relations Marketing Executive: Deepak Kumar and Rayyan Khan
Business Development Executive: Thilakh Rajavel

First published: April 2023

Production reference: 1100323

Published by Packt Publishing Ltd.
Livery Place
35 Livery Street
Birmingham
B3 2PB, UK.

ISBN 978-1-80461-954-4

www.packtpub.com

To my parents, Robert and Vera, who instilled a life-long love of learning and who supported me in many steps of my journey. To my wife, Joanne, who has helped me become a better person, and to my sons, who are starting their own journeys but who have always made me proud.

– Paul Browne

Foreword

With the explosion of interest in **Artificial Intelligence** (**AI**) in recent years, I am more convinced than ever that the rules-based approach to AI alongside machine learning is the most accessible route for Excel users. That's based on my own, and my team's, work with business users like you, looking to capture business knowledge and rules in a way that can be easily shared and executed. Right now, the community is especially excited about the next generation of tools, making it easier than ever to deploy decision and machine learning models together.

It has been about 15 years since my first code contribution was accepted by the Drools project team – a brand new parser for the **Drools Rule Language** (**DRL**) that landed just in time for Drools 5. Since then, I have had the privilege to learn and work with the most brilliant engineers in the industry and the opportunity to collaborate with an amazing open source community.

Drools was already a widely used and mature open source rule engine. The community was about to release Guvnor, a set of integrated tools to support users managing their business rules, life cycles, from authoring to packaging to deployment.

But so much more has happened since. The Drools engine not only evolved but also helped advance the whole field of rule engines and expert systems with the introduction of the PHREAK algorithm. Drools was also one of the first to introduce a unified programming model for business rules and workflow working side by side, sharing the same concepts and APIs.

Outside the runtime engines, the tools also dramatically expanded. Guvnor evolved and became Business Central, a full **Business Rules Management System** (**BRMS**). Business Central had the ambitious goal to provide a user-friendly interface where developers and business practitioners could collaborate; progress was made, laying a solid foundation for future improvement.

In parallel with all these advances, the community itself evolved – from the single Drools project to a family of leading open source projects that play a role in delivering solutions around business automation and artificial intelligence named KIE (Knowledge Is Everything, pronounced the same way as the word key (/kē/) in English).

One turning point in the business rules and BRMS landscape was the introduction of the **Decision Model and Notation** (**DMN**) specification by the **OMG** (**Object Management Group**). This powerful spec defines a graphical notation for decision models and a set of semantics for decision modeling and runtime execution.

Today, DMN is already widely recognized as a leading standard for decision modeling and is used by organizations around the world to manage their decision-making processes. Moreover, the decision management discipline associated with AI has become more popular than ever, driven by the power of the DMN standard. Another advantage of the DMN is that it's vendor-neutral, and it's possible to find a variety of training material, books, methodologies, and other content from practitioners not limited to any specific vendor.

Drools introduced official runtime support for DMN a couple of years after the first release of the spec. Since then, the team has joined the OMG to help shape the spec's future and shift all high-level representation of business rules and decisions investments to it. With this strategy in place, and as the DMN spec increased in popularity, the KIE community was ready to start a new cycle of innovation…

Kogito began as an initiative, which later also became a project. All KIE technologies were containerized at this point, and all investments had cloud-first in mind. However, the team felt the need to go one step further: we needed a new initiative to rethink business automation in a cloud-native fashion.

A new set of tools also emerged from this initiative. First, the **Business Process Model and Notation (BPMN)** and DMN editors were extracted from Business Central and made available as extensions for VS Code. And the team didn't stop there – we were motivated to make the KIE technology more accessible, and that's when we introduced dmn.new, incorporating a runner that creates a dynamic data-input modeling experience inspired by spreadsheets.

And this is where Paul's new book comes in handy: Paul is a long-time community member with a talent for decoding the universe of business rules, decision management, and AI for practitioners and advanced Excel users using accessible language. With the content of this book, you'll add new powerful tools to your tool belt.

Very few technologies survive and can claim relevance for an extended period without a continuous track record of innovations. This community owes much of its success to its ability to foster a warm and welcoming environment. Mark Proctor, a long-time friend and mentor, has played an integral role in leading the community.

The KIE community has been fortunate to attract, build, and retain many other talented individuals, starting with Edson Tirelli and Kris Verlaenen, who laid the foundation for its success—followed closely by Mario Fusco, Maciej Swiderski, and I, who have continued to expand and bring new ideas and perspectives. And now we have the rise of a new bright generation that includes names such as Eder Ignatowicz, Tiago Bento, Matteo Mortari, Daniele Zonca, Enrique Gonzales, Tibor Zimányi, and Ricardo Zanini, who represent the future of the community and are poised to help it continue to thrive for years to come.

And just now, the KIE community is starting a new exciting chapter with IBM joining Red Hat in the stewardship of the community. I'm personally excited to share this part of the new chapter. KIE is in the process of moving to a new home: the Apache Software Foundation. At Apache IBM, Red Hat and the wider community (including you) will have the opportunity to expand the boundaries of business automation and AI even more, together!

Alex Porcelli

Chief Architect for IBM Process Automation and Decision Manager Open Edition

IBM Business Automation

Contributors

About the author

Paul Browne is a product and program manager currently working for Europe's largest VC by deal flow. Most recently, he led a team from three partner institutions that won an EFMD award for ecosystem development, training over 100 eurozone companies to implement digital solutions together. This continues Paul's previous work leading business and technical projects in the public, financial, and life science sectors across Ireland, the UK, the US, the Netherlands, Belgium, and New Zealand.

Paul's qualifications include a degree in European business and French from Ulster University and more recent certifications in finance (ACCA), procurement (CIPS), and business strategy (ESMT). He has technical certifications from Microsoft, Oracle, and IBM and holds a master's in advanced software engineering from University College Dublin.

Paul is also the author of *JBoss Drools Business Rules*, by Packt Publishing, and has lectured in Excel and Visual Basic at third level.

I would like to thank the Drools, KIE, and Kogito communities, and the teams at Red Hat, IBM, and Microsoft for delivering great AI and business automation solutions, and for their ongoing support in writing this book.

About the reviewers

Karina Varela has worked with enterprise technologies for over 10 years, focusing on cloud solutions, Java technologies, and the open source culture.

Her solid knowledge is built on practical experience in development, architecture, delivery, and troubleshooting production applications and products. Having worked at Red Hat, the biggest open source company in the industry, not only does she bring a vast understanding of the open source model and the open communities but she is also largely involved in the delivery of architecture and the delivery of mission-critical software in multiple sectors around the globe. She has also been awarded the Red Hat champion recognition.

Karina is well recognized within the Java community for articles and blogs, books, talks at international tech conferences, open source contributions, and active nurturing and management of communities such as SouJava.

Filippe Spolti is a software engineer and an open source and cloud enthusiast. On a day-to-day basis, he works with Kogito Engine for Serverless Workflows. He worked on OpenShift V3 in its early stages, helping to bring middleware products to the cloud. He was also a technical support engineer who helped customers to solve issues and contributed to several open source projects, more recently with CNCF Serverless. He contributes to local conferences in Brazil as a speaker and track coordinator. He holds a bachelor's degree in information systems and specializations in software engineering and information security and wrote the book *WildFly: New Feature*, and has helped other authors to be successful with their books.

Sharing knowledge is rewarding and it also requires dedication and a little time away from family and friends. I am thankful for the support they have given me in recent years.

Nishant Ravle is an IT professional with more than 16 years of IT experience in BPM, SOA, and middleware technologies. He has extensively worked on Oracle and IBM product stacks. Currently, he is in the field of software consultancy and corporate and online training.

Nishant's technological expertise spans primary skills and expertise in business process management and the service-oriented architecture domain, developing BPM processes using IBM BPM, Oracle BPM, jBPM, Camunda BPM, and Activiti BPM in on-site assignments in the UK, Norway, Oman, Malaysia, South Africa, Dubai, Kenya, and Qatar for requirement gathering, development, consulting, architecting, and training.

Niall Browne has worked extensively with Excel and web technologies. He studied maths and psychology at Dublin City University and has a keen interest in coaching and sports analytics. Most recently, he was a member of the team at The Mill in Drogheda, which co-created a financial payments project with PFS.

Table of Contents

3

Your First Business Rule with the Online KIE Sandbox   45

Part 2: Writing Business Rules and Decision Models – with Real-Life Examples

4

5

6

Calling Business Rules from Excel Using Power Query   127

Part 3: Extending Excel, Decision Models, and Business Process Automation into a Complete Enterprise Solution

7

Using Business Rules in Excel with Visual Basic, Script Lab, or Office Scripts   159

8

Using AI and Decision Services Within Power Automate Workflows   183

9

Advanced Expressions, Decision Models, and Testing   211

Part 4: Next Steps in AI, Machine Learning, and Rule Engines

10

Scaling Rules in Business Central with Docker and the Cloud   239

11

Rules-Based AI and Machine Learning AI – Combining the Best of Both   267

12

What Next? A Look inside Neural Networks, Enterprise Projects, Advanced Rules, and the Rule Engine   295

Appendix A

Appendix B

Appendix C

Preface

Think about a world without Excel. That's just impossible for me.

Satya Nadella, Microsoft CEO

Most of us agree with Microsoft CEO, Satya Nadella. If you include similar products (and Google doesn't release the exact figures for Sheets), there are over a billion of us who can't do without Excel or a similar spreadsheet to organize our daily work and our professional and personal lives.

But you're a special member of this billion-strong group. You're a member of the group of Excel Power users that push the limits of this tool. You're the person that colleagues go to with the trickiest Excel problems, and you get them fixed. You're the person that knows it can be done in Excel, even if you need to delve into the furthest corner of the web to get the answer. You're the person with the key knowledge that your business runs on – all captured in the trusty Excel file format.

If you're reading this book, you know you have a problem. Excel will always be a core part of your working life – but you know it can be better. You've lost track of the hours spent searching to find a mistake in a sheet that somebody else introduced. You're tired of having to explain to colleagues how the sheets actually work, and you suspect they're not listening in order to avoid being burdened with maintaining them. In a world where AI is popping up everywhere, your current Excel solution may require just a bit too much human intervention.

This book suggests a better way by building on your existing knowledge of Excel.

Who this book is for

While there are a billion people who will benefit from reading this book, it is written with three key groups in mind:

- Excel Power users who have reached the limit of Microsoft Office 365 and are wondering what's next, especially as AI tools are becoming more and more powerful.

- Business analysts and knowledge workers looking for a tool to capture their knowledge and deploy it as part of enterprise-grade systems.

- People who are joining an existing rules, AI, or workflow project using decision models, as many of the tools will already be set up; they will find the introduction to DMN and FEEL particularly useful.

Other people will also find the book useful, such as machine learning experts looking for a rules-based safety net for their predictive models. The book will also have value for developers who are looking for a more structured approach to implementing AI and business logic, no matter what language they use.

When you should read this book

The quick answer to when is now. More and more businesses are moving online and adopting digital tools – and that's even before you consider the wave of disruption that AI is hit most office-based jobs with.

Excel is a great starting point for this move, but sooner or later, you will need a pathway to more powerful solutions. This book gives you one clear pathway. It has the added bonus that capturing your knowledge in a when ... then format separates the business knowledge from the technical implementation, making your investment much more likely to last into the future.

What this book covers

Chapter 1, Wrestling with Excel? You Are Not Alone, outlines the problems you might face in Excel, but reassures you that you are not the only person to encounter these issues and shows how an AI-based rules approach can help.

Chapter 2, Choosing an AI and Business Rules Engine – Why KIE and Drools?, shows why the rules engine and AI tools from the KIE project are the best choices for you as an Excel user, and welcomes you to an open community supported by IBM and Red Hat in which you can get ongoing support.

Chapter 3, Your First Business Rule with the Online KIE Sandbox, dives into writing your business rule and creating your first decision model in the online KIE Sandbox using a classic Hello World example.

Chapter 4, More Decision Models, Business Rules, and Decision Tables, expands your knowledge of decision models and builds out a working chocolate shop example to show more of the tools available.

Chapter 5, Sharing and Deploying Decision Models Using OpenShift Cloud and GitHub, looks at making your decision models sharable, allowing other people to run them in the cloud, and using online tools to collaborate with colleagues on the model's design.

Chapter 6, Calling Business Rules from Excel Using Power Query, links Excel to our AI, rules, and decision tables using the Power Query tool built into Excel.

Chapter 7, Using Business Rules in Excel with Visual Basic, Script Lab, and Office Script, gives three alternative script-based methods to give you more choices on how you link Excel with your business rules.

Chapter 8, AI and Decision Services within Excel and Power Automate Workflows, introduces Microsoft's business automation tool and shows how we can use our models to make decisions at key points in a flow.

Chapter 9, Advanced Expressions, Decision Models, and Testing, explores the full power of the expression language built into KIE and introduces the scenario testing tools so we can guarantee our decision models behave as we expect.

Chapter 10, Scaling Rules in Business Central with Docker and the Cloud, demonstrates the power of the KIE and Kogito decision-making tools, leveraging containers to increase our deployment options and editing capability.

Chapter 11, Rules-Based AI and Machine Learning – Combining the Best of Both, introduces the other main part of AI and shows how we can use the tools in KIE and Azure ML Studio to deploy both machine learning and rules-based decision models alongside each other.

Chapter 12, What Next? A Look Inside Neural Networks, Enterprise Projects, Advanced Rules, and the Rules Engine, expands on the previous chapters and gives key areas for future learning with practical first steps on neural networks, Enterprise Java projects, and ethical, explainable AI.

Appendix A, Introduction to Visual Basic for Applications, introduces just enough **Visual Basic for Applications** (**VBA**) so that those of you who are new to the language can understand the VBA examples in that section of *Chapter 7*.

Appendix B, Testing Using VS Code, Azure, and GitHub Codespaces, introduces the **Visual Studio Code** (**VS Code**) editor from Microsoft – while it is more advanced than the tools in the main chapters of the book, many of you will appreciate its power for testing and building projects in Azure and Codespaces.

Appendix C, Troubleshooting Docker, supports the instructions given in *Chapter 10*; most of you will not need this and will experience a smooth Docker installation – but it is good to know there is support here if needed.

To get the most out of this book

Just like knowing how to open the hood (bonnet) of your car to replace the oil and spark plugs, being able to look under the hood of Excel will give you a lot more power. This book will take you through this step by step and explain things in a way that an Excel Power user can easily understand. But be aware that you will sometimes get oil on your hands – not everything will be as tidy as the way Microsoft delivers the Office apps.

These are the requirements to get the most out of this book:

You should be familiar with Excel – for example, know what a spreadsheet is, how to open files, input formulas, save and rename files, and so on. It is not necessary to be a Power user (for example, using advanced formulas, Visual Basic for Excel, or other scripting tools), but having tried these tools will help you appreciate the full power of business rules we are giving you in this book.

You should be very familiar with using a web browser. While the book describes Business Central and Azure Web Portal in a way that is no more complex than a typical travel booking site, a moderate amount of web literacy is assumed, as we focus on the pages, not the browser.

You should be comfortable with breaking a big problem into smaller problems and solving each in turn. Most Excel users will do this naturally when writing formulas, and the book assumes you will use the tools described to solve your problem rather than expecting a full ready-to-go solution.

For *Chapter 10*, you should know how to install software on your computer. Full instructions are given to install Docker Desktop, which is a convenient container giving you the confidence that the examples will work on your computer exactly as they do in the book. You will need to download and run a graphical installer and troubleshoot minor issues (for example, if you need an admin password to proceed with the installation). We do give alternatives, as not every computer setup is the same, and sometimes things just don't work.

You should be comfortable asking for help. This could be as simple as googling common error messages to find how other people solve the problem, reading documentation (pointers provided!) as you write your own business rules, or even asking more technical colleagues or open source community members nicely for support.

While the book assumes you have no coding experience and always gives a simple, non-technical route, there are (additional) appendices that will allow more technical colleagues to support you if you want to explore these areas.

For a technical book, the list of must-have tools is surprisingly short, since we use freely available online tools where possible.

In fact, it is possible to get a lot of value from the book with only a web browser. However, since Excel (both laptop and online) is available as a free trial from Microsoft, we highly recommend installing it, as you will learn so much more – especially in *Chapters 6* and *7*.

Requirement	Additional Details
Modern web browser and reasonable speed internet connection	Chrome, Edge, and Safari are all confirmed as working, with Firefox also likely to be compatible shortly.
Microsoft Excel and Office 365	Alternative options are given in *Chapters 6*, *7*, and *8*, but you are recommended to sign up for the free trial of Office 365 and Power Automate.
Credit card and cell (mobile) phone	All products used are the free versions, but a credit card and cell phone may be needed to verify identity when signing up for OpenShift and Azure.

The most demanding chapter (in terms of the hardware specifications needed to run the tools) is *Chapter 10*, where we use Docker – most laptops sold in the last 5 years will be able to support it, and alternatives (such as using the cloud instead) are given.

If you are using the digital version of this book, we advise you to type the code yourself or access the code from the book's GitHub repository (a link is available in the next section). Doing so will help you avoid any potential errors related to the copying and pasting of code.

Download the example code files

You can download the example code files for this book from GitHub at `https://github.com/PacktPublishing/Business-Rule-Engines-and-AI-for-Excel-Power-Users`. If there's an update to the code, it will be updated in the GitHub repository.

We also have other code bundles from our rich catalog of books and videos available at `https://github.com/PacktPublishing/`. Check them out!

Download the color images

We also provide a PDF file that has color images of the screenshots and diagrams used in this book. You can download it here: `https://packt.link/EAEVJ`.

Conventions used

There are a number of text conventions used throughout this book.

`Code in text`: Indicates code words in text, database table names, folder names, filenames, file extensions, pathnames, dummy URLs, user input, and Twitter handles. Here is an example: "The formula to match with the first 10,000 customers is `Customer.Number < 10000`."

A block of code is set as follows:

```
let
    // "SourceUrl" with quotes needs to match the named range on
our Excel sheet. You may need to change {1} to {0} depending on
when your first line begins
    pSourceUrl = Excel.CurrentWorkbook(){[Name="SourceUrl"]}
[Content]{1}[Column1]
in
    pSourceUrl
```

When we wish to draw your attention to a particular part of a code block, the relevant lines or items are set in bold:

```
let
    // "SourceUrl" with quotes needs to match the named range on
our Excel sheet. You may need to change {1} to {0} depending on
when your first line begins
    pSourceUrl = Excel.CurrentWorkbook(){[Name="SourceUrl"]}
[Content]{1}[Column1]
in
    pSourceUrl
```

Any command-line input or output is written as follows:

```
curl -X 'POST' \
  'https://dmn-dev-sandbox-yu88rl6qu490-crt-openshift-dev.apps.
sandbox.x8i5.p1.openshiftapps.com/Customer Recommendations/
Product Recommendation Service' \
  -H 'accept: application/json' \
  -H 'Content-Type: application/json' \
  -d '{
  "Customer": {
    "Number": 0,
    "Name": "string",
    "Date of Birth": "2022-10-23",
    "Country of Residence": "string",
    "Special Requests": "diabetic",
    "Previous Orders": [
      0
    ]
  }
}'
```

Bold: Indicates a new term, an important word, or words that you see onscreen. For instance, words in menus or dialog boxes appear in **bold**. Here is an example: "Click **Done** at the bottom right of the screen to save the code and exit the screen."

> **Tips or important notes**
> Appear like this.

Get in touch

Feedback from our readers is always welcome.

General feedback: If you have questions about any aspect of this book, email us at customercare@ packtpub.com and mention the book title in the subject of your message.

Errata: Although we have taken every care to ensure the accuracy of our content, mistakes do happen. If you have found a mistake in this book, we would be grateful if you would report this to us. Please visit www.packtpub.com/support/errata and fill in the form.

Piracy: If you come across any illegal copies of our works in any form on the internet, we would be grateful if you would provide us with the location address or website name. Please contact us at copyright@packt.com with a link to the material.

If you are interested in becoming an author: If there is a topic that you have expertise in and you are interested in either writing or contributing to a book, please visit authors.packtpub.com.

Share Your Thoughts

Once you've read *AI and Business Rule Engines for Excel Power Users*, we'd love to hear your thoughts! Scan the QR code below to go straight to the Amazon review page for this book and share your feedback.

https://packt.link/r/180461954X

Your review is important to us and the tech community and will help us make sure we're delivering excellent quality content.

Download a free PDF copy of this book

Thanks for purchasing this book!

Do you like to read on the go but are unable to carry your print books everywhere? Is your eBook purchase not compatible with the device of your choice?

Don't worry, now with every Packt book you get a DRM-free PDF version of that book at no cost.

Read anywhere, any place, on any device. Search, copy, and paste code from your favorite technical books directly into your application.

The perks don't stop there, you can get exclusive access to discounts, newsletters, and great free content in your inbox daily

Follow these simple steps to get the benefits:

1. Scan the QR code or visit the link below

https://packt.link/free-ebook/9781804619544

2. Submit your proof of purchase
3. That's it! We'll send your free PDF and other benefits to your email directly

Part 1: The Problem with Excel, and Why Rule-Based AI Can Be the Solution

The first part of the book builds the case, showing how an AI and business rules approach can help solve the problems you are encountering in Excel.

This section includes the following chapters:

- *Chapter 1, Wrestling with Excel? You Are Not Alone*, outlines the problems you may be facing in Excel, but reassures you that you are not the only person to encounter these issues and shows how an AI-based rule approach can help.

- *Chapter 2, Choosing an AI and Business Rules Engine – Why KIE and Drools?*, shows why the rules engine and AI tools from the KIE project are the best choice for you as an Excel user and welcomes you to an open community supported by IBM and Red Hat where you can get ongoing support.

- *Chapter 3, Your First Business Rule with the Online KIE Sandbox*, dives into writing business rules and creating your first decision model in the online KIE Sandbox using a classic Hello World example.

1

Wrestling with Excel?
You Are Not Alone

If you read the *Preface*, you will know that a lot of people use Excel, being one of them, and that you are not the only person frustrated with the limitations of it as a tool.

Based on the fact that you have read on, you must now know that this book can help you. But before we can go into how exactly it can help, it's worth exploring in detail the problems we're trying to solve. In this chapter, we'll cover the following:

- Why do you use Excel?
- Enterprise solutions and the gap between them and Excel
- What's your real business problem?
- What is artificial intelligence and which type can help you best?
- Practical artificial intelligence and business rules
- Splitting Excel into different pieces

Why do you use Excel?

If you ask most of the billion Excel users around the globe, most of them will say they use Excel for these two main reasons:

- As a convenient place to store information – more structured than using post-it notes, but flexible enough to evolve over time
- A convenient way to exchange information – because everybody else uses it

If you are an Excel power user, you'll add a third reason:

- You use Excel to process important information. And your organization depends on the knowledge you have in your head to get the process right

In working with Excel, you and your colleagues are using it as the core engine to drive your business. Let's look at a couple of real-world examples.

Excel as the engine room of the business

There are many important jobs in every business (I'm using *business* as shorthand for *any organization*). But those jobs will grind to a halt without a way of capturing, processing, and sharing information. On the surface, it looks like Excel does these tasks very well:

- If you work for a medical company, you might use Excel to capture orders for vaccines, process them to forecast demand, and then use Excel to share orders with various plants worldwide

- If you're in the aircraft leasing industry, you might use Excel to track how many planes you have placed with airlines worldwide, process the information to calculate different risk scenarios (for example, a major war breaking out), and then use Excel to share information with the banks that are funding you

- If you're a small business, you could use Excel to track salary information, process it to calculate payroll taxes due, and carefully share the relevant information with each employee

The following diagram shows how you use Excel in each case:

Figure 1.1 – How you use Excel

This diagram is so simple that you've probably never needed to think about it – you take some information in (for example, from a spreadsheet), process it (apply hand-crafted formulas or review it manually), and then share it (maybe save it to an internal drive or SharePoint for others to use).

And that is the core of the problem – your processing is bundled up with how you gather and share your information. This workflow is great for getting started, but sooner or later, you're going to run into problems as each of the steps in *Figure 1.1* gets in the way of each other. We'll look at how you might encounter this problem in your daily work, before beginning to talk about ways of solving it.

Day-to-day Excel problems

How you use Excel is unique to you. But I'm guessing that you've run into several of the following common problems:

- A large part of your day involves repeating tasks in Excel by hand. This includes capturing information by manually copying details from one sheet to another.

- Emailing Excel files back and forth, not being sure whether you're using the latest version, and losing information by editing the wrong version.

- Wondering whether your formulas may have been broken by other users and spending hours rechecking them.

- You use complex Excel formulas that no one else can really understand without spending hours drilling down into them. Formulas within formulas combined with more formulas. Sometimes, even those who write them can't really remember how they work.

These pain points are particularly harsh in a regulated environment (for example, financial or medical/life sciences) where data integrity and auditing how decisions are made are required. But these pain points also exist in sectors such as manufacturing and management, where the consequences of decisions made on faulty spreadsheets can get very expensive very quickly.

The core part of most of these problems is that the file that contains the information is the same file that contains your functions for processing that information. What if you could separate them?

One solution – separating information and processing instructions

One way of solving this problem is to use two Excel files – one data source containing the information we want to work with and the other for processing the instructions or business logic.

Figure 1.2 gives an example:

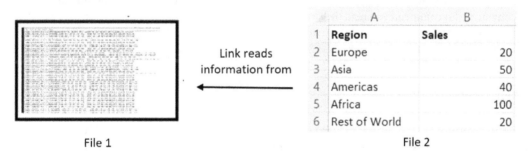

	A	B
1	**Region**	**Sales**
2	Europe	20
3	Asia	50
4	Americas	40
5	Africa	100
6	Rest of World	20

Link reads information from ⟵

File 1   File 2

Figure 1.2 – Separating information and processing instructions

This diagram shows a solution, used by many Excel power users, to separate the original information from the formulas that act on this information:

1. File 1 contains the information, and only information. You can share this file with other people and allow them to edit it.

2. File 2 contains the processing instructions (formula), often a summary page or report that can be printed.

3. The two files are linked using the standard Excel formula for linking spreadsheets, similar to the following:

```
=[Workbook_name]Sheet_name!Cell_address
```

This solution is better – you can pass around the first file, knowing that your formulas can never get broken (either by accident or deliberately). The second file contains all your important formulas. It's not perfect – updating the two files can be tricky, and it's easy to break the link (for example, by saving the files in the wrong place).

It's a start toward a solution. In fact, most enterprise computer systems separate the information and information processing in this way. They will often refer to the information you're working on as **data** and the processing instructions (for example, Excel functions) as **code**.

If you've ever written your own functions or macros in Excel, using **Visual Basic for Applications** (**VBA**), you'll have come across these terms before. You'll see the terms data and code a lot in the coming chapters. We'll also be talking about enterprise solutions as we move through the book – it's worth reminding ourselves what they are.

Keeping it simple and secure

If this simple solution solves the problem for you, use it. More information on how to use a formula to reference a cell in another Excel file or spreadsheet is available on the Microsoft website.

In fact, if there is one thing we recommend you take away from this book, it's don't fully trust any spreadsheet that another person can edit (even if it's password protected). If you aren't convinced, I recommend you read the story of how one trader almost put a major international bank out of business by fraudulently manipulating Excel – `https://www.amazon.com/Panic-Bank-John-Rusnak-Million/dp/0717135632`.

Enterprise solutions

One core promise of this book is to build on your existing knowledge of Excel and help you find solutions that are more scalable, robust, and supported by a wider team. By this, we mean the following:

- **Scalable**: Whatever we build can be used by tens or hundreds of users simultaneously, manipulating a very large dataset.

- **Robust/durable**: What we build can be left to run by itself, since it won't easily break and highlights any errors using tests that can be run automatically.

- **Supported by a wider team**: Most Excel sheets are maintained by only one person. What if they leave? The solutions we build should be understood by many people.

Typically, these are called enterprise solutions. In your organization, you're likely to have several of these, supported by an internal or external IT team. Let's look at a couple of examples.

Examples of enterprise solutions

We gave an example before of a company using Excel to track salaries paid to employees and manage the taxes to be paid. But unless you're an early-stage start-up, you're likely to find another way of doing this – using a pre-built solution. If you Google the term `Payroll Software`, you will find hundreds of examples of it, and many will be tailored to the tax system of the country that you live in. In general, for a generic requirement such as this (since every company has to comply with the same local laws), you're better off using an *off-the-shelf* solution.

This is great if you're a business such as a fast-food franchise. Headquarters will tell you what enterprise systems to use and then charge you for using them. But most businesses do things slightly differently as they try to win new customers. Even if 80% of their requirements (HR, property management, and finance) are the same, these businesses are likely to have some things that they need to do differently.

One example might be a home loan lender who focuses on lending to workers in the *gig economy* with a fluctuating income. It may decide to build its own system to approve these loans since the decision-making process is different from banks that lend to people with a stable 9-5 job.

For these bespoke requirements, its IT department will often build the solution using a language such as Java, C#, or Python. They'll build on top of standard libraries and tools such as Oracle, Microsoft SQL Server, and even cloud-based services (e.g., from Amazon). If it doesn't have the skills in-house, it may contract an external company to build the system.

Simple then – we just get our IT department to rebuild our Excel sheets in an enterprise software solution. Obviously, it's not quite as simple as that; otherwise, 1 billion people wouldn't still be using Excel.

It's probably worth underlining that we think Excel is a great tool and should be used alongside your set of enterprise solutions. Not only is it incredibly flexible and puts the power in the hands of business users but it can often also fill the gap as a good-enough solution while your IT team builds something longer-term. Either way, now that Excel is a first-class programming language, don't be afraid to use it. Just know that this book gives you a roadmap to build from your current Excel sheets when you need something better.

> ### What is a first-class language?
> For more details on what this means, see the following link. In general, don't let anybody intimidate you into thinking that Excel isn't a proper solution – `https://www.microsoft.com/en-us/research/podcast/advancing-excel-as-a-programming-language-with-andy-gordon-and-simon-peyton-jones/`.

The chasm between Excel and enterprise solutions

So, why doesn't your IT department just build a shiny new solution to solve all your Excel problems? It turns out there is a bit of a chasm between Excel and true enterprise solutions. We'll cover three gaps that you may already have run into.

Gap 1 – the need to code

Coding or programming is being able to write instructions in a language that a computer can understand. It's not difficult – you're doing it already in Excel. The set of functions, numbers, graphs, and so on that you put in Excel are instructions to the computer to produce the result you want.

You've already done the hardest bit – breaking down a larger problem into smaller ones that the computer can then work through. But like Excel, even if coding is easy to do, it is harder to do well. It can take commercial developers (including your colleagues in the IT department) several years to fully master their craft.

Gap 2 – business experts and tech experts are now two different people

As an Excel power user, you're likely to be a business domain expert. You might be the person who knows everything about the forecasting demand for umbrellas in the mid-west region of the United States. You could be the person who knows how to tweak expenditure on online and traditional advertising to make the most sales in India. Or you could be the person who knows how to forecast the demand for spare computer parts in Europe for the next five years.

This business knowledge is valuable as it is the one thing your business cannot do without.

Very few people have this business knowledge and are also able to code. It's not impossible, it's just that mastering two things (business knowledge and coding) is more difficult than one. Also, both disciplines lead to different career paths, so being skilled in both is tricky.

That's OK. Two people can work together to build the solution. But having two people working on the solution leads to *gap number 3*.

Gap 3 – knowledge disappearing into code

Take a look at the following mortgage tool (a home loan calculator, available at `https://www.drcalculator.com/mortgage/`) shown in *Figure 1.3*:

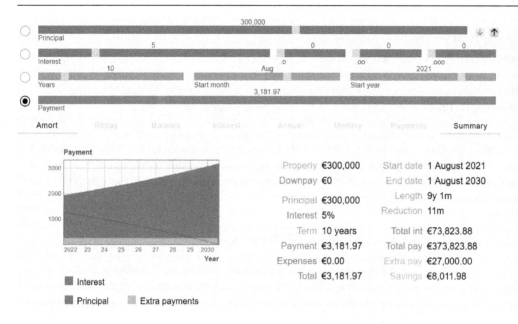

Figure 1.3 – A web-based home loan calculator

It's a pretty straightforward system – you put in the amount of money you want to borrow and what the current interest rate is, and it calculates how much you need to repay every month. Play around with it – especially the bit where paying off a small amount of money early can save you large amounts over the lifetime of the loan.

When they built this home loan website, you could imagine a business expert setting out the rules for the calculator, and a technical colleague building these rules in code. What if you want to see whether they have done the job correctly? Easy – you just look at the code, right? You'll see that it's not so simple when you look at the following code sample:

```
(window.webpackJsonp=window.webpackJsonp||[]).
push([[19],{"3X0S":function(n,e,t) return d.fc(n),d.
Wb().sliderButton(0,0)}),d.Kb(2,"ion- this.updateAll()}
radioChange(n){"ion-radio-group"===n.target.
localName&&(this.m.getCalcMode()!==+this.radioValue?(this.
radioClicks=0,this.g.getShowCalcModeMessage()
&&this.c.showCalcModeDialog(this,+this.
radioValue),this.m.setCalcMode(+this.radioValue))
...
```

Don't worry if you can't understand this – that's the point. Without extensive testing, it's very difficult to check whether what is happening in the code is what you intended. It'd be even worse if you were returning to update this calculator after a year or two of working on other projects and had forgotten the work you did previously on the project.

> **But why don't we build this in Excel?**
>
> As an Excel power user, when you saw the mortgage calculator website, you probably thought *I could build this in Excel*. And you probably could. But as you add more features, your Excel sheet will become so complicated that other people will have difficulty reading it, a bit like the code sample. This is where the solutions that this book proposes come into play.

What if there was a halfway house – allowing you to capture your business knowledge in a way that the computer could understand, but was still human-readable? This book proposes business rules as part of the solution. But to explain why (and how), let's put Excel to one side and look at the business problems you're trying to solve.

What's your real business problem?

We talked earlier about Excel being the engine room of many businesses. Somebody (a client or an employer) pays you to use it for a reason. The knowledge you have embedded in your spreadsheets helps the business save money or make more sales. If you work with an organization that saves lives, the knowledge you have embedded in your spreadsheets could get people the right medicine at the right time.

The knowledge you have embedded is the important part. Spreadsheets are just convenient tools to capture and share that knowledge. Since most businesses have intense (and growing) competition, how well you capture and manage that knowledge dictates whether your business will survive and grow or shrink and close in the coming years.

Spreadsheets are convenient tools, but they are not perfect. In fact, if your organization relies heavily on Excel, it is likely that most people haven't (yet) thought about how to capture and maintain the business knowledge that's core to a company's survival. The very same senior managers would be horrified if they didn't have a list of buildings owned by the company. But there is complacency in listing and managing intellectual property, which is often several times more valuable.

What these business problems look like in real life

Without a systematic way to capture and manage your company's business knowledge assets, you're going to run into these kinds of day-to-day problems. Ask yourself the following questions and consider how many apply to you:

- Do you find that you can never get enough good people to join your team? Either it's difficult to recruit people with the right skills, it takes too long to train them with the knowledge that they need, or when they are trained, they move on to other jobs, taking their knowledge with them.

- Do you get complaints from customers that they get different answers depending on who in your team they ask? Even worse, have you found customers repeating the question to different team members until they get the answer that they want?

- Is there one key team member who you can't afford to lose – the one person who knows how the system really works? If you answered *no* to this question, is it possible that you've overlooked a key team member and will only realize the gap when they leave?

- If you're that key team member with the key knowledge in your head, it feels pretty good, right? Or it would feel good if you weren't getting asked basic questions most of the day, getting in the way of you doing your *real* job…

- If your organization is project-based, do the project teams capture the knowledge coming out of each project so it can be used in their day-to-day work? Or does each effort tend to start with a *blank sheet* as the team finds it difficult to capture and reuse knowledge from previous projects?

- Do you have process and procedure documents that have been left sitting unused and not updated on a shelf? Is there a temptation to not use or update these documents as the team is *too busy* and you promise yourself you'll get around to updating it sometime later?

- If you changed these process documents, would anybody notice? Your team members aren't machines – they won't just execute a new process if the document changes. But what if you could (gently) check that what is in the process was actually being implemented?

- Are edits tracked so that people can agree on what changes need to be made to the process? Just as important, if things go wrong, can you trace back to the change that broke it? When the fix is made, are you sure people will use the correct version of the process?

- Are the right people carrying out the right tasks? This used to be easier to manage when everybody worked in the same office. Now, with hybrid working, and teams being dispersed across different continents and different companies, do we know whether people are doing the right thing at the right time?

- In general, sharing information is much more powerful than keeping it a closely guarded secret. But sometimes, key information needs to be kept under wraps (for example, the percentage discount you give to key customers). The ability to edit this information (for example, changing the level at which this discount applies) needs to be more closely controlled. Is this the case in your company?

It's no surprise that in a book with *business rules* in the title, we're advocating for a solution involving rules to capture, share, and manage your business knowledge effectively. But to explain how we can do this, let's introduce one of the hottest topics nowadays – **Artificial Intelligence (AI)**.

Artificial intelligence and which type can help you best

On a bad day at the office, you've probably had the great idea of either cloning yourself or one of your key team members. That way, you could leave your clone working away while you do more important things, or just take a break at the beach.

Just to be clear, this book does not recommend cloning humans as a practical solution!

What is possible is applying recent advances in AI to the problem. Surely if we live in a world of almost self-driving cars, we could train a computer to capture and process the knowledge in our Excel sheets, in a way that can solve many of the problems that we've talked about?

Will AI take my job?

You may read this and think, *if a computer can do my job, what am I going to do?* With almost every bit of automation in the last 200 years, about 80% of your job can be automated, and it's normally the boring and repetitive bits. If the boring bits are automated, it leaves room for the 20% that is really interesting to expand – hopefully leaving you with a more interesting job!

It turns out (no surprise, since *AI* is in the title of the book) that we can teach computers to help us in this way. But since there is so much buzz around AI, it's worth being a bit more precise about the type of AI we're proposing to use to solve the problem.

What is artificial intelligence?

There are many formal definitions of AI, but I particularly like the definition from John McCarthy, the Stanford professor that originally came up with the name – `http://jmc.stanford.edu/artificial-intelligence/index.html`. Broadly speaking, it is teaching computers to do tasks normally carried out by humans. Most people include the following as examples of AI:

- A computer learning to identify tumors in X-rays
- A computer applying a set of knowledge to a problem to propose a solution (for example, a streaming site suggesting movies you're most likely to want to watch)
- A computer understanding your search phrase well enough to suggest documents on a similar topic
- A computer evolving programs generation after generation to attempt to find the best match for the problems (genetic algorithms)

If you notice, these four examples are in very specific areas. While AI has made great advances in recent years, these are often across deep verticals, and AI often lacks general *common sense*. Humans will not be replaced anytime soon, even if some of the specific tasks we do will be.

Since AI is good at specific verticals, we need to decide which specific tools can help us solve our problem. We'll focus on three main areas that you'll likely have come across already.

> **More reading on AI**
>
> We're focusing, in this section, on *AI for Excel power users*. It won't surprise you that, with such a hot topic, there are many books on these and other AI-related techniques – with many going into very powerful but niche technical details. The Packt website has many suggestions: `https://subscription.packtpub.com/search?query=artificial+intelligence`.
>
> If you're interested in "how we got here" and more details on AI concepts, *A Brief History of Artificial Intelligence* by Michael Wooldridge (Flatiron) provides a good summary. In this book, we'll concentrate on practical tools that you can use now in your work based on a rules-based AI approach.
>
> We'll return to the area of machine learning in *Chapter 11*, when we explore other types of AI tools in a little bit more detail.

Artificial intelligence type one – machine learning

If you've only heard of AI in the last couple of years, most likely you're thinking of the machine learning part of AI. Broadly speaking, if you (like Google, Microsoft, or Amazon) have access to hundreds of thousands (or even hundreds of millions) of samples (for example, pictures of traffic lights, samples of handwriting, or the purchase history of millions of people), then you can help a computer to *learn* the appropriate response.

Hopefully, people working in the machine learning field won't be insulted when I describe neural networks and other techniques to achieve this as a *load of fancy math*. It's even possible to implement simple versions of these networks in Excel – take a look at *Chapter 12*. Of course, for most practical purposes, you'd use tools more optimized for machine learning.

The math theory behind these tools is truly impressive, as are the breakthroughs in thinking in recent years. These tools have progressed and been packaged so that they can solve off-the-shelf problems for a non-technical user. We'll use them as part of our wider solution in a later chapter.

However, your problem is likely not one that can be solved with a fully off-the-shelf solution. If it was, you'd be using one of the pre-built solutions we mentioned earlier, instead of your own Excel spreadsheets.

Another issue is that traditionally, neural networks have found it very hard to explain how a decision is made – you know the samples used to train the network, you know the output, but you can never be completely sure how it came to the answer it did.

A final issue is that you're unlikely to have the millions of samples needed to effectively train a neural network. More likely, you'll have several hundred samples (for example, of a home loan application) and a human expert with the knowledge in their head.

Artificial intelligence type two – natural language processing

What if the business expert could *talk* to a computer in something close to normal human language, and have the computer understand what that expert meant? Until recently, this was the stuff of science fiction – humans previously needed to use a more constrained language with perhaps about 100 words, used in a very specific order. If you're not a programmer, think of how you'd talk to a 2-year-old child.

Recently, researchers solved this problem by using millions of documents to train different neural networks. You've probably used the results of these, for example, Google Translate. More recently, *GPT-3* and Microsoft tools such as *Copilot* (https://copilot.github.com/) have shown great promise in translating from normal English into Java, Python, and other computer code that computers can execute.

While I think these tools will evolve rapidly, and welcome anything that gives more people the ability to program, we've just duplicated the problem that we ran into before with the web-based mortgage calculator. Whether it's a colleague or a computer writing the code for us, once our knowledge is *translated* into code, it becomes much more difficult to check whether this code accurately represents the business rules we want.

What we really want is a way to keep our business rules simple, and for the computer to learn how to apply these rules to our current business problem.

Artificial intelligence type three – rule based

Some of the first attempts at AI consisted of making statements that were known to be true and letting the computer *figure it out* from there. Examples of these statements for a car-driving computer could include the following:

```
When the driver says "go" start the engine.
When there is a stop sign and there are humans on the road,
then stop.
When there are no stop signs and the road is clear, then
accelerate to 50km/h.
When there is a person visible in the road, then the road is
not clear.
```

Based on what we've said about other approaches, you may notice some things straight away:

- These rules are written in something close to an English language format, even if they follow a slightly formal when … then structure.

- These rules did not need hundreds of millions of examples to create. It just took one author (who passed his driving test a long time ago) to write them, and a second person to review them to make sure they made sense.

- To us as humans (and hopefully expert drivers), these rules are clear. If we need to change the rules (for example, if the law changes the speed limit), they are easy to review and edit.

- The rules are independent of each other. If we edit the speed rule, we don't need to revisit our rule about the stop signs. We let the computer worry about the interactions between the rules, which makes the rules themselves much easier to understand

- While the rules are clear, we probably want to test the outcomes. For example, when the car is moving at 50 km/h and somebody steps out into the road, rules 3 and 4 are no longer true – but will the car actually stop (we have no specific rule telling it to do so)?

Truth maintenance

Withdrawing a rule when it is no longer true is called **truth maintenance**. In this case, it should cause the *when the road is clear* rule to be withdrawn and the car comes to a stop.

Would you trust this rule? Most business rules will be more explicit – and include a rule such as *when there is no explicit signal to drive, then stop*. Even then, it is vital to scenario-test the rules – a topic we will cover in *Chapter 9*.

Most Excel spreadsheets, while they may contain hundreds of business rules, are actually a lot simpler than our driving-based example. We've never had to teach an Excel spreadsheet how to recognize a stop sign. We've also never connected an Excel sheet to a car accelerator to make it move forward.

This is just as well, since rules-based AI performs much worse at these general tasks. Can you imagine the hundreds of rules you'd need to describe traffic signs, and even then not be sure whether you've described them all? It's a pretty open-ended problem. But for problems that can be fully written down (for example, the laws governing how to drive correctly), rules-based AI is a good match.

By definition, problems that you can describe in Excel can be fully written down, making them a good match for rules-based AI.

So, for most Excel applications, rules-based AI is what we're going to be able to make the most progress with, and it's the one we'll focus on in this book. We'll revisit complementary approaches later in the book, in *Part 3, Tools to Extend Business Rule Engines and Excel into a Complete Solution*, just to make sure we're getting the full picture.

Types of AI working together

If you really are building a self-driving car, then I highly recommend you read the other AI books from Packt. But otherwise, it's a good example to show the different types of AI working together. You would use natural language processing to listen to driver commands (*drive to the restaurant*). You would use neural networks in computer vision to recognize road signs. And you would use rules-based AI to guarantee that you followed all relevant driving laws (*stop at the stop sign*).

Our self-driving car example highlights two more benefits of the rules-based approach:

- The rules we are applying are pretty clear – they're not hidden in obscure code or buried in the weightings of a neural network. This clarity extends to bias. If there is bias in our rules (they are written by humans after all), we can at least examine and challenge them. This is not always true for other types of AI, especially if they are trained on biased data.

- We can almost guarantee that certain business rules will apply in certain situations. The *almost* but not certainly being able to guarantee the behavior is due to the interplay of different business rules. But we can test for this and modify our business rules as appropriate.

Both these strengths address the weaknesses of the neural network AI approach in particular. This is not a book written for Google or Tesla AI engineers, but if you are one, consider using rules-based AI as a safety net underneath the systems you are developing!

As great as the rules-based approach to AI is, we still need something to run these rules (we'll talk more about rule engines shortly). While we haven't yet addressed some of the problems we highlighted previously (for example, change tracking), we'll see later how the tools around a rule engine will help us solve that problem as well. Before that, it's worth looking more at what a business rule is in more detail, as it's core to this approach to AI.

Practical artificial intelligence and business rules

The preceding business rule examples deliberately used a when ... then format. This was no accident; the format gives clarity about the knowledge we are trying to share with the AI system.

The when ... then format

Let's highlight the key format for writing business rules:

```
When "something is true" then "take some action"
```

This is a very simple concept, so simple that if you're an Excel power user (or have programmed in other languages), this is something that might trip you up.

In Excel, the flow is important – one cell references another, which might reference a third cell – but the order in which the values will be calculated is guaranteed. Likewise, in computer languages such as Java or VBA, statements are executed strictly in the order they are written (with options to loop and call functions).

A business rule can activate any time the "when" part is true – there is no guarantee of the order the rule statements will fire in.

The reminder is that we use when not if – when the first part of the rule is true, we should try to ensure that the then action is taken. Most programmers will struggle with this subtle difference – they are used to controlling *if* the code should branch, instead of trusting the rule engine to decide *when* something is true and that it should be executed on their behalf.

To an Excel user, this sounds like a recipe for chaos. Obviously, once we start executing these rules, we need some sort of engine to manage all of this for us. The engine will decide the following:

1. Which rule(s) are activated and which have valid conditions and therefore should be fired.

2. If more than one rule is ready to fire, which one goes first.

3. If a rule is no longer true before it has fired, to remove it from the list.

4. Repeat the steps from *step 1*, unless there are no more rules ready to fire.

Thankfully, and as we'll see soon, there are ready-to-go rule engines that can effectively manage all of this complexity for us.

```
When "something is true" then "take some action"
```

By the time you have written many hundreds of business rules, you'll see that this simplicity makes the rules easy to maintain. At the same time, how the rules interact can give you some very sophisticated results.

Don't believe me? Let's take a look at a real-life situation that shows the power of this format.

Triage – life or death business rules

Imagine you are standing in the Accident & Emergency section of your local hospital when a major incident occurs. Ambulances are bringing in victims with different levels of injury and the doctors in the hospital are getting overwhelmed by the number of people arriving. More help is on its way, but by the time they arrive, it could be too late for many people.

You ask whether you can do something, anything to help, weakly mentioning the basic first aid certificate you got many years ago (having covered nothing like situations like this). You get handed a set of cards like the ones represented in *Figure 1.4* and are told to follow the instructions:

General Practice - Staff Emergency Guideline	**Abdominal Pain**	General Practice - Nurse Triage Guideline	**Swollen Limb**
	1. **Alert the Practice Nurse and/or GP immediately** for additional triage and advice		If **any** of the following symptoms **call Ambulance via 000**:
	2. Call Ambulance via 000 if requested by Practice Nurse/ GP or if no GP present		• Gasping for breath at rest or difficulty speaking (phrases only)
	3. Assist patient into most comfortable position (usually with knees bent)		• Associated onset of chest pain
	4. If trained apply oxygen if available via a therapy mask (≤ 94% SaO2)		• History of severe allergic reaction or anaphylaxis
	5. Watch for deteriorating level of consciousness		• Coughing up red/pink froth
	6. Stay with patient until assistance arrives		If any of the following symptoms present, **direct patient to ED** consider **Ambulance via 000** if Symptoms severe:
	7. Retrieve patient record for further information		• History Of recent surgery to the affected limb
	8. Consult appropriate guidelines for additional guidance e.g. **Collapse/Semi-Conscious, Severe Pain or CPR chart**		• Sudden onset of a cold limb
			• NO pulse or feeling present in limb
			If none of these symptoms present consider making an **Appointment for the patient today or within 24 hours (Cat. 6)**
			If unilateral leg pain in the absence of injury consider asking patient to **Come to the Practice Now (Cat. 5)** if unable to comply consider **referral to ED or After Hours GP Service < 2 Hours**

Figure 1.4 – Manchester triage system cards

In total, there are 84 cards like those shown in *Figure 1.4*. While these cards are written for nursing professionals, they are so clear that even an untrained person can follow the when … then format:

```
When there is Abdominal Pain … then take the medical action listed
```

You are never going to be able to replace the years of training and experience of surgical and nursing staff. But in a situation where all of those staff are busy, they have successfully shared their knowledge with you using these cards. Or they've shared enough knowledge that you can make a difference to the people who need help.

> **More on the triage system**
>
> Details of the Manchester triage system and the PDF shown in *Figure 1.4* can be found here – `http://www.gptriage.info/practice-nurse-triage-guidelines.html`. Both documents are great examples of business rules and are frequently updated and revised with best practices – but they are medical guidelines, so take care in reading them if you are slightly squeamish.

Thankfully, our particular example is unlikely to happen to you. But there is a reason why people make a considerable effort to capture their knowledge as a set of business rules:

- The intended audience for these cards is highly trained medical professionals. But as *best practices* change over time, capturing such knowledge on the cards allows everybody to review and agree on the best treatments for each situation and continuously share this knowledge.

- While we all would like to be treated by the best surgeon, during an emergency, the best support available is often from the person that gets to you first. Having these cards means that *knowledge is shared*.

- Many people will be involved in treating a patient during their time in the hospital. *Consistency* is important – not having to recheck the work of your colleagues means professionals can focus on their part of the patient's medical treatment.

Business rules in your organization

You probably have (or should have) paper-based business rules in your organization. Some examples could be safety guidelines for visitors to a construction site, a checklist before running a major event (such as a product launch), or even anti-fraud guidelines to be followed during an audit.

Where these business rules become really powerful is when we have them not only documented but also available for automated execution. This means that the rules don't just exist *on paper* – you guarantee that what is documented is also what is executed and applied. This increases the importance of getting the rules "correct," which reinforces the value of having a centralized source of rules that can be discussed and agreed upon with appropriate updates whenever best practices evolve.

Every organization will have its own rules, it's part of the reason why an organization exists. To make sure the idea is clear, here are other examples we can consider:

- When a new employee starts, then add health and safety to the required training list

- When a new employee starts, then issue them a badge

- When a badge is issued, and the employee is a new start, then send the employee an email with instructions about the new starter discount at the canteen

- When a badge is used for the first time to pay at the canteen, then give a 10% discount on this order

Typically, there can be hundreds of such business rules, but the when ... then format makes them easier to review and maintain.

Just from reading the preceding four rules, you can see how the condition of one rule firing (the then part) would trigger other rules to fire in a cascade. Note that they don't necessarily have to fire in order (the first two could be valid at the same time). You may also have spotted that the third rule has an and clause – both parts must be true for the rule to fire.

We'll cover these and many more powerful and clearer ways to write business rules in later chapters. But first, since we can only get so far running business rules on paper, there must be a better and faster way of running these rules, right?

A business rule engine you already own

It is no surprise that there is a way to automatically run these business rules. It's called a **rule engine**. What may surprise you is that you already own a (very simple) rule engine in Excel. Take a look at *Figure 1.5*, showing a feature of Excel that you may have used many times – **conditional formatting**.

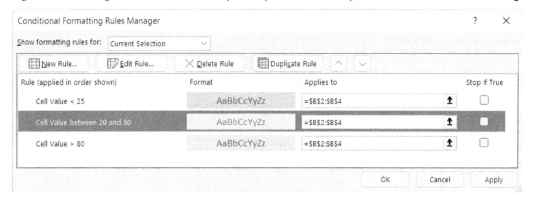

Figure 1.5 – Conditional formatting rule editor in Excel

This editor can be found in Excel under **Home** | **Conditional formatting** dropdown | **Manage Rules**.

In this particular example, we have three rules:

- When the value is greater than 80, then set the cell to green

- When the value is less than 25, then set the cell to red

- When the value is greater than 20 and the value is less than 80, then set the cell to yellow

An important note for readers paying attention – notice that the last two conditions overlap. What color will Excel choose for cells with a value of 22? *Figure 1.6* shows the result:

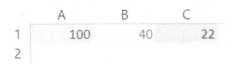

Figure 1.6 – Conditional formatting rules applied to a spreadsheet

As expected, the cell with a value of **100** is green, and the cell with a value of **40** is yellow. You may (or may not) be surprised to see the cell with the value **22** is red. How did the formatting rules decide which of the two possible rules to apply?

The answer, in this case, is **salience**. When there is a conflict between rules (that is, more than one rule can fire), the Excel conditional formatter executes the action of the first rule it finds. This is why the cell with a value of **22** is formatted in red (as that rule is higher up in the list). More powerful rule engines give much more efficient ways to resolve conflicting rules. For now, a good habit would be to keep the rules as simple as possible, trust the rule engine to sort out any conflicts, and validate results when possible.

> **Other rule engines in Microsoft Office 365**
>
> If you've become a fan of hidden rule engines within Microsoft Office, take a look at the *Inbox Rules* feature in Outlook. It also contains a rule engine to help you respond to your many emails.

Don't use Excel as a rule engine

We don't recommend using Excel as a rule engine. While the when part of the conditional formatting rule can hold some logic (users can use pretty much any formula in Excel), the then part is much more limited – it only allows setting the cell color or formatting. This results in limited interaction between the rules – the result of one rule firing cannot create or change conditions for other rules to start.

More powerful business rule engines

So far in this chapter, we have described the problems you may have encountered using Excel, and how AI and, in particular, rules-based AI might be able to help solve these problems. These ideas are not very useful without a tool to implement them, and you will be glad to know that more powerful rule engines exist.

We will not go into too much detail (yet) on these rule engines, since we'll start covering that in the next chapter. For now, we just want to prove that they exist, they are easy to use, and they follow the same when ... then format that we introduced earlier. *Figure 1.7* gives an example of one more powerful business rule engine:

RecommendedProduct *(Decision Table)*

F	Customer.Country of Residence *(string)*	DayCalc(Customer.Date of Birth) *(string)*	Customer.Number *(number)*	RecommendedProduct *(string)*	annotation-1
1	-	-	<10000	"Silk Tray"	Only first 10000 custom
2	"SA"	-	-	"Lumpy Fruit and Nut Bar"	
3	"UK"	"Friday"	-	"Crunch Bar"	
4	"US", "JN"	-	-	"Peanut Candy"	
5	-	-	-	"Milk Chocolate"	

Figure 1.7 – A guided business rule editor

Figure 1.7 shows a sample business rule written in the guided editor that we'll see in *Chapters 3* and *4*. It uses the when ... then format that we're now familiar with. The first three columns of the table are the when condition and the fourth is what action happens as soon as the condition is met.

Remember that this is a web-based editor, so it's easy to use. These rules are saved in executable format, being ready to run in a rule engine.

Even without explaining the rule in detail, it is pretty easy to figure out what would activate it and then what will happen when it does. When a person resides in a particular location, then recommend them a particular chocolate (candy) bar.

> **Where is the information stored for our rules?**
>
> If you have an Excel background, where you're used to referring to values in other cells such as =A4, you might wonder where values such as Country of Residence are coming from in the preceding example. For the moment, think of it like a named range in Excel – a convenient name to make things clearer.

As we begin to look at more powerful tools such as rule engines, it turns out there is a lot of hidden power from understanding details such as "where is the data stored" or "where is the data coming from." The best way to introduce this concept is to understand some more of the very clever things Excel does for use.

Splitting Excel into different pieces

We use Excel so much that we don't pause to think how powerful it is. While it looks like a single block, Excel can be broken down into many different components. *Figure 1.8* shows one simple way of breaking out Excel into different parts.

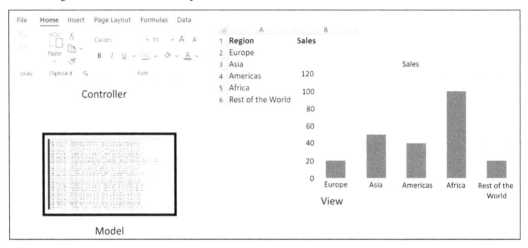

Figure 1.8 – Excel broken into simple model, view, controller pieces

This pattern is a way of breaking up Excel into more simple parts, each with one key job to do:

- You give commands to Excel using the **controller**. Typically, this means clicking on a command in the toolbar, on the menu, or elsewhere on the page, which makes Excel do *something*. This *something* usually changes the model.

- The **model** is how Excel stores its data. If you've imported CSV or other non-Excel formats before, you may have a clearer idea of this. These formats are *pure data*, without any functions or VBA code.

- Excel can present this data as one or more views. When the model updates, the view updates automatically. In this example, there are two views, both showing different representations of the same model – one showing sales by region in a table format and the other as a graph.

Since Excel is composed of *many different parts*, many being behind the scenes, we can pick and choose the parts we want to use. This book proposes replacing the *controller* with a business rule engine solution that updates the Excel model (data file). That way, instead of having to use lots of repetitive clicks to get the output we want, everything can be automated, and we can still view the output in Excel.

This is a more sophisticated version of the solution we introduced back in *Figure 1.2*. It allows us to split our data in Excel from our business rules in a separate file, which makes for a more robust solution. In *Chapter 8*, we'll see how we can combine lots of different approaches (manual Excel edits and automated business rules) in one workflow.

> **Design patterns**
>
> Some people would consider the way we have described Excel as being close to the Model View Controller design pattern. The key point is to think of Excel not as one monolithic block but composed of many different components. This book proposes swapping out and upgrading some key components while keeping the rest that are still familiar and useful to us.

Other solutions are available

You may be surprised to read this in a book about rule engines and AI, but other solutions are available. These solutions could be as follows:

- **Code-based**: For example, learning a language such as Python gives you tools to script and automate many Excel tasks. While great for repetitive tasks, be careful that you don't encounter the *knowledge disappearing into code* problem we described earlier.

- **No-code or low-code tools**: For example, Microsoft Power Automate. These allow you to chain a lot of simple steps together in a workflow. Business rule engines complement this approach really well, when you have a step that needs to make a more complex decision. We start looking at Power Automate (using it with rule engines) in *Chapter 8*.

- **Pure AI and data science**: We mentioned before that rules are only one of the many types of AI. Excel has some great statistical model features and extensions, and Python will give you even more. We recommend this approach when you don't have the answer, but you do know that the answer is hidden (somewhere) in the large amount of data that you have.

More likely than not, the best solution for you will contain all of these elements. We'll cover more of these approaches in the second half of this book. We'll give you a flavor of what tools are available and how they can combine to enhance a business rules and Excel-based approach.

> **Future proof investments**
>
> Banks were early adopters of technology, and they bought mainframe technologies when they first appeared. Their business rules were written in COBOL (an early type of programming language). The trouble is their business knowledge disappeared into code – and now several banks are stuck using the old-style mainframes. This means job security if you are a COBOL programmer, but it's tough on banks competing with new Fintech startups.

The when ... then format is much more readable. While business rule engines and rules standards will continue to evolve, in a worst-case scenario, the rules are self-documenting and can be rewritten with whatever new approach appears. Will people still understand your spreadsheets as clearly in 10 years?

Summary

In this chapter, you learned that you are not alone in your frustrations with Excel, but that it is far too important of a tool to abandon. We looked at enterprise solutions that can solve some of the problems you are facing, but often these have an overly large gap to bridge before they are useful to you. Trying to bridge this gap, we looked at the core business problems we might use Excel for and discovered that AI, and in particular a rules-based approach, might be able to help.

One good surprise is that business rules are very familiar, and we might have used them already without knowing it. We discovered that Excel is actually a much more powerful tool than we give it credit for and that we don't need to fully replace it, just upgrade certain parts – if we aren't afraid to delve under the bonnet. We also mentioned that while other solutions are available, an approach based on business rules is a good investment since it has a large element of future-proofing built in.

We promised practical solutions to Excel problems as part of this book. The next chapter begins to deliver on these as we move from the *idea* of a business rule engine to one that we can actually download and run.

2

Choosing an AI and Business Rules Engine – Why Drools and KIE?

In the previous chapter, you saw how a *rules-based AI* approach could help solve your Excel problems. However, you're not going to get very far without choosing a full *business rules engine* to execute your rules.

This chapter takes you through potential rule engine solutions available on the market and chooses one that we will use throughout the book. It also shows you why it's important to think not only about solving your immediate problem but also about how you're going to work with colleagues and scale your solution in the future. To do this, we are going to do the following:

- Understand the different types of people reading this book and find out which group you fall into

- Look at many of the available rule engines and evaluate them against our criteria

- Explain why open source provides a huge advantage for support and how it helps confirm our choice of which rule engine to use now

- Understand enterprise software better and understand where rule engines fit in the wider range of business solutions, so we know our choice is a good one for the future

- Learn how to ask for help in the open source world

- Introduce the projects to support running the rule engine samples

- Look at four different ways we can host and run our business rules

By the end of the book, you will be able to use the KIE/Drools rules engine to build more powerful solutions, extending what you can do in Excel. Since a large part of deploying these extended solutions in real life will involve working with colleagues, it is helpful to start with understanding the kind of reader you are.

Are you reading this book for personal or business reasons?

It is very likely that you'll find yourself fitting into one of the following categories:

- **Personal use or exploration**: You own the laptop that you are trying out these samples on, and your main aim is to improve your skills. While you have complete freedom to install software (a good thing), you do not have an IT helpdesk to turn to if things go wrong (not so good).

- **Business user**: As one of the first people in the organization to try AI and business rules, you're still driven by the need to improve your skills, but you may also have a business problem in mind. More likely than not, there will be restrictions on the software you can install on your laptop. On a positive note, there is an IT helpdesk to support you. While your colleagues may not understand business rules engines, they can help you work through these instructions to set one up.

- **Business user, joining an existing rules project**: You've been handed this book by the team running the business rules project to help you get up to speed. It is likely that they have much of the technical setup already completed. It is still worth reading this chapter so you know more about the technologies they have chosen.

No matter what situation you find yourself in, this book will walk you through the instructions step by step. First, we need to choose a business rules engine to install.

Which business rule engine to use

We saw in the previous chapter that rules engines can be embedded in many places that you don't expect (such as Excel and Outlook). There are hundreds of rule engine-like projects out there. So, how do we filter through these to pick one that can run the *hands-on* examples in this book? We'll do this filtering based on the following criteria:

- We need a good user interface for editing rules, aimed at business users. This rules out *Jess* and *Prolog*, which are very powerful but need a lot of technical knowledge.

- The main focus of the product should be rules. For example, we'll see other products later in the book that use workflows (for example, *Microsoft Power Automate*). These are great for doing steps in order but don't have as powerful decision-making capabilities.

- Since you're in *learning* or *trying things out* mode, you want it not only to be free to download but also free from hefty license costs in the future. We'll explain later how open source is a good fit for this, but for the moment, it rules out fully commercial vendors such as *Trisotech*, *TIBCO*, and *FICO*.

- The program must be available to be downloaded and installed by an Excel power user. This excludes *Microsoft Biztalk Server*, which is a very powerful product but needs to run on the Server version of Windows.

- If we're investing time into learning a product, we want one that has been around for a while and has an active community – increasing the chances it will last into the future. This excludes many of the smaller hobby or proof-of-concept rule engines.

- If all goes well, we might persuade colleagues to adopt the rule engine, which is easier to do if it comes from a *big-name* vendor. This rules out smaller vendors such as *Hyperon* (`Hyperon.io`), which is probably the harshest exclusion, since it is a very capable product with an active team behind it.

KIE and Drools backed primarily by Red Hat and IBM meets all of these criteria, making it our choice for running most of the book's samples. KIE and Drools gives us the following:

- **A Business Rules Management System (BRMS)**: A lot of the alternatives we discarded had a core rule engine but not much more. Since KIE and Drools gives us the core engine *and* rule authoring tools, it is much easier to write and manage our business rules.

- **An editor for Decision Model and Notation (DMN)**: An industry-standard way of modeling rules, it means that a lot of what you read in this book is applicable to other tools. KIE Sandbox, the VS Code plugin, and the Business Central web-based editor mean that you have access to more powerful diagnostic tools, over and above this standard.

- **An Apache 2.0 license (open source)**: We'll talk about open source later in this chapter. The key message is that this license gives you a wide choice of where and how to deploy your business rules without having to pay upfront.

What's in a name – KIE, Kogito, or Drools?

In this chapter, we've used the terms KIE, Drools, and Kogito almost as if they were the same project. While the three projects work very closely together, it's useful to note that there are fundamental differences:

- The original business rules community project is **Drools**. While it is possible to interact directly with Drools (and many advanced projects do so), we take the easier approach of using the tools provided by KIE. The Drools home page can be found at `https://www.drools.org/`.

- **KIE** (or **Knowledge is Everything**) is the umbrella project of which Drools is now part. For example, it provides KIE Sandbox, which we'll use to edit rules and decision models starting in *Chapter 3*. It also provides other knowledge management tools, such as integrating machine learning and rules, which we'll cover in *Chapter 11*. The KIE home page can be found at `https://www.kie.org/`.

- The **Kogito** project empowers KIE solutions with cloud capabilities. It allows Drools and the other KIE projects to be first-class citizens in cloud environments, which we'll leverage when deploying our rules in *Chapters 5* and *10*. The Kogito home page can be found at `https://kogito.kie.org/`.

As an umbrella project, KIE provides several other tools that we don't cover in this book. **OptaPlanner** is a project that leverages Drools, which could be described as a much more powerful version of the Solver tool in Excel. **jBPM** is a business process management tool (or workflow engine) that allows us to orchestrate key business steps in the right order. We'll meet jBPM again briefly in *Chapter 8*. More information on both tools is available on the KIE home page.

Finally, IBM and Red Hat have released commercial versions of most of these products. You may see the name **Red Hat Decision Manager** or **IBM Decision Manager Open Edition**. For simplicity, we won't use these corporate names, even though most of what we discuss in this book covers these products as well.

Now that we understand the KIE, Kogito, and Drools projects better, let's confirm that we've made the right choice to select them as our rule engine.

Why choose KIE and Drools as our Rule Engine?

Let's go over our criteria again and explain how KIE and Drools meet each of them:

- KIE and Drools give us several options to edit rules, in particular, a powerful but simple-to-use web-based editor aimed at business users.

- The Drools component of KIE is a very sophisticated rules engine. While it integrates into a wider toolkit, it can also be used standalone.

- KIE and Drools are available as open source technology. This means you can try it out for free, without needing to commit to paying either now or in the future.

- KIE and Drools are Java based, so will run in a variety of environments. It's also extendible, for example, to make it work easier with Excel.

- Drools (one of the core components of KIE) has been running as an extremely active open source project since 2001 and has recently delivered several key upgrades through the Kogito initiative.

- KIE and Drools is backed by Red Hat and IBM, growing through community collaboration. *Nobody ever got fired for buying IBM products* used to be a saying in the IT industry. Bringing up IBM will help if you're talking to colleagues to bring them on board with your solution.

> **I need to use another rule engine – what now?**
>
> From reading the preceding list, and even doing a Google search of the products, you will see there are many different *flavors* of rule engine, often packaged as part of a bigger enterprise solution. While we highlighted KIE as the most powerful one that is also easy to get started with, rest assured that much of what you'll learn in this book can be applied to other products.

You can understand why we're such big fans of KIE and Drools. But two of the previous points appear to contradict each other. How can KIE be supported by both a vibrant community and a major multinational corporation (that is, Red Hat and IBM)? To explain this, and why it is a good thing, we need to look at the Red Hat and IBM business model.

Open source and the Red Hat and IBM business model

Imagine you've bought a piece of land and are building your own house. In theory, this is easy. Standard plans are available on the web, including architectural drawings, lists of the materials you need, and videos on how to put it all together. For the trickier parts (plumbing and electrics), you can hire a suitably qualified person, give them instructions, and ask them to complete that piece.

You could call these instructions **open source** – you might have heard the term before. In the software world, it's where all of the necessary instructions to build products such as Kogito/Drools are freely available on the web. Even better, because the instructions can be run by a computer, with the right setup, you can push a button and everything builds itself. Easy – in the same way building a house is easy *if you know what you are doing*.

So, why do people often choose not to build their own software, or build their own house?

Sometimes you want something already built – just turn the key and it's ready to go. Sometimes you don't have the time or skills – it's nice to buy something somebody else has already made. And sometimes you need a guarantee that everything will work in the way you expect it to – where the reassurance that comes from paying a major vendor (such as Microsoft for Excel, or Red Hat and IBM) means you get more sleep at night.

This is how Red Hat makes money. It makes the plans for its software freely available on the web to increase the number of people using it. But if you need something prebuilt or with added support, you can buy a corporate-level subscription. It's a very successful approach. IBM paid about $34 billion to acquire Red Hat in 2018, and its value has increased since.

For you, deciding to use a Red Hat product such as KIE and Drools means two good things:

- You can freely download and use the software, knowing that you'll never be surprised with a bill at any point. The main websites for this approach are www.drools.org and https://kogito.kie.org/.

- If you or your colleagues need the comfort of corporate-level support, that's available for you as an optional commercial support contract. The main website for this offering is https://www.redhat.com/en/products/process-automation.

Most readers of this book will never need commercial support from IBM and Red Hat. But even so, it's good to know that it is there. So, let's focus on what benefits KIE being open source brings to you.

How KIE being open source helps you

In some ways, Excel spreadsheets (the file, not the Microsoft program) have their source open for viewing. Since most spreadsheet files aren't password protected, if you have a copy of somebody else's spreadsheet, you can often open it and learn how it works.

Within reason (for example, if you work at the same company as the creator), you can update the Excel sheet and make it even better. This is useful, for example, when the original author has left the company and the sheet is vital to keep the business running.

Open source means that you have all the details of the software design available to you, instead of just downloading the end product as a binary file that you cannot change. It means that you can modify, build, and run the software both now and in the future – even if the original vendor goes out of business.

Open source is supported by a set of tools to allow the easy sharing and building of these source files into usable software. While there are software license agreements, the focus of these is to ensure the source remains open and supported by an active community, both now and in the future.

Red Hat gives a lot more detail on the background to the open source movement, the types of licenses, and what it means for us at `https://www.redhat.com/en/topics/open-source/what-is-open-source`. The Kogito/Drools rules engine is made available under the standard, business-friendly Apache license. This license guarantees you access without requiring you to share any changes you make to it.

When you think about it, this *access to the source* is unusual for much of the software world. You don't normally get to take things apart and make them better. But having open access means you have a range of support options. If you don't like the support from the main vendor, you are free to get help elsewhere from a range of community and paid-for options.

So, for most people reading this book, the advantages of open source are as follows:

- A community of people to help you solve your problems as you try out Kogito (building a proof of concept)
- Gives you a roadmap and long-term access to the Kogito tools when you commit to using Kogito long-term in production (for example, using it in real-life business situations)

From proof of concept to production, and everything in between

When starting with Excel, we often start *playing* with it to find a solution to an immediate problem. If it works, we quickly use it in our day-to-day tasks without giving it much thought – often on the same laptop. That's a great way to respond to problems quickly, but often we find ourselves *breaking* an existing Excel sheet to introduce new features.

With enterprise software (such as KIE and Kogito) these steps are similar but much more formal. For much of this book, we're at the **proof-of-concept** stage, playing with Kogito to see whether it can help us.

In the final chapters, we discuss how to deploy a Kogito-based solution in **production** for real-life use, on a different computer, with the help of experienced colleagues. Before we get to that point, those colleagues will help us to move the solution through formal **development** and **testing** phases to ensure the project does what we need it to do.

While some contributors view open source as an end in itself, we take a more pragmatic approach in this book. Let's focus on three advantages – how open source can be more secure, how open source can give you additional support, and the specific resources that KIE/Drools make available as an open source project.

Open can be more secure

The technologies and solutions proposed in this book are secure...not because I say they are, but because you (and your colleagues) can audit where the software and solutions come from. You'll get a lot of reassurance from the following:

- The project's source code is viewable, so you can inspect the code before you run it
- The projects are often sponsored by major vendors such as IBM (Red Hat) and Docker, with a lot of documentation on how to set up a secure production environment using these technologies
- The samples run within containers, so you can limit access to other resources (less harm if things go wrong)

However, it is important to remember that *the examples in this book emphasize ease of use over security*. For example, the version of the KIE Sandbox rules editor that we will use has no username or password. This is great (as it's one less thing to stop you from running the sample), but please have a conversation with your IT colleagues when you decide to move from trying things out to using it as a day-to-day business system. A best practice to follow is setting up a fresh, secure environment for you to deploy your work into. Instructions on how to do so can be found are on the project site. See the KIE, Kogito and Drools Resources section.

Asking for help in Drools (or in any open source project)

Knowing **where** to ask for help in the open source world is easy. We'll introduce the main websites of the three projects we will use later in this chapter. Since most open source projects are hosted on a platform such as GitHub.com, once you get used to its layout, you'll find it very easy to navigate.

For the moment, think of GitHub as a more powerful version of OneDrive or SharePoint, with a community wrapped around it. *Figure 2.1* presents a screenshot of the Drools (rule engine) home page on GitHub. All projects hosted on GitHub will follow this format:

Looking under the bonnet (hood)

Whenever I buy a car (automobile), I typically open the bonnet (or hood) and look at the engine bay. I don't know why I do this – I won't be doing my own repairs. Maybe I look to reassure myself that the engine exists, it looks clean, and I can identify where to add oil and water.

Keep this in mind when you look at the following screenshot. It's good to know where our more technical colleagues will be working. But really, what we're looking for is the two or three user-friendly links that we can actually use.

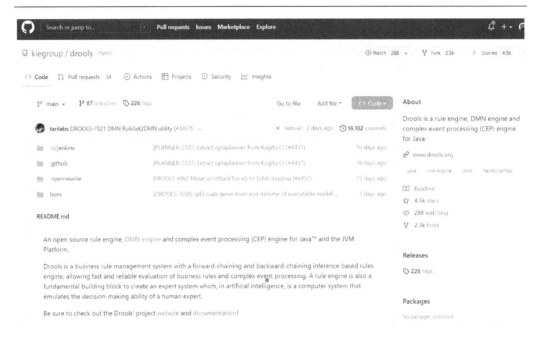

Figure 2.1 – Drools home page on GitHub

We've simplified this screenshot of `https://github.com/kiegroup/drools` as there are a lot more files and folders on the home page of GitHub (the folder icons at the middle left of the screen). These files allow you to modify and build the Drools/Kogito rule engine completely from the source if you want. We are not going to be doing this in this book, so let's look for the information on this page that we need to use:

- At the top right is an **About** section giving a one-line summary of the project. Since it describes the project as a **rule engine**, we know we're in the right place. It also links to the main project site (`drools.org`), which we'll explore in a couple of minutes, and gives mailing lists for user support.

- At the bottom left is the `readme.md` – a more detailed description of the project. It repeats the link to the website but also shares more links to the documentation for the project.

- At the top left are tools for collaboration (such as **Code** and **Branches** or **Main**). We won't be going into this in detail, but if you do want to know more about how hundreds of people across the world can use these tools to work together on a complex product, take a look at the Packt book by George Lomidze, *Git and GitHub: The Complete Git and GitHub Course*, available at `https://www.packtpub.com/product/git-and-github-the-complete-git-and-github-course-video/9781800204003`.

- On the right of the page are measures of project activity, such as people watching, stars, forks, and releases. Not surprisingly, this is a very active project – we wouldn't ask you to invest your time in anything less.

- This is not shown, but in the bottom right are the contributors to the project. At the time of writing, there are more than 200 contributors, which makes it one of the most active projects on GitHub. It's good to see there are *real people* behind the project.

We'll come back and use GitHub in more detail as a place to save our business rules in *Chapter 5*. There, we'll have the chance to get familiar with the standard GitHub page layout.

The best way to ask for help in the open source world

While it's easy to find *where* to ask for help, I don't want to leave you with the impression that these 200 contributors are just sitting there waiting for a call from you. While they are passionate about the KIE project, these are busy people, all with a day job (like you). Knowing *how* to ask for help will get you better results. In one line, a little humility and a lot of trying to solve the problem first will go a long way.

> **Try it on your colleagues**
> The following *how to ask for help* steps are equally valid when it comes to working with your colleagues on the IT helpdesk as when reaching out to the open source community.

The following are the steps to follow when you run into an issue. It is possible that you've already asked for help on Excel community forums in the past. If so, none of the following steps should appear unfamiliar to you:

1. Always assume that it is your mistake, not a problem in the underlying project you are using. Ninety percent of the time, when you work through it step by step, you'll find a spelling error, a problem with an internet connection, or some simple misunderstanding. You will lose a lot of credibility if you approach the project developers with something that turns out to be your fault and is a very simple error.

2. **Read the Fantastic Manual** (**RTFM**) is age-old advice, with the addition of **Search the Fantastic Web** (**STFW**). While the material we are working through in this book is new to us, plenty of people have tried similar things before. Take your time to read this book and the online documentation and double-check any other instructions you are working through.

3. Google any error messages. Error messages make for great search terms as they are often very specific. The search engine will suggest plenty of pages with areas worth investigating to help solve your problem.

4.   Turn it off and on again. It is only half a joke that your IT helpdesk will ask you to restart your laptop to resolve a hard-to-fix problem. A less radical approach is to close and reopen the individual pieces of software (for example, the web browser, or restarting the Docker desktop service). Modern software is complex with many moving parts that are easy to get out of sync with each other. Reopening them gives them a fresh start, and makes it more likely all the different pieces will line up correctly.

5.   Make sure you are looking in the right place for help and information. Remember that this book combines several different projects and technologies (Excel, Drools, Docker, Azure, Power Automate and OpenShift, Visual Studio, and others). Asking an Excel-specific question on a Drools mailing list is unlikely to return a response.

6.   Look for similar problems. When you are searching mailing lists and the web, be open to reading about problems that are similar but not an exact match for your current issue. Some of the steps taken to solve that other project may also help you.

7.   Two pairs of eyes are better than one. I've lost count of the number of times a colleague spotted the issue within a couple of minutes of looking at my project. This is also true where they don't have expertise in that technology – a fresh approach is sometimes enough. At the very least, having to talk through what you are doing and the Q&A that follows will unlock several suggestions that will get you nearer to a solution.

8.   Make your question standalone. Very few people will have the exact same setup as you do. The more that you can remove special setup steps when asking your question, the bigger the pool of people that will be able to help. It's even better if you can include steps to reproduce the problem (as a step 1, 2, 3 format or a code sample).

9.   Make your question smart. You're asking for help, and the community is under no obligation to respond to you. Taking the time to make your question clear and concise will increase your chances of success. A well-known guide in asking smart questions, by Eric Raymond, can be found here: `https://github.com/selfteaching/How-To-Ask-Questions-The-Smart-Way`.

10.   Check again. Before you ask the question, go through all the preceding steps and document the steps you have already taken. This will give you credibility in asking your question, and avoid the frustration of getting back suggestions that you've already attempted.

11.   Now, and only now, post your question and wait. Since you're looking for community support, you need to be prepared for a delay in receiving an answer (if at all). You may not receive a complete answer, but steps toward a solution. For some people, this is fine. But if responsive support is a must for you, it might be worth looking at the commercial support options from Red Hat and other vendors.

You'll notice that we haven't (yet) supplied you with the actual locations to ask questions. We'll share those shortly. The open source community is friendly but might have been worn down by lazy questions in the past. So with a bit of thought, your question will stand out and get answered.

When you find a solution (or part of one), share it back via the mailing lists or help forum for that community. While this is good karma, on a more practical level, it will help bolster your reputation in the community and make it more likely that you will get help in the future.

Now that you know how to ask questions, let's look at one of the places we can ask questions related to the Kogito/Drools project.

KIE, Kogito, and Drools resources

We've touched on a lot of aspects of the Kogito/Drools project already. We've seen the various components of the project, alongside the Drools rules engine. We've seen the dual nature of the open source and commercially supported projects from Red Hat and IBM. We've also seen the Drools GitHub site as a jumping-off point to learn more about the project and ask for help.

While this book will walk you through everything you need to get started with business rules, we want to give you resources to learn more, explore, and ask questions about the KIE/Drools rules engine.

Before you follow the upcoming links, remember that the documentation is written for people already familiar with business rules and the underlying technologies. It will become more accessible to you as you work your way through this book. Just don't be overwhelmed by the complexity and detail of information being shared on these sites now:

- As we saw in our previous look at the GitHub site for Drools, the main Drools site is `https://www.drools.org/`.

- The navigation bar at the top of this site contains links to the overall umbrella community (KIE). Many of these links (but not all) are relevant to the business rules engine – for example, the Kogito project home page at `https://kogito.kie.org/`.

- More information on the corporate version of this product, Red Hat Decision Manager, can be found at `https://developers.redhat.com/products/red-hat-decision-manager/overview`, which is especially useful when making the business case to colleagues for using a rules-based solution.

These three links are the most likely to stay relevant, while the following links might change over time. If any of them are broken, you should be able to search for the updated one:

- Since the starting point for readers is KIE Sandbox, the resources listed on the main KIE page are probably best to look at first: `https://kogito.kie.org/get-started/`. This lists the main guides, examples, and technical documentation for the project.

- The Kogito documentation is updated with every release and goes into more detail about the features we highlight in this book. It's available online at `https://docs.kogito.kie.org/latest/html_single/`.

- Remember that underneath, Kogito uses the Drools rules engine to power the decision services. There is a lot of rule engine documentation on the site at `https://www.drools.org/learn/documentation.html`. Over time, this documentation is becoming more business user friendly, but some of it may be more suitable for technical developers.

- There are a lot of useful videos on the site at `https://www.drools.org/learn/video.html`, as well as videos hosted on the KIE YouTube channel at `https://www.youtube.com/channel/UCUjeymTM-TrwHs36388VRbw`.

- We talked earlier about how to interact with and ask questions on open source project mailing lists. The main Drools lists are `https://groups.google.com/g/drools-setup` and `https://groups.google.com/g/drools-usage`. There is a more technical-focused Kogito mailing list at `https://groups.google.com/g/kogito-development/c/18JqnqyITQA`.

- Other good sources of help are listed on the Drools site at `https://www.drools.org/community/getHelp.html`. One key external support site is Drools on Stack Overflow, with good instructions on how to interact with people via the site: `https://stackoverflow.com/questions/tagged/drools`.

- You're unlikely to use it at this point, but as well as the source code hosted on GitHub, instructions on how to build the project from the source can be found at `https://www.drools.org/code/sourceCode.html`. Likewise, the project developers have a live chat channel (similar to Teams/Slack), which can be found at `https://kie.zulipchat.com/`. While it's good to know where they are, most readers will not interact directly with them. Instead, let's remind ourselves that IBM and Red Hat sponsors the project and offers support options at `https://www.drools.org/product/services.html`.

Some of the resources we've just highlighted will only make sense as you explore future chapters. Come back to this section on a regular basis as you work through this book; you'll get more out of it each time. There are also a huge number of other tutorials on the web, written for various levels of technical ability, which are worth exploring as you move through the chapters.

Contributing back to the community

Even if you are not a developer, you can contribute back to the open source community. This could be as simple as posting the answer (once you find it) to a question that you may have previously put on a mailing list. Or it could involve filing a bug report (if requested by the team), or writing and updating the documentation.

As an Excel power user, your skills and time are valuable. All it takes is a willingness to learn how the project works and find an area that needs your help. The diversity of skill sets is what makes open source projects work.

Now that we understand more about Kogito as open source enterprise software, let's take a look at the kind of solutions that it helps us build.

How to design and build enterprise solutions

You saw in the previous chapter that in solving your problems with Excel, you were taking steps toward more robust enterprise-type solutions. We explained that unlike Excel, enterprise solutions are built by many people, but can also be used by many people at one time.

As you evaluate whether KIE/Drools can solve your immediate problems with Excel, you need to know that it will continue to solve your problems in the long term. That's why we're including this section – just enough about designing and building enterprise solutions. It should assure you that you have a roadmap to deploy and support Kogito as part of a bigger system over the longer term.

Already in this book, you have seen hints that the enterprise software world is similar but also very different from the Excel world:

- In the previous chapter, we broke Excel down into three parts (model/data, as well as view and controller). Whatever enterprise system we build using Kogito, will need to have all three parts.

- In this chapter, we mentioned that unlike the more casual approach in Excel, enterprise systems move through a life cycle of proof of concept, develop, build, test, and production. There will be formal processes and a team to move between each.

Let's look at those key parts in more detail, so you understand how Kogito/Drools fits into the bigger picture. Let's start with the team you will be working with.

Working with a team

At the start of this chapter, we asked about your current situation – whether you're working in a corporate environment (with or without official support) or you are at an earlier stage of personal learning, but still likely to apply those skills in a business environment.

Whatever your situation, you've probably noticed that instead of working on a single file, supported by one person, we're gradually moving to a system that is supported by an entire team. It's worth taking a while to examine the different roles in this team to help you work better with them:

- **Business knowledge expert**: That's you. You understand how the business runs (or wants to run) so the team can translate the process into the appropriate technology.

- **Software architect**: Sketches out the design of the software solution and makes key decisions on the tools and technologies to use.

- **UX or user interface specialist**: Responsible for designing all elements of the system that interact with the user, to make it as easy to use as possible.

- **Developers**: Write the complex part of the system in languages such as Java, C#, and Python.

- **Testers**: Try to break the system once it is nearly complete. While other team members may not fully appreciate this, they will be secretly glad since the earlier a problem or bug is found, the easier and quicker it is to fix.

- **Project managers**: Responsible for the entire team delivering the entire system on time, on spec, and on budget.

- **System or cloud administrators**: Responsible for the infrastructure to run the system in the development, test, and production phases. Often, they will be the first to flag issues that happen when the system is running *in real life*.

It is possible for several of these roles to be combined into smaller projects. Alternatively, larger organizations may have teams that split these roles. Either way, your role as a business knowledge expert is crucial to the entire team and a good business expert is invaluable to delivering a system that allows the organization to run effectively.

What software architects do

Just like architects design houses, enterprise software architects design enterprise software. Both are great jobs, with many highly skilled and very opinionated individuals. Some software architects may be upset by the one-size-fits-all enterprise solution I have presented in the following diagram.

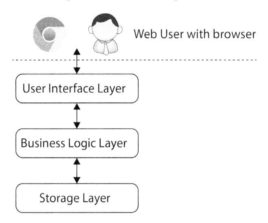

Figure 2.2 – One-size-fits-all enterprise software diagram

Figure 2.2 is simple but shows what most systems do: take information from a user, process it in some way, then store it somewhere. Splitting the design into three layers like this makes it easier to understand what each layer does:

- The **user interface layer** communicates to and from a *real* person. Normally, this is a web page. But if we wanted to change to a voice interface (such as Amazon Alexa) or a 3D avatar, we would only have to change this layer.

- The **business logic layer** is where we do something with the user information. It might use the dates selected to suggest flights, update your bank balance, or carry out any other process you need to run the business.

- Unless you want to forget everything within a couple of seconds, your enterprise software needs a **storage layer**. Traditionally, these were databases such as Oracle or Microsoft SQL Server (think of a much more robust and bigger version of Excel). More recent technology is optimized for the cloud and can handle hundreds of millions of users. The point is we don't care too much about the technology, just as long it stores and retrieves the information when we need it.

In general, each layer does one thing and one thing only. While this diagram suggests that everything runs on one computer, it doesn't have to. Each layer could be in its own container (more about those soon) hosted in a different data center in a different country.

Not surprisingly, we're mostly concerned with the business logic layer in this book, as that is where the Drools rules engine will be deployed. But when we introduce our examples, we will need to provide you with a user interface and a storage layer to get you started.

No doubt you are reassured by having a long-term roadmap for deploying your business rules. But it is worth reminding ourselves that many software architects have only dealt with systems where the business logic layer is coded in languages such as Python, C#, and Java. Remember the problem of *business rules disappearing into code* that we discussed in the previous chapter? That's exactly the same problem.

If you need to convince your software architect colleague to use a business rule engine in the business logic layer, talk them through the following points:

- **Separation of layers**: Tools and frameworks exist for storing data and creating user interfaces. Rules engines give a similar framework for the business layer. It makes it less likely that code will leak across the different layers. This is a key topic for enterprise architects, who try to design systems where each component does one thing and does it well.

- **Knowledge management**: Business rules, in other words, knowledge, are the core of any big enterprise software. In the approach proposed by this book, rules can be written by business users, and this same rule file can be managed and executed, avoiding errors from miscommunication. Rule engines can be the natural home to manage all of the knowledge essential to your business. You'll be able to code business rules that say *what to do*, not *how to do it*, in a human-readable format.

- **Versioning and authoring**: The tools that come with Kogito/Drools allow business knowledge to be tested and deployed on a separate timeline to code deployment. For example, in an online home loan application, the lending rules could be updated independently of changes to the website. This allows the business to react quickly to a changing environment without the risk of introducing new bugs.

- **Speed and scalability**: When deploying in the cloud, time (and computing resources needed) is money. The way rule engines work is mathematically more efficient than human-written code since they are based on the PHREAK algorithm (an evolution of Rete) for DRL-based rules and efficient algorithms in the DMN engine, for fast and effective decision-making.

- **Auditing**: Unlike other types of AI, rule systems are designed to explain how and why a particular decision was made. While this is also possible with handwritten code, in practice, it's quite difficult as you often need to examine log files line by line for the same information

We've spent a couple of pages thinking long term to confirm that our choice of the KIE/Drools rules engine is worth investing our time to learn. We have confirmed that it can solve problems for us now and give us a scalable path to continue using it in the future.

But we have a more immediate problem. We're at the *proof-of-concept* stage and we don't yet have a full team of people to help us to build one. We need to introduce supporting projects to fill this gap so you can easily run the book samples.

Containers supporting Kogito, KIE, and Drools

This book focuses on rule engines. But it is also a key aim of the book to help you on the journey from using Excel-based solutions (running on your desktop) to more powerful enterprise solutions that can be used by many people at once. Containers make this journey easier, so let's take a quick look at what the technology is and how we will use it.

> **Do I really need to learn about containers?**
>
> The quick answer is no. This is a book about Excel and the Kogito/Drools rule engine, and you'll get value in your day-to-day work even if you just focus on those areas.
>
> But a likely outcome is that other people will be interested in what you have done and will want to contribute to and/or run your business rules. Container technologies help you collaborate and deploy your rules more effectively.

In some ways, you've already used something similar to containers when you've used Excel. For most spreadsheets, you can just share them with somebody else – and know that they work, regardless of the particular setup they have on their laptop. This is also (mostly) true even if they are using another type of spreadsheet – for example, OpenOffice or Google Sheets. All the complexity of the software is hidden by Excel acting as a container for you – it just works. Your colleague can view the spreadsheet just as you made it.

With Kogito, KIE, and Drools, we're using much more complex software once we progress beyond the first examples with the online sandbox (in the first half of this book). So, I have a challenge as an author – how do I get this software into your hands in an easy-to-use way? Let's work through the options step by step:

- The easiest option for you would be for me to personally install the software on your laptop. But since there is only one of me and thousands of readers, that is not really a realistic solution.

- The next approach would be to give you a detailed set of instructions to follow. You're an Excel power user and would have a reasonable chance of getting it right – if everything goes smoothly.

But what if something goes wrong in more than one of the 20 steps that this would take? Every single computer setup is different, and there is no way of giving simple instructions to cover all possibilities.

- The final option is to pull together a package of tools needed to run the samples in the book – let's call it an **image**. We could then give you this image to drop into a preprepared space on your laptop (let's call it a **container**). If the container was more than just a place to store files, but could somehow guarantee that the image would run exactly the same way on all machines, that would be an ideal solution. This is what **Docker** and other containerization technology give you.

Containers take their name from the shipping containers you see on the backs of trucks, trains, and cargo ships. They have a similar purpose of moving software around. So long as everything fits in the container, everything works – the same crane can load and unload containers from a ship, no matter what is inside of it.

Containers are a big deal

It's hard to underestimate how much of a big deal the containerization of software is.

For example, in a previous version of a similar book, the technology to run the samples took 2-3 hours to install if everything went correctly. But despite it being aimed at a more technical audience, things could go wrong – in part because everybody's laptop has a different setup.

Under the covers, the container approach enables us to use the KIE Sandbox software that we'll use to write our first rules in the next chapter and allows us to start writing rules in 2-3 minutes.

We'll return to containers in more detail in later chapters, since we want to give you a smooth path from running and editing rules locally to deploying your rules in a robust, scalable production environment.

Containers are now widely used. So, while we've chosen Docker (as it has the most user-friendly desktop tools), there are alternative tools listed at `https://opencontainers.org/`, including *Podman*. As you'll see in *Chapter 10*, we can also run the same containers in the cloud with Microsoft Azure, Red Hat, Amazon, and Google. We'll see more about Docker as we install it and use it to run samples in later chapters.

Before we end the topic, it's also worth underlining the security advantages of containers – especially if you need to ask permission from colleagues to install Docker. Containers (as their name suggests) are fully isolated from the computer running them. Even though you might feel you can trust me as an author (after all, we're well into the second chapter of the book), and you can inspect both the contents and the source code running in it, Docker will still isolate the code in its own container, giving you another layer of security.

> **Windows, Mac, and Linux**
>
> Because we're using Docker and containers, all the samples used in this book will run on recent versions of Windows, Mac, and Linux (so long as your machine meets the Docker hardware specs). Our detailed instructions for installing Docker will focus on Windows, but alternative instructions are freely available on the web for Linux and Mac machines.

Now that we've met the supporting technologies, let's look at the choices they give you to run these book samples.

Four different ways to work with business rules

Now that we know about containers, let's look at the four main ways we will use them to run business rules as we work through this book. Remember that unlike Excel, the choice of tool to edit rules is separate from the choice of engine to run the rules. We present the four main choices here in a way that keeps things simple, but you still have the option to pick and choose between them.

These options start with the simplest and work up to the more powerful. This is in line with our journey from Excel to enterprise-grade solutions. In all four suggestions, we continue to use Excel from our laptop and call the business rule engine no matter where it is located:

1. **Editing in KIE Sandbox online, using KIE extended services on your laptop as the engine**: This is the solution we start with as it is the easiest to use. It hides a lot of the complexity, which is great for getting started, but works best for single users.

2. **Editing in KIE Sandbox online, running our rules in the cloud using OpenShift**: We'll introduce this approach in *Chapter 5*, taking advantage of the integration between KIE and OpenShift. *Appendix B* gives a variation on this – where we use codespaces (hosted in the Azure cloud) to do something similar but using VS Code as the editor.

3. **Hosting both the editor and the engine in containers on your laptop or another computer that you have access to**: Once you have Docker installed, getting the Kogito container image running in it is easy. We cover it as a stepping stone toward deploying your rules in the cloud using a provider other than Red Hat (e.g., Microsoft, Amazon, or Google). Containers may also be the preferred way for your IT department to deploy the KIE tools and the Drools rules engine on-premises in your organization (keeping all your knowledge in-house). We cover this approach in *Chapter 10*.

4. **The final method is to set up the technology stack yourself**: This is relatively straightforward if you have the technical knowledge (or know a colleague that does). We won't go into detail, although some hints are given in *Appendix B*. Full instructions are available at the KIE and Drools links we shared earlier. This gives you full control of how you deploy your business rules.

Four different ways to run the book's samples might appear a lot, but every reader's computer is different, and there are billions of combinations of hardware, software, and configuration that make it impossible to test them all.

For example, some organizations may block you from downloading and running an `.exe` file (which is needed for the first option, using KIE Sandbox). In this case, users may skip ahead and use the cloud approach to run the samples. By giving four alternative options, we make it much more likely that every reader will be able to run the samples.

Some self-assembly required

IKEA furniture is renowned for its design, but also that it comes flat-packed with some self-assembly required. Often, I don't manage to get it right the first time, but I'm willing to try again and ask for help if needed.

KIE, like other enterprise software, is similar. You need to follow the instructions to get it up and running. While these steps aren't difficult, this will feel very different from the Excel world (where it came prebuilt for you). If self-assembly isn't for you, that's OK; you should be able to get to the end of *Chapter 9* without too much difficulty. At that point, hopefully, we will have convinced you that the power of business rules makes the effort worthwhile.

Summary

In this chapter, we learned more about you as a reader and the amount of support that might be available to you from your colleagues as you work your way through this book.

We looked at the different business rules engines available and why we recommend Kogito/Drools to work through in this book and saw a glimpse of some other interesting projects from Red Hat. Since open source is a key part of this decision, we looked at the support available from the community and saw resources where we can learn a lot more about the technology.

As we will be investing significant time in the KIE project, we provided reassurance of the long-term benefits to you and your team in deploying it as part of a wider software solution. This included understanding how enterprise solutions are both more powerful and more complex than Excel, the team of people that work on them, and how KIE and Drools fit into this overall enterprise solution.

Finally, since not everybody will have this team around them as they read this book, we looked at containers as a supporting technology. That allows us as Excel power users to quickly get up and running, while still giving us a roadmap so that we can deploy what we are learning in a real-life business environment.

The first two chapters introduced the problem with Excel, and how business rules might solve them. So, you'll be glad to hear that in the next chapter, we get to write our first business rule.

3

Your First Business Rule with the Online KIE Sandbox

In the first two chapters of this book, we looked at the problems that you often face when working with Excel, and how AI tools such as rule engines (in particular, KIE and Drools) can help solve them. But this is a practical book, so it's about time we got hands-on and showed you how to write rules using the online KIE tools.

In this chapter, we'll write our first business rule – a variation on the classic `Hello World`. We'll use the KIE Sandbox Extended Services to allow us to run the rules we write in the online editor. We'll introduce Decision Models as a visual format for capturing decisions and business rules and begin to expand our first rule so we can glimpse the power of the rules-based approach. Finally, we'll explore other elements of the KIE Sandbox user interface, so we'll have a good foundation for the more sophisticated rules we'll write later on.

The following are the concepts we will cover in this chapter:

- Writing our first business rule online
- Running and validating our rules in the KIE Sandbox Extended Services
- A more in-depth look at decision models
- A tour of the KIE Sandbox user interface
- Working to improve the Decision Model for our Greetings example
- Other interface elements in the KIE Sandbox

The KIE community collaborators and leads on the Red Hat and IBM teams have put a lot of effort into the tools to make them easy to use. So, let's get started by using the freely available online version of the KIE sandbox that they have set up to help us get started.

Writing our first business rule

Now that we are ready to write our first business rule, getting started is as simple as opening your browser. Most modern browsers will do – Chrome, Safari, or Edge. At the time of writing, the current version of Firefox is missing a feature to run the KIE Sandbox, but this is likely to be resolved soon. In your browser, go to `http://dmn.new` (mirrored at `https://sandbox.kie.org`). You should see a page similar to the one shown in *Figure 3.1*:

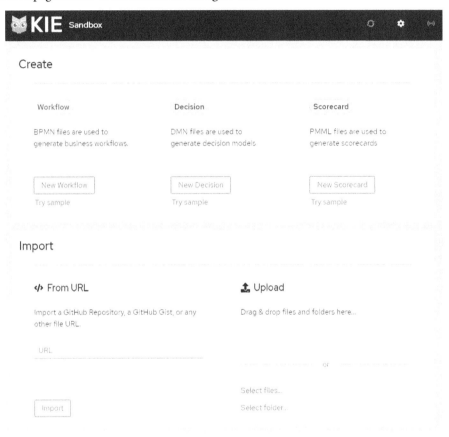

Figure 3.1 – KIE Sandbox home screen

A lot of time is being invested in evolving the KIE editors, so there may be some differences between this screenshot and what you see on your laptop. However, there's no need to worry since the decision editors are based on the DMN standard (more on that soon), so any differences will very likely be cosmetic.

On the KIE Sandbox home page, there are three options:

- We'll touch on workflows in *Chapter 8, AI and Decision Services within Excel and Power Automate Workflows*

- Scorecards are related to PMML and machine learning, a topic we will cover in *Chapter 11*
- Right now, we're interested in decisions/rules

Click on **New Decision** (shown in *Figure 3.1*) and the KIE decision editor, similar to *Figure 3.2*, will appear:

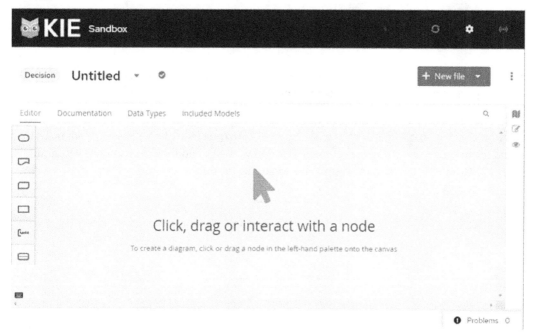

Figure 3.2 – KIE decision editor in the KIE Sandbox

We know we're in the right place, as it says **Decision** underneath the KIE logo in the top-left corner. There's a lot to see on this screen. We'll introduce the various elements in this **user interface** (**UI**) as we work through the Hello World sample in the next couple of pages.

> **Take the tour**
>
> You may see a pop-up menu in which KIE offers to take you through a 5-minute introduction tour. It's worth spending a couple of minutes playing with that tour as another way of getting used to the screen. Clicking **Skip Tour** will take you back to the main KIE decision editor.

KIE Sandbox uses responsive web design to provide the best possible screen layout. It does mean that if your browser isn't full-screen (like in the previous screenshot), you won't see all the available options. Maximize the windows and you will see the additional options that will be useful later – these are highlighted in *Figure 3.3*:

Figure 3.3 – KIE Decision editor with full menu options

Since we have an empty canvas (the main white area on the screen in *Figure 3.2*), there should be a message saying **Click, drag or interact with a node**, so let's do that to get started.

Take a look again at *Figure 3.2*. On the left-hand side, you'll see a series of different shapes. If you move your cursor over them, you'll get a description of what each one is (we'll go through them in this and the next chapter). Drag the rectangle (DMN Decision), and then the rectangle with round corners (DMN InputData) onto the canvas so it looks like the following figure:

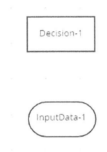

Figure 3.4 – Data and decision nodes

Don't worry if the positions don't exactly line up, but getting a layout similar to *Figure 3.4* will help you follow the next steps. Let's go through what each of those shapes (nodes) is:

- **InputData**: We need some way to map this decision model and tell KIE Sandbox what information we'll be passing as inputs. This node, when we have edited it slightly, allows us to do that.

- **Decision**: The entire point of using a decision tool such as KIE Sandbox is to design and run business rules in an automated manner. As well as describing the details of how the decision is made, Decision nodes also specify the names and types of input. Since Decision nodes also specify the type and name of output data, they can also function as **Output Data** nodes, returning information to the user.

This model looks pretty but isn't very descriptive. Double-clicking on each shape will allow you to edit its name. Since DMN is designed for business users, you can call them pretty much anything you like (there are fewer restrictions in naming than in Excel), but for this example, it's easier if you use `greeting` as the Decision node name, and `name` for the InputData node, as in *Figure 3.5*:

Figure 3.5 – Named nodes

Great – it is now much clearer that we're expecting a name to be passed in (the rounded box), and we'll make a decision on which greeting to reply with (the rectangular box).

While it's obvious in this simple diagram, we still need to tell KIE explicitly which data is used in the decision. We can do this by drawing an arrow from the `name` (InputData) node to the `greeting` (Decision) node.

Start by clicking on the `name` node so additional icons appear around it, as in *Figure 3.6*:

Figure 3.6 – Editing a node

We'll come back to the other icons later, but for now, click on the arrow button (**Create DMN information requirement**). This allows you to draw an arrow from the data to the `greeting` node. The direction of the arrow is important, so make sure your diagram looks like *Figure 3.7*:

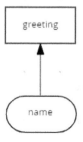

Figure 3.7 – Connecting the nodes

Based on what we can see in the diagram, KIE now knows we want to feed a name into the greeting decision. But we still haven't told KIE how it's going to make its decision – let's fix that now. Click on the rectangular box greeting node, as shown in *Figure 3.8*:

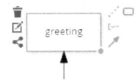

Figure 3.8 – Editing node properties

Then, from the icons that appear, click on the *Edit* icon (the square with the pencil, on the middle left). The screen will change to something like the screenshot in *Figure 3.9*:

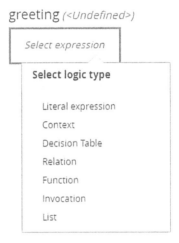

Figure 3.9 – Editing the Decision node type

You may need to click on the **Select expression** box to view this drop-down menu to display the different logic types available. Select **Literal expression**.

A quirk of the editor

Be careful – in the current version of KIE Sandbox, there is no way to change the logic type once you have chosen it.

If you do choose the wrong type of expression, you'll need to go back to the main decision diagram, delete the entire greeting node, and then create an entirely new one (including renaming the node and connecting the InputData node to it).

We'll run through the different logic types later but think of this as being similar to a function you'd type into Excel. You should see the **Literal expression** editor as shown in *Figure 3.10*:

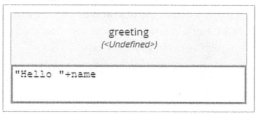

greeting *(Literal expression)*

greeting
(*<Undefined>*)

`"Hello "+name`

Figure 3.10 – Expression added to decision node

In *Figure 3.10*, we've already entered the formula into the box – we've used the `"Hello "+name` function.

Like in Excel, when typing the expression, be careful to get the spelling right, pay attention to the double quotes, and make sure the name matches what we called our InputData node. There should be a pop-up suggestion in the boxed editor to guide you as you type.

> **Boxed expressions and FEEL**
>
> Typing a formula into a box like this should feel familiar – it's very Excel-like. Not surprisingly, they are called **boxed expressions**. The language that boxed expressions use is called **Friendly Enough Expression Language** (**FEEL**) – a standard originally from Oracle. You'll see in the next chapters that it is very powerful. But for the sake of this example, just understand that it is similar to, but not exactly the same as, Excel functions.

When you've finished editing, click on the **Back to Untitled** link to return to the main decision diagram. While you've edited the decision criteria (and the expression has been saved), the diagram will still look like *Figure 3.7* earlier. Don't worry, you can click on the node, then edit again; you will see the expression has been successfully saved.

Having a graphical editor is great, as it is so easy to understand the diagram. However, one downside is that following graphical instructions can be tricky – especially as getting one step wrong can lead to you getting very different results.

For that reason, the Decision Model samples in this (and all the chapters) can be found on the book's GitHub page (`https://github.com/PacktPublishing/Business-Rule-Engines-and-AI-for-Excel-Power-Users`). The *Uploading decision models from other sources* section later in this chapter shows how to load these samples into your local sandbox (hint – it's pretty easy!).

We have successfully designed our first `Hello World` rule in the web editor. But to run it, we have one program we need to download first.

KIE Sandbox Extended Services

Excel is very convenient – it bundles the application to edit and execute your formulas into one package. Most enterprise software (including KIE/Drools) split these into separate steps – you edit the rules in one tool, and then make a conscious decision to execute them, often using a separate software package. While a bit more work, it does mean that you don't accidentally *break* something when editing, which makes your rules solution more robust.

So far in this chapter, we've been using the online KIE editor. But we need a way to execute our decisions and rules. For that, we need KIE Sandbox Extended Services.

Browsers have come a long way in the last 20 years – to the point that it's easy to forget that the KIE Sandbox editor isn't a native desktop app. While tools such as WebAssembly have the potential to make the experience smoother in the future, it is difficult to make a complex, enterprise-grade piece of software such as KIE or Drools run completely in the browser. Or at least make it run in the browser so that it behaves *exactly* as it would when deployed by your enterprise IT team. This is important, as you don't want any surprises with rules behaving differently at that point.

Thankfully, the KIE team has a very good solution – they have taken the essentials of the rules engine and packaged them so they can easily be downloaded and run. This means we can get instant feedback as we edit our rules, and know that the rules will run in the same way when we deploy our full solution later. This packaged version is called **KIE Sandbox Extended Services**, and we'll download it in the next section.

> **It pays to be cautious – but you may need to ask for permission**
>
> One word of warning – while no installation is needed, on Windows, the extended services are packaged as a `.exe` file. While we trust where this file is coming from (see the *Open can be more secure* section in *Chapter 2, Choosing an AI and Business Rules Engine – Why Drools and KIE?*
>
>), Windows is a lot more cautious, since `.exe` files are very powerful and could cause damage in the wrong hands. This applies to most software, and not just the tools from KIE.

From experience, most issues that you will encounter with the next section will be because downloading or running `.exe` files has been blocked for security reasons by your IT department. There are alternatives, such as deploying into the cloud (which we will cover in *Chapter 5*, and again in *Chapter 10*). But the edit-rule, test-rule cycle enabled by KIE Extended Services is so productive, it is well worth asking for permissions to run it.

Let's walk through the steps to download, answer some simple security questions, start the extended services, and then connect to KIE Sandbox.

Downloading and running KIE Extended Services

KIE Sandbox Extended Services is packaged to make it as easy to use as possible.

At the top right of the KIE Sandbox web page, you should see a message similar to *Figure 3.11*. You may need to maximize the KIE Sandbox window in order to fully see it.

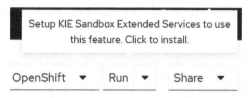

Figure 3.11 – Reminder to install Extended Services

This warning message only appears if you don't have KIE Extended Services installed. Thankfully, **Click to install** is the first step in fixing it. After seeing a screen explaining what Extended Services are (click on **Setup** to move to the next step), you should see a panel similar to *Figure 3.12*:

Figure 3.12 – KIE Sandbox Extended Services download screen

This is the KIE Sandbox Extended Services setup screen, which allows you to select the appropriate package to download. Select your operating system, then click on **Download** to get the file you need.

> **Want a direct link to download?**
>
> The download URL in KIE Sandbox links to `https://github.com/kiegroup/kie-tools/releases` – normally, you take the most recent version, although you have the option to choose the earlier one. The source code for building the Extended Services tools is also on this site, should you or your IT colleagues wish to audit it for security reasons.

When the file has been fully downloaded, go to where you saved it, then double-click to open and run it. Again, it's worth remembering that some IT departments may block you from doing this. If this happens, you'll see an error message, and you will need to get in touch to request that they remove any blocks.

Even if you have permission to run it, Windows will double-check that you know what you are doing. On Windows 11, you will see a screen like in *Figure 3.13*; other versions of Windows will have something similar:

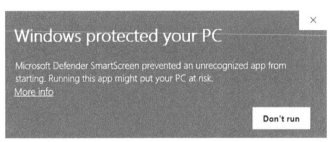

Figure 3.13 – Windows 11 EXE warning screen

If you get a warning screen like this one, click on **More info**. You should have the option to run anyway.

You may also get a warning from Windows Defender (or similar antivirus software), as shown in *Figure 3.14*:

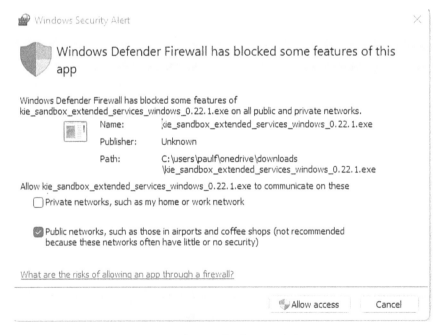

Figure 3.14 – Windows Defender permission screen

KIE Sandbox Extended Services is, in effect, a mini web server (so that the online editor can communicate with it), so it needs to communicate over the network. This is okay, so you can confirm this with Windows Defender by clicking on the **Allow access** button.

Thankfully, these security checks need only need to be done once. If you see two screens like *Figures 3.15* and *3.16*, everything is working okay.

Figure 3.15 – Confirmation in the editor

Figure 3.15 shows the confirmation message in the KIE Sandbox editor that everything is running okay.

```
C:\Users\paulf\OneDrive\Dow   X   +  ˅                                                      —   □   ×
Server started: 0.0.0.0:21345
msg: __ ___ __ _____  ___ ____ _____
msg: --/ _ \/ / / / _ \ / _ \/ //_/ / / / _/
msg: -/ /_/ / / / / _ \/ _  _/ ,< / / / /\ \
msg: --_____/ |_/_/_/|_\____/___/
msg: 2022-08-26 18:12:07,099 INFO  [io.quarkus] (main) jitexecutor-runner 1.12.0.Final native (powered by Quarkus 2.3.0.
Final) started in 0.105s. Listening on: http://0.0.0.0:55999
msg: 2022-08-26 18:12:07,099 INFO  [io.quarkus] (main) Profile prod activated.
msg: 2022-08-26 18:12:07,099 INFO  [io.quarkus] (main) Installed features: [cdi, hibernate-validator, resteasy, resteasy
-jackson, smallrye-context-propagation, smallrye-health, smallrye-openapi, vertx]
200 -> 200 OK
```

Figure 3.16 – Extended Services running

Figure 3.16 shows the console window that opens in the background. Two key messages are `Server started` at the beginning and `200 -> 200 OK` at the end, which show that the necessary service has started.

Troubleshooting KIE Sandbox Extended Services

I'll repeat it – by far the most likely cause of problems is security restrictions by your IT department. If you are having issues with installation, try the download process again (paying attention to any warning messages), and contact your colleagues to get the necessary permissions to run.

If this isn't the case, take a look at the *How to ask for help* section in the previous chapter. It's also worth trying the following additional steps:

- Look in the console window (*Figure 3.16*) for any helpful error messages.
- Reboot your laptop (obviously, this also restarts your browser). After every reboot, you need to find the KIE Sandbox Extended Services file, and double-click on it to start it manually. It does not run automatically by default.

- Open a web browser and point to the page `http://localhost:21345/ping` – this communicates directly with the KIE Sandbox service. If everything is running okay, you should see a message:

```
{"App":{"Version":"0.22.0"},"Proxy":{"IP":"0.0.0.0",
"Port":21345,"InsecureSkipVerify":false},
"Modeler":{"Link":"https://kiegroup.github.io/kogito-
online/#/"}}
```

For most of you, things will run smoothly – so we can get on with running our first rule!

Running our first rule

Now that we have Extended Services running, the KIE Sandbox web page will communicate automatically with it in the background. Clicking on **Run** at the top right of the Decision Editor should now make the panel appear as shown in *Figure 3.17*:

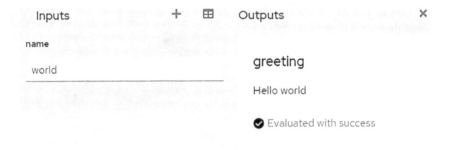

Figure 3.17 – KIE Extended Services input and output

In this screenshot, we have already populated our input values (we have put `world` in the **name** field). Every time we make a change, our decision/rules run (extremely fast) and we get our response back: **Hello world**.

Congratulations! You have just successfully drawn your first business rule, as part of a decision diagram. And you have successfully executed that model, using the KIE/Drools rule engine (packaged as part of KIE Sandbox Extended Services).

What is happening behind the scenes – KIE Sandbox and Services

It's not strictly necessary to understand the chain of events that happened when you updated the value of the **name** field. But in future chapters, we will be calling rule engines from Excel, so being curious about what is going on is a good thing.

So, what is happening between the browser and your newly installed KIE Extended Services as you enter values on the KIE Sandbox page?

1. When you edit a value in the input field, an event is triggered in the browser.

2. The KIE Sandbox web page (using standard JavaScript) translates the input values into a format known as **Javascript Object Notation (JSON)**. It also includes a copy of the Decision Model (in XML format) that needs to be executed. More on both of these formats later in the book.

3. The KIE Sandbox web page calls the extended service, passing the values to it. This process is similar to opening a web page in the browser.

4. The extended service (powered by KIE/Drools) compiles the Decision Model into a format it can work with. The KIE/Drools engine then executes the diagram, passing the input information (name) to it.

5. The result is passed back to the KIE Sandbox web page and processed so that the results can be displayed.

If you're curious about seeing these steps in action, the developer tools in your browser will allow you to peek behind the scenes in more detail. We don't need to do this, since KIE handles all the details for us.

Some of you may be keen to jump in and call this process from Excel, so take a look at *Chapter 6*, where we start linking Excel with the KIE/Drools rule engine. But for now, KIE Sandbox gives us a powerful environment to edit and run our decision models.

If we are going to be editing more decision models to write our rules, it's worth looking at them in more detail.

More on Decision Models

Since we jumped into our example and focused on getting a working business rule, we only got a hint of what Decision models are. Officially called **DMN**, the three key benefits are as follows:

- **Decision models are accessible to business users**. You could share the `Hello World` example with a colleague and have them understand what is going on – without any technical training.

- **Decision models are executable**. Unlike other diagrams, there is no need for a technical colleague to translate them into executable code. We might take this for granted in Excel, but it's a radical idea. In other solutions, the diagram and the code often drift apart, so we can never be totally sure of the business decision-making process. Since Decision Models are executable, we don't have that problem – what is in the diagram is how the decision gets made.

- **Decision models are an agreed standard**. You've probably already scrawled similar diagrams on a whiteboard in your office, but by writing them in the agreed **Object Management Group (OMG)** format, you know that there is a range of vendor tools (not just KIE/Drools) that can execute them. This guarantees your business models are usable in the longer term, and the time you spend learning the notation will prove worthwhile. More information on the OMG format is available at `https://www.omg.org/dmn/`.

Decision Models are graphical and easy to understand, but there are a few common misconceptions to highlight as you look at Decision Models for the first time.

Decision Models aren't workflows

Despite the arrows on a Decision model, they are not a workflow.

If you're a business analyst, you may be familiar with workflows or process flows. These flows are a set of steps that happen over time and are often paused when waiting for human or external input. An example of a workflow might be a health insurance claim, which might be on hold for days (or weeks) while the doctor sends a medical report. Once the report has been received, execution of the workflow picks up at the next step and the payment might be made.

By contrast, decision models happen all at once – like our previous example, this can be very fast. Our aim is to apply all the business rules we can, making a decision based on the information we have available.

However, Decision Models and workflows *can* work well together.

Decision Models are often employed to make key judgments at particular steps in a workflow. For example, in a health insurance workflow, there may be a key step where we decide to pay the medical claim, using information that has been submitted. This is often a yes or no decision, and the workflow will branch depending on the answer from our Decision Model – to send a payment cheque if the answer is yes, or a letter to explain why the claim has been declined if the answer is no. In *Chapter 8*, we will talk in more detail about how to use Decision Models at key points in a workflow, as combining the tools gives us a lot of power.

Differences between Decision Models and business rules

We'll also need to keep in mind that Decision Models and business rules are similar but not exactly the same thing. A bit like an Excel graph and an Excel table, both can show the same underlying information, but are optimized for slightly different things, as in these examples:

- Decision models are a highly graphical format. You can represent rules in this format, but there are many other ways of writing business rules – you will see this with decision tables in the next chapter, and we'll touch on the Drools DRL format later in the book in *Chapter 12*.

- A rules engine such as Drools is not the only way of executing a Decision Model. It is pretty effective, and the one we focus on in this book.

- Some of the expressions available in FEEL used by Decision Models can be executed but not optimized by the business rule engine. In practice, you value this flexibility and will only be concerned if your FEEL expressions become too complicated to understand. At that point, you could rewrite your expression into a Decision Table format (which are business rules). We will cover Decision Tables in *Chapter 4*.

- In Decision Models, the focus is on the decision to be made, and only then on how we make that decision. In our previous example, you created the Decision node first (*respond to greeting*) and only then created the rules on how to make that decision (*answer Hello + name*). It is possible to use KIE/Drools to create business rules without any graphical Decision nodes. The business rule engine then has complete freedom to decide when to fire – a more powerful approach for some applications where there are hundreds of thousands of business rules.

In practice, Decision Models are so simple to understand and the graphical editor is so powerful that they make an excellent entry point into the world of business rules. Just keep the subtle difference in mind as you explore further outside of this book.

A tour of the UI

Our `Hello World` example is a great start, but obviously, Decision Models and rules can do so much more. Let's expand our `Hello World` example a bit more and explore KIE Sandbox along the way.

To start, you may have noticed a blue box marked **Problems** at the bottom right of the KIE Sandbox decision model screen, as shown in *Figure 3.18*:

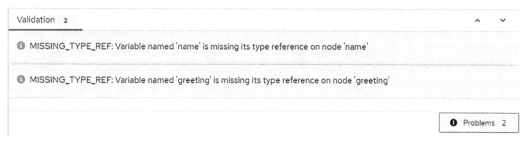

Figure 3.18 – Issues highlighted by KIE

This screen shows when you click on the **Problems** button. But what do these messages mean? What is a variable, and how can it be missing a type reference? Let's explain what variables and types are.

What is a variable?

You have almost certainly typed a formula into Excel to add two cells together – something such as = A1+B1. In this case, you're telling Excel to go to the box (cell) named **A1**, take the value found there, and add it to the value that Excel finds in box (cell) **B1**. If the values in the boxes (cells) change, the result returned by the formula changes. Think of **A1** and **B1** as variables.

If you have used **Named Ranges** in Excel, you're a step closer to how Decision Models, KIE/Drools, and most other modern computer languages use variables. Your variables can be called whatever you like – in this case, the person's name.

The Input nodes in our decision diagrams are a type of variable, but there are other ways of creating them, as we'll see in the next chapter.

What is a type?

In general, Excel manages data types pretty well for you. Most of the time, you don't need to think about it – you can put any value (number, text, or Boolean such as true and false) into a cell and Excel will do its best to work with it. The FEEL language used by KIE allows something similar – it's called an **Any** data type.

Sometimes in Excel, it is better to specify the type of variable (or cell) we use – for example, to tell Excel that it is a *date* and not a *number* that we are dealing with.

KIE is similar. While you can use the Any data type, it is much better to specify the data type you are using. This helps KIE reduce hard-to-find errors in our business rules. As well as the many data types that we may be familiar with from Excel, KIE has a lot more powerful data types, which we'll explore further in *Chapter 4*.

Thankfully, these errors are only warnings and do not halt the decision model from producing a result. These error messages are a nudge for you to do the right thing. Let's keep KIE happy and specify the data types in our example.

How to fix these errors

Go to our Decision Model and select the name input node, as shown on the left-hand side of *Figure 3.19*:

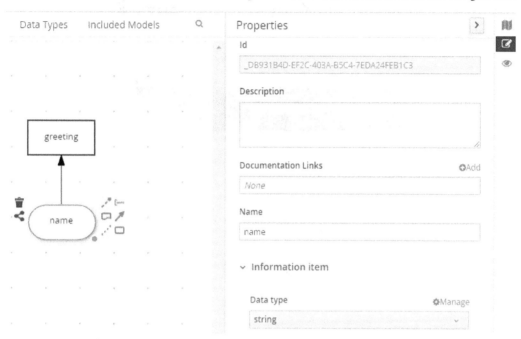

Figure 3.19 – Changing the name data type to string

In this figure, we've already clicked on the *Properties* icon at the top right of the screen to bring up the **Properties** panel on the right-hand side.

We then set Data type to **string** (bottom right of the figure). *String* is just another name for a piece of text.

As soon as we make this change, one of the errors should disappear from the **Error** panel, since we told KIE to expect this node to supply strings as an input type.

It's a similar process for the greeting node (right-click the node, edit properties, and set Data type to **string**). The second warning error should be cleared since we told KIE that this decision node takes text as its input type.

Giving our Decision Model a name

Up to now, our Decision model has been called **Untitled**, but we can do better. Double-click on the name **Untitled** at the top left of the screen, which gives you the option to rename it `Hello World`, like in *Figure 3.20*:

Figure 3.20 – Changing the name of our DMN Model

If you want to export a copy, click on the **Share** button at the top right of the screen, as we saw in *Figure 3.3*. As shown in *Figure 3.21*, this will allow you to download a copy of the current diagram as a DMN file:

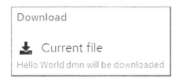

Figure 3.21 – Downloading the DMN diagram

If you want, you can open the downloaded file in Notepad or a similar editor (the layout used is XML). The format of the file is part of the OMG specification for Decision Models, meaning that you should be able to execute this DMN file in a tool from another vendor. Behind the scenes, the XML format enables the advanced code editing and collaboration techniques we will cover in *Chapter 5*.

But in practice, you'll work mainly with the graphical editor, and the main use of this download function is that it makes it easier to share Decision Models with colleagues.

Previous autosaved decision models

You notice that we talked about *exporting* and not *saving* the Decision Model. This is because KIE autosaves the DMN Model in browser storage, which is a standard feature of most modern web browsers. This means that even if we close the browser and reopen it, it will not disappear.

Let's try this – close and reopen the browser at `https://sandbox.kie.org/#/`. If you look toward the bottom of the main KIE home page, you will see something like *Figure 3.22*:

Figure 3.22 – Recent models

As you create and edit more Decision Models, the list of recent models will grow. While browser storage is pretty robust, it's unique to each browser. If you use Chrome and Edge on your laptop, each will have its own **Recent models** list. While this is good enough for us now, we'll see a more sharable, more robust model storage mechanism in *Chapter 5*.

Uploading Decision Models from other sources

Before we leave the KIE Sandbox home page, it's worth highlighting a feature that we skipped over earlier. On the right-hand side of the screen, there are options as shown in *Figure 3.23*:

Import

</> From URL

Import a GitHub Repository, a GitHub Gist, or any other file URL.

URL

Import

⬆ Upload

Drag & drop files and folders here...

or

Select files...

Select folder...

Figure 3.23 – Importing and uploading DMN Models on the KIE Sandbox home page

These options allow you to import a previously created Decision Model from a URL (web address) or upload a file already on your computer. As we move through the rest of the examples in this book, we'll typically provide a file with the completed result to make it easier to follow along. This screen will allow you to easily import these sample files to your local KIE sandbox.

Let's continue to build on the example we just created.

An improved Decision Model for greetings

Now that we know we can import samples, we can move a little bit faster in the next couple of pages. We'll still work through the sample instructions step by step, and we'll probably learn more by doing this, but we have the safety net of importing the final decision model in case there is any step that is not completely clear.

Our `Hello World` Decision Model is good, but we know we can do more with it. Let's try something a little bit more sophisticated. We'll give you two options on how to follow along with this sample.

Option 1 – importing the sample

While I hope you follow the step-by-step instructions that we list in the other options, here is the shortcut to import the sample decision model:

1. Go to the GitHub book samples page at `https://github.com/PacktPublishing/AI-and-Business-Rules-for-Excel-Power-Users` and download the `03_sample_02_Good Morning.dmn` model to your laptop.

2. To download it, click on the filename in GitHub; a web page will open showing the file. Click on the **raw** button on this page to see only the file contents, no formatting.

3. Right-click on the **raw** contents in the browser and select **Save page as...**. When choosing a filename, check that you have **all files** rather than **txt** selected, since this will cause problems with the filename later.

4. Open Windows explorer, making sure that **view... file extensions** is checked in the menu. Go to where you saved the file, and double-check that the file didn't get **.txt** added to the end.

5. Open the KIE Sandbox home page like in *Figure 3.23*. Click on **Select files** and choose the decision model you have just downloaded.

6. Click **ok** to import the model – you should see a decision model like in *Figure 3.24*.

It's still worth reading the step-by-step instructions to understand how we built this decision model.

Option 2 – step-by-step instructions

Our step-by-step instructions start with the Hello World Decision Model that we last saw in *Figure 3.20*. We're going to make the following changes to it, to give us a Decision Model like in *Figure 3.24*:

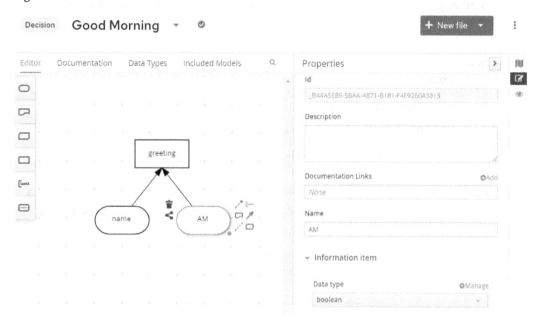

Figure 3.24 – Adding a second data node

To do this, follow these steps:

1. Double-click on the Decision Model name, and rename it to Good Morning.

2. Add a new Data node to the diagram (drag and drop from the menu on the left).

3. Double-click on this Data node and rename it AM.

4. Select the AM Data node, click on the Arrow node that appears, then drag the arrow to connect it to the greeting decision node. Be careful of the arrow direction – it should go from the AM node to the greeting node.

5. Select the AM Data node, and then click on the *Properties* icon (top right of the screen), to show the **Properties** editor panel.

6. Using the **Properties** editor, change **Data type** for the AM Data node to **boolean**.

> **Boolean data types**
>
> You've probably used Boolean data types in Excel – they are either `True` or `False`. Like in Excel, there is a third Boolean type of empty, where no value has been supplied.
>
> Sometimes, the impact of an empty value shows up as a `Required Dependency ... not found` message, which disappears when we pass in a value. Keep this in mind as we run the sample.

Now that we are supplying additional information to our decision node, we want to update our decision to take advantage of it. To do this, follow these steps:

1. Select the `greeting` Decision node in our Decision Model.
2. Click on the **Edit** button that appears on the middle left as a context menu.
3. Using the boxed editor, update the expression to `if AM then "Good Morning "+name else "Good Afternoon "+name`.
4. The result should look like *Figure 3.25* – note that the editor has captured the text, but won't show all of it on screen unless we drag the right-hand side of the boxed editor to expand it:

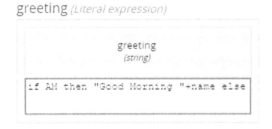

Figure 3.25 – Updating the decision expression

5. Click on the **Problems** tab at the bottom left of the screen to see whether KIE has highlighted any issues. A major source of errors is getting the characters for the quotes around the text wrong – it's the same double-quote character you use in Excel.

No doubt you're keen to try out these changes. Like a previous example, click on the **Run … as Form** menu at the top right of the screen and enter some values like in *Figure 3.26*:

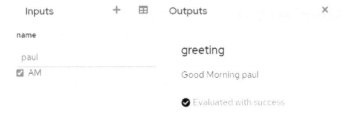

Figure 3.26 – Updated input/output form

On the **Inputs** side, you'll see that our two inputs are automatically listed – a textbox for entering a name and a checkbox for our Boolean **AM** value. Like before, when we update the values, the decision model evaluates them and outputs a value – in this case, a time-appropriate greeting.

In our Decision node, the expression box used a FEEL expression (`If ... Else`) to decide whether to say **Good Morning** or **Good Afternoon** based on whether the **AM** box is checked or not.

> **What is greeting (null)?**
>
> You may have noticed that before you input any values into the form, there may be a message in the output, something such as **greeting (null)**.
>
> This is because of the empty value in our Boolean – because we pass in an empty value, KIE doesn't have enough information to make a decision. Rather than KIE hiding this issue, it tells us by passing back the null message.

This is still a relatively simple example – we're only scratching the surface of the FEEL expression language. We haven't get begun to chain multiple decision nodes to make more complicated decisions. And we haven't yet introduced decision tables that split our business decisions into very simple **when … then** rules. But you can already begin to see the power of taking something normally crammed into a hard-to-read Excel expression and editing it as a much clearer Decision Model.

We'll cover all of those items in the next chapter. But before we got onto more powerful tools, it's worth completing our tour of KIE Sandbox, as there are several other features that we will find useful.

Other UI elements in KIE Sandbox

On the Decision Model page of KIE Sandbox, if we click on the *Decision Navigator* icon (the flag-like icon at the top right), KIE will show **Decision Navigator**, like in *Figure 3.27*:

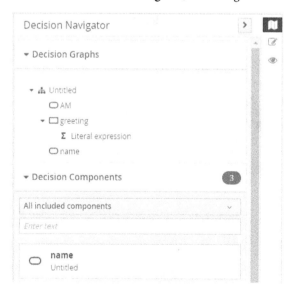

Figure 3.27 – Decision Navigator view

The **Decision Navigator** view is another layout to represent the same Decision Model – this time, as a tree-like structure. All the nodes are the same, but it is easier to see the content of the nodes (for example, when we use a literal expression to make our decision). Clicking on the elements in **Decision Navigator** will jump to the relevant part of the diagram.

Also on the right-hand side of the screen is **Explore diagram**. The icon looks like an eye, as highlighted in *Figure 3.28*:

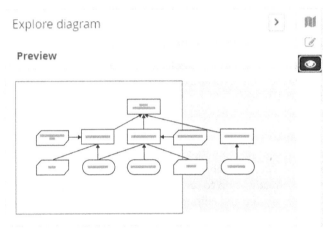

Figure 3.28 – Explore diagram

Explore diagram is really useful for exploring larger decision models – which is why *Figure 3.28* shows the more complicated sample Decision Model that comes with KIE. While you can't read the text on the individual nodes, it allows you to zoom out and see the bigger picture.

Returning to the Decision Model editor, just underneath our model name, you'll see four tabs, as shown in *Figure 3.29*:

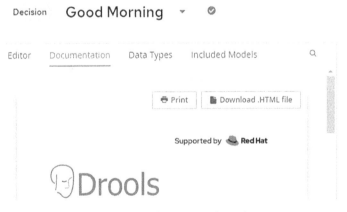

Figure 3.29 – Documentation tab

Let's look at the tabs:

- **Editor** is the visual decision model editor that we've been working with throughout this chapter.

- **Documentation** summarizes our decision model into an easy-to-export format (such as PDF). We can share these PDF docs with the wider team and check for agreement on business decisions.

- **Data Types** allows us to build more complex data types, which we will explore in the next chapter. We touched on these in our examples.

- **Included Models** allows us to include other decision models that we can use to build our business decision. We don't need to cram our decisions into one Decision Model.

Finally, the down arrow beside our model name at the top is a shortcut that allows us to quickly navigate between other Decision Models we have created.

Note – KIE Sandbox is only a sandbox

To be more precise, KIE Sandbox Extended Services is only a development tool. It's easy to be impressed by the fluid nature of editing decision models, and you should be! The KIE Sandbox editor is one of the best, most robust, implementations of the OMG Decision Model standard and shows the time and effort the IBM and Red Hat teams have put into it.

However, please remember the runtime (KIE Sandbox Extended Services) is only a convenience to help you evaluate your decision models as you build them. It can only run on your local machine, accessible only to you, so it's not suitable for deploying as a stable solution. In *Chapters 5* and *10*, we will show you how to run your business rules in a truly robust, scalable, enterprise solution.

Summary

We achieved a lot in this chapter – we went from talking about business rules as an abstract concept, to executing business rules using hands-on tools such as KIE Sandbox.

Along the way, we saw how Decision Models are another way to represent our business rules, and their highly visual format meant that we could quickly build two samples. We downloaded and ran KIE Sandbox Extended Services to evaluate our Decision Model and saw some of the different data types on which we can base our decisions.

We took a tour of the UI to understand how we can import and export decision models, and where to access previous models that KIE has autosaved for us. We also saw some of the other views of Decision Models, which are especially useful when sharing them with colleagues for validation.

However, there were several key points in the chapter where we understood Decision Models, rule engines, and the FEEL expression language are much more powerful than we've previously explored. Let's stay within KIE Sandbox for our next chapter and do a deep-dive to explore the power these tools give you.

Part 2: Writing Business Rules and Decision Models – with Real-Life Examples

This section builds on the Hello world example we saw earlier, working with colleagues to build useful business rules and decision models and linking them back to Excel for day-to-day use.

This section includes the following chapters:

- *Chapter 4, More Decision Models, Business Rules, and Decision Tables*, expands your knowledge of decision models, building out a working chocolate shop example to show more of the tools available.

- *Chapter 5, Sharing and Deploying Decision Models Using OpenShift Cloud and GitHub*, makes our decision models sharable, allowing other people to run them in the cloud, and looks at using online tools to collaborate with colleagues on the model's design.

- *Chapter 6, Calling Business Rules from Excel Using Power Query*, links Excel to our AI, rules, and decision tables – using the Power Query tool built into Excel.

More Decision Models, Business Rules, and Decision Tables

In the previous chapter, we wrote our first business rule using *Decision Models* in the KIE Sandbox. While it gave a friendly greeting, that business rule wasn't very powerful. This chapter will explore other features of KIE to write more powerful business rules that solve more real-life problems.

Along the way, we'll explore different formats for storing information. We'll use the tools in KIE Sandbox to model these formats, making it a lot easier to understand the data we're working with. We'll create our first **Decision Table** and see how these are a very powerful way of expressing business rules. We'll explore other node types to help us process information and help prepare it for the decision tables. Finally, we'll combine all of these node types to create a very powerful decision-making example.

Our aim is to capture our business decision-making processes to provide a useful service. For that, we will cover the following main topics:

- Make your decisions easy to talk to
- A more powerful Decision node – Decision Tables
- Other types of Decision Nodes
- Adding nodes to support our Decision Table
- A more sophisticated Decision Table
- Rule matching and HIT Policies
- A safer Decision Table example

Let's start by thinking about how we can make our decision service easy to work with.

Make your decision service easy to work with

You might not have realized it, but in the previous chapter, you wrote your first decision service. When running our *Greeting Example* in the KIE Sandbox, we supplied inputs (a name and if it was morning or not), made a decision, and then shared the output (**Good Morning** or **Good Afternoon**).

While we can't see many colleagues signing up to use this particular service, this will change quickly as we move into the more sophisticated examples in this chapter. It's worth thinking now about what other people need to know when using our service:

- How we make a decision – in general, the **Decision Model and Notation** (**DMN**) format makes this pretty clear. It is certainly much clearer than other solutions (such as functions hidden in code or in Excel).

- The data needed to be passed into the decision service, and the format of the data we get back from it.

In our greetings service, we expected a String (`Text name`) and Boolean (whether it was morning – `true` or `false`). But Decision Models allow us to be a lot more specific about the type of data we pass in and out. This is a good thing, as it makes it easier for people to use our service.

Before we begin to specify the data we expect to pass into, and back out from our Decision Service, it's worth thinking about how Excel models data.

What shape is your data – tables or trees?

Excel is brilliant – you've never really needed to think about the shape or structure of your data. All Excel data is table based on a grid-type layout. A typical example would be *Figure 4.1* – a table of customer information that we might have if we were running an online chocolate shop:

Customer Number	Customer Name	Date of Birth	Country of Residence	Special Request
1029	Jane Smith	10-Mar-2001	Netherlands	
2219	Sita Patel	18-Apr-1998	New Zealand	Vegan
8781	Joseph Okoru	22-Sep-1963	Sri Lanka	
1123	Peter Murphy	04-Nov-02	United States	

Figure 4.1 – A very simple customer table

It's pretty simple, and in real life, we'd have more columns than the ones listed here – perhaps to store emails, shipping addresses, and similar information. But it's good enough to demonstrate the grid-type layout that Excel encourages you to use. And there are obviously more sophisticated sheets – for modeling company financial projections, where an entire sheet would represent one company, instead of the one-row-per-client layout we show here. But our simple example is enough to show the limitations of grid-based data.

Of course, like most Excel sheets, it's not a true grid – the values for **Special Requests** are optional (it can be empty). A bigger problem, that you've probably already seen in your own Excel sheets, is that additional data that doesn't quite fit into the grid pattern. For example, if we also want to track customer orders in this spreadsheet, we have three options:

- Add in another column for the first order, yet another column for the second order, and so on – we risk ending up with a very messy spreadsheet.

- Or we could add another row (duplicating customer numbers) and put separate order details in each row we add. This gives us space to store more information but makes it difficult to update customer-level information (such as name).

- Or, we could create a separate table for orders and cross-reference them using **Customer Number**. If you've ever used SQL databases, you'll be familiar with this approach. But having information in two places makes it difficult to view information all in one go.

The point is that the grid shape of our data doesn't quite fit.

What if we tried a different, tree shape for our data instead? *Figure 4.2* is one line of our customer table in tree (**JSON**) format:

```json
{
    "CustomerInfo": {
        "Customer Number": 1123,
        "Previous Order": [
            "ord001","Snap Crackle Bar",
            "ord002","Turkish Delight"
        ],
        "Customer Name": "Paul Murphy",
        "Special Request": "lactose intolerant",
        "Date of Birth": "2001-11-02",
        "Country of Residence": "United States"
    }
}
```

Figure 4.2 – One customer in JSON format

If you've seen a JSON file before, the layout will be familiar, but let's highlight some key features of this file format: we've indented the text to make the tree-like structure clear:

- This file is just a text file with an agreed layout. It's similar in many ways to a **comma-separated values (CSV)** file – another type of text file with an agreed layout.

- You can open and edit JSON files in Notepad or another text editor. *Figure 4.2* with color highlighting is from VS Code (we'll use that editor again in *Chapter 12*).

- Each value is named – so it's very easy to identify key pieces of information, such as customer names.

- While we show only one line from our customer table (since the tree format isn't as compact as a grid/table), it is possible to repeat our `CustomerInfo` entries as many times as needed.

- The types of information (text, numbers, and dates) are easier to infer from this format as well. You can also see where we have created our own data structures (the main `CustomerInfo` structure, which contains strings, numbers, dates, and a second custom order structure).

- The tree structure is much more flexible. For example, we've been able to add multiple orders for this customer. Because each value is named, it's ok to omit the optional **Special Requests** field, and the file will still be readable.

While JSON is designed to be easy for us humans to read and easy to edit, the good news is that we will almost always have a sample file to start from. For example, the preceding JSON format was actually generated by the KIE Sandbox. We'll show more of that in *Chapter 5* when we connect the KIE sandbox to the cloud.

> **More on JSON**
>
> In the previous section, we introduced *just enough JSON* to model the data our decisions need. But JSON is a format that is widely used and you're likely to encounter it again. If you're interested in learning more, one of the better guides is from Microsoft at the following link: `https://pnp.github.io/blog/post/introduction-to-json/`.

Since we know that there are more powerful data formats available and that the KIE Sandbox has a Data Type Editor to specify those formats. So how do we use this editor to make it clearer to other users of the Decision Service the format of data we expect input and the type of data we will pass back as a result? We'll work through an example to model the customer data in the editor.

Modeling our data in the KIE Sandbox

To start modeling our data:

1. Open the KIE sandbox at `sandbox.kie.org`.
2. On the home screen, create a new **Decision**
3. In the new decision model, click on **Data Types**. You should see a screen like the one shown in *Figure 4.3*:

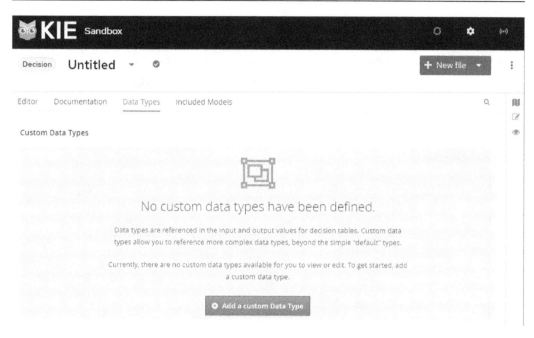

Figure 4.3 – Data Type editor in KIE

4. Click on **Add a custom Data Type** – the blue box near the bottom of the screen.

5. Enter the name `tCustomer`. While we can choose almost any name we like, the `t` at the start (which stands for type) will make it easier to distinguish this as a data structure later on.

> **What is a type?**
>
> Think of a type as a cookie cutter. With one cutter, we can cut out and bake as many cookies as we want.

6. In the drop-down menu, we choose a data type of **Structure**. The screen should look similar to *Figure 4.4*:

Custom Data Types

Figure 4.4 – New Data Type

7. Our **tCustomer** is equivalent to one line in the earlier Excel spreadsheet. We still need to tell KIE about the individual pieces of information within each customer type. Click on the pencil icon to add a customer number of a **number** type, then click on the tick icon to save.

8. Click on the + icon (underneath the customer number) to add the following types in turn, as shown in *Figure 4.5*:

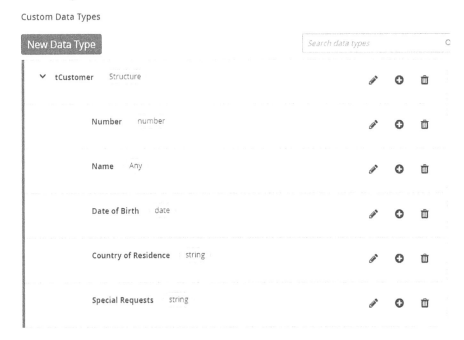

Figure 4.5 – Custom Data Types

Congratulations – you've just created your first **custom data type** in the KIE sandbox. Now that we've created a **custom data type**, let's see what it looks like in a Decision Model.

> **Is customer name really needed on our data type?**
>
> In real life, we're unlikely to pass in personally identifiable information such as customer names. This is because our decision service doesn't store any information – it just makes a judgment on the information you pass to it.
>
> You shouldn't (for many reasons) make a decision based on a single customer name. A more likely scenario is that for very important customers, you might create a **Special customer** Boolean field.
>
> These design choices are especially important when we begin to consider the ethical use of customer data, which we'll touch on in the next chapter.

Using our complex data type in a decision model

To start using our **tCustomer** data type in a decision model, do the following steps:

1. Start by returning to the **Model Editor** screen by clicking on that tab.

2. In the editor, drag an **Input data** node and call it **Customer** – remember our cookie customer example? **tCustomer** is the cutter, we're going to use it to create an actual customer shape.

3. Click on the properties icon (remember – it's on the top right of the editor). In the **Properties** pane, specify that we want to use the **tCustomer** data type we just created. It should look similar to *Figure 4.6*:

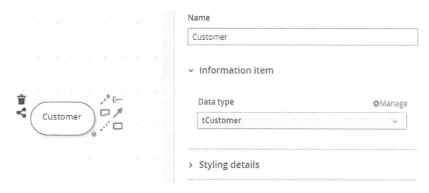

Figure 4.6 – Using our data type in a Decision Model

We mentioned before that structured data types like **tCustomer** are part of a *contract* with people calling this decision service. To demonstrate this, if we click on the **Run .. as form** button, we can see that KIE has automatically generated a data input form based on our structured data type, as shown in *Figure 4.7*:

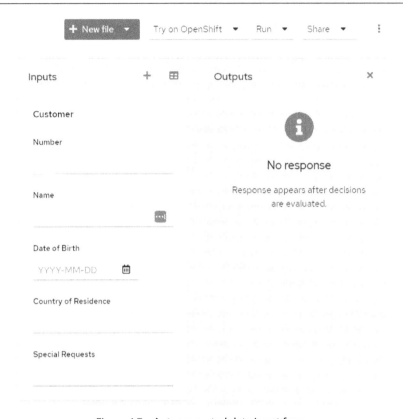

Figure 4.7 – Autogenerated data input form

Of course, because we specified neither the output nor the data type of that output, KIE hasn't (yet) been able to autogenerate that. That will change as we continue to build our decision model.

Describing our data better using constraints

In describing the shape of our data, it is useful not only to describe the information we are gathering but also the values that we will accept. It may be that in our **Special Requests** field, we only recognize health or diet requirements (such as diabetic, vegan, or lactose intolerant). KIE allows us to specify these constraints on our data type. Let's add some data constraints to our data model:

1. Return to the KIE data type editor and navigate to the **Special Requests** field (*Figure 4.8*). Click on **Add Constraints** for this field:

Figure 4.8 – Adding constraints to our data type

2. The **Data type constraints** screen appears. In *Figure 4.9*, we've already selected **enumeration**, which allows us to specify a list of values. And then we entered the text that is acceptable for use in our **Special Request** field: **diabetic**, **vegan**, or **lactose intolerant**. Note that it is also possible to enter the list of values as an **expression** type (if you choose this route, the Sandbox will give you an example to help guide you).

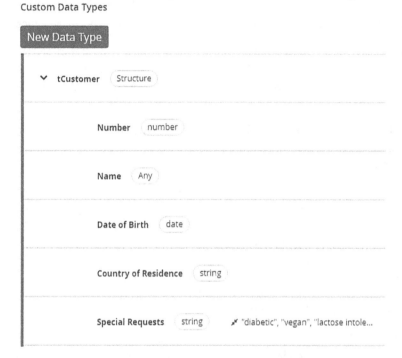

Figure 4.9 – Complex data type with constraints

3. Remember to click **OK**, or the green arrow in the constraint editor to save our updates.

When we go back to the **Run** menu, you'll see (*Figure 4.10*) that KIE has recognized the new contract and updated the user interface so that you can only select values that align with this restraint:

Figure 4.10 – Updated data input form suggesting constrained values

You'll notice that our sample (as modeled in KIE) does not yet match the Customer (with Orders) we modeled in JSON and Excel. Since you've already used the data type editor, creating an order object and nesting it within the customer is easy:

1. Create the **tOrder** type, with the fields you need.

2. Edit the **tCustomer** data structure and add a (Previous) **orders** field using this **torder** type.

3. Edit the **list** slider, which allows us to add multiple previous orders per customer.

As before, the auto-generate form on the **run** screen will update – try it out! The downloadable copy of the data type we created is available as `04_Customer_Data.dmn` on the book's GitHub page `https://github.com/PacktPublishing/AI-and-Business-Rules-for-Excel-Power-Users`.

Downloading it will make it easier if you don't want to work your way through all these steps – but remind yourself of the GitHub download instructions we gave in the previous chapter to avoid the most common mistakes.

Just because you can create extremely complicated custom data using the editor doesn't mean that you should. Let's think about what makes for a good design.

What makes a good custom data type?

Since you're building a service that other people (including you in the future) will use, it pays to make it as easy to use as possible. There are entire books written on good data design, but at this stage, a couple of simple guidelines will go a long way:

- It's better to follow how people talk in day-to-day business – customers, delivery addresses, orders, product recommendations, and other similar terms. Familiar, clear names makes it easier for people to understand since you mirror the way they already think.

- Several simple data types are better than one large complex one. Not only are they easier to understand, but it makes it easier to reuse your decision service.

- Data modeling can get very complicated very quickly. Copying existing spreadsheets and systems is a good start. Consistency is better than the confusion of having a slightly different data model.

- Keep the names simple – our type used **number** instead of **customer_number** since it was already clear from the context that it was associated with a customer.

Above all – don't be afraid to experiment. At this stage in the book, we're prototyping – playing with the technology with a focus on learning. And at some point, we will probably (re)start with a *clean-sheet* design. This clean-sheet design will be built a lot faster as we will have a much better idea of what we are doing at that point.

Now that we can use data types to specify the data we expect to be passed in, let's use it in a more powerful Decision Model using Decision Tables.

A more powerful Decision node – Decision Tables

In *Chapter 1, Wrestling with Excel? You Are Not Alone*, we introduced business rules as decisions we can make using a when … then format, for example; When time is AM - say Good morning.

We are likely to have more than one business rule - otherwise, why bother using a rule engine? Decision tables are just a format to write multiple, similar business rules in a table format, like this:

First	Input Value 1	Input Value 2	Output
1	When value1 = "Something"	AND value2 > 100	"Matched"
OR 2	When value1 = "Completely different"	AND value 2<100	"Different match"
OR 3	-	Value 2 = 100	"Match on number only"

Table 4.1 – Business rules mapped as a simple Decision Table

Where are the **Input Values** coming from? That's the data model we constructed earlier. The arrows we use to wire different nodes together mean that KIE knows what data is available for use by the decision table (and will try to autogenerate the table for you).

Drools (the rule engine underlying KIE) takes these input values and tries to find the line in the Decision Table with the best match. There are different methods (**HIT Policies**) for finding the best match. We'll use **First** in our example since it is simple to understand, but we'll come to policies for matching later.

When it finds a match, the value in the **Output** column is returned. We can have more than one output value, but we're keeping things simple here.

Note that not all values need to be provided. The hyphen, -, in line three of *Table 4.1* tells KIE not to match in this column for this rule. There are a range of **friendly enough expression language** (FEEL) expressions we can use in the values we want to match, which means that any text we want to match has to be surrounded by quotes.

We don't actually use **AND** or **OR** in our decision table syntax – they are implied by the layout of the table. We include them here for clarity. Likewise, we just write **something** as the pattern we want to match (see *Table 4.1* - the first column of our first rule).

Now that we've understood the idea of a decision table, let's capture our first decision table using the tools in the KIE Sandbox.

Our first Decision table in the KIE Sandbox

The graphic editor in the KIE Sandbox makes creating our decision table easy. We'll start using the data model we created in our previous exercise earlier in this chapter. This is also available on the samples page as 04_Customer Data.dmn.

To add a Decision Table to this decision model:

1. Open the model in the KIE sandbox and rename the decision model to **First Decision Table**.

2. In the editor view (which should currently be blank), drag and drop a data node. Call it **Customer**.

3. Open the **Properties** view for this node and set the data type to **tCustomer** (the data structure that we created earlier in the chapter). This is shown in *Figure 4.11*.

4. Back in the main model, drag and drop to create a decision node. Call it `Recommended Product`.

5. Link the two nodes with an arrow (right-click on the **Customer** node to view this option). Your decision model should look similar to *Figure 4.11*:

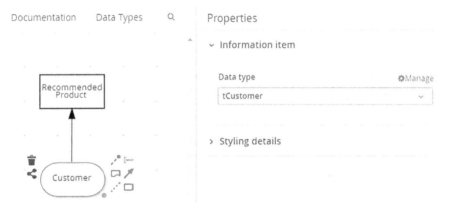

Figure 4.11 – Linked data input and Decision nodes

Our data and decision nodes must be linked before taking the next steps. If not, KIE is not able to autogenerate the fields on the decision table since it won't know what information is being passed in.

Let's now create a decision table within our **Recommended Product** Decision node:

1. Select the **Recommended Product** Decision node and click **Edit**.

2. In the screen that appears, select **Decision Table** as the type of expression we want to use. Remember – we don't get a chance to change this later – so if you get this wrong, you'll need to delete and create a new decision node.

3. You should see an empty decision table similar to *Figure 4.12*. We have deleted some of the autogenerated columns and resized the column widths to make this screenshot clearer:

RecommendedProduct *(Decision Table)*

U	Customer.Country of Residence (string)	RecommendedProduct (<Undefined>)	annotation-1
1	–		

Figure 4.12 – Empty Decision Table

Now that we have created an empty decision table, let's populate it with some values, as shown in *Figure 4.13*:

1. **HIT Policy** (top left of the table in *Figure 4.13*) – To change this value, double-click and change to **First**. This makes our example easier to understand (use the first rule if more than one matches).

2. Output column (**RecommendedProduct**). Left-click to give it a type of String, since we're going to be recommending names of different chocolate (candy) bars.

3. To add more lines, right-click on the table, then choose **Insert below** from the menu.

4. Double-click on a cell to edit its value. When entering text values, remember to put quotes around them (otherwise, KIE thinks it's a variable), and remove any hyphen that KIE may have added to denote an empty cell that it can ignore:

RecommendedProduct *(Decision Table)*

F	Customer.Country of Residence (string)	RecommendedProduct (string)	annotation-1
1	"SA"	"Lumpy Fruit and Nut Bar"	
2	"UK"	"Crunch Bar"	
3	"US","JN"	"Peanut Candy"	
4	–	"Milk Chocolate"	

Figure 4.13 – Decision Table with input and output values

Many of the lines follow the same pattern, which is the ideal use case for Decision tables. When we match **SA** as a **Country of Residence**, then we recommend a `Lumpy Fruit and Nut Bar` – these samples are based on real consumer data.

Notice that there are different expressions based on FEEL to help us match values. For example, for the multiple values separated by a comma (`"US"`, `"JN"`), either of the patterns will match and trigger our rule.

Let's test by running our Decision model – click on **Run** in the top right of the screen. Entering US as a value will gain us a product recommendation of **Peanut Candy**, as shown in *Figure 4.14*:

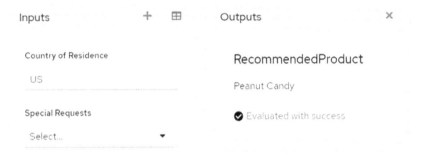

Figure 4.14 – Running the Decision Table

Try some of the other country values to confirm that the results are as expected. It's worth playing around with the decision table a bit to get a good feel for how they work.

Some more things to know about Decision Tables

Decision Tables are valuable because they summarize a lot of business rules in one place. While it is possible to model without tables, you would need a lot of smaller nodes and have to click into each node to see the logic. That is a much harder model for a user to understand.

Once you understand the repetitive format of any Decision Table (including the data it expects in and out), it is very easy to scan through the table and understand the various decisions being made. Many Decision Tables can run to hundreds or thousands of lines, so this is a key feature.

> **Warning – a Decision Table is not an Excel sheet**
>
> While the grid layout is familiar, a decision table is not an Excel Sheet. The contents of the boxes are only patterns that we look to match against incoming data. A Decision Table has quite a strict template about what information it expects and where.
>
> The matching patterns can be quite sophisticated but not quite as powerful as the Excel formula. We saw a glimpse of this in our match against either US or JN in our previous example, and we'll learn more about FEEL expressions in *Chapter 9*.

KIE also has an incredible time-saving feature around Decision Engines – it can analyze the rules you are writing and highlight any gaps in them. This is especially powerful when we specify the range of input and output values when working with numbers or constrain the list of valid text as we did with our **Special Requests** data type. KIE knows you should write rules to address each of the **diabetic**, **vegan**, or **lactose intolerant** values. If you don't, KIE will give you a warning (not an error) in the **Problems** tab on the editor.

The more specific we can be in matching our rules, the easier it is for KIE to highlight any gaps we might have. Changing the HIT policy to match the **First** business rule made our sample easier to understand, but you can see KIE gives a warning that you should consider a more accurate HIT policy.

Decision tables are also fast. Because they are business rules written in a When... Then format, Drools as a business rule engine can optimize the rules and will actually get faster over time. *Chapter 12*, *Inside the Rule Engine*, explains the mechanism behind this, but for now, consider Decision Tables as your go-to solution when modeling decisions.

Decision Tables as your go-to solution (other nodes are available)

It is possible to use other types of nodes to make a decision. For example, our greeting example in *Chapter 3*, *Your First Business Rule with the Online KIE Sandbox*, made a decision based on a simple FEEL expression. In real life, we would not use a Decision Model or rule engine for such a simple example.

Using Decision Tables as the default option for expressing our business rules makes it easier to understand what the other nodes and expressions do:

- We use Decision Tables to express the business rules that make decisions
- We use other nodes to prepare data to feed into the Decision Table

We can see this pattern in our simple example that we populated from *Figure 4.11* onwards – the **Customer** data node defined the type of information we expected and the rules Decision Table in the **Recommend Product** node made the decision. So, what are the other types of nodes that can help prepare our data?

More nodes that you can use

We've already covered the nodes that you will use most often to model your decisions. But there are several other nodes worth exploring. *Figure 4.15* showcases the different types of nodes available in KIE decision models:

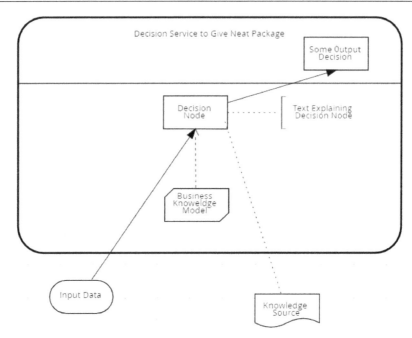

Figure 4.15 – The different Decision Model nodes in KIE

Of all the nodes we see in *Figure 4.15*, we've already used Data and Decision nodes. But there are some other types that we'll need soon:

- **Text** nodes allow us to add comments to our Decision Models to explain what is going on. They are for information only and not evaluated.

- **Knowledge Source** nodes also gives additional information but refers to an external source. For example, we might use a Knowledge Source to link to the document certifying which of our products are OK for each medical condition. They are for information only and are not evaluated.

- **Decision Services** nodes help since our Decision Models can get quite complicated. Decision Service nodes allow us to *wrap* this complexity to hide some of the internals, making it clearer what input and output we expect.

- **Business Knowledge Models** allow us to call external rules. These could be Decision Services, other Decision Models, an external system (via Java), or an external AI model. We can also use them to define reusable functions using FEEL, which we cover in more detail in *Chapter 9*.

We'll use these nodes in examples throughout the book. But while we've used Decision Tables, there are still some types of Decision nodes we haven't explored – let's take a look at them now.

Other types of Decision Nodes

We've already created two types of decision nodes – the Decision Table that we used earlier in this chapter and the literal expression we used to generate our greeting in *Chapter 3*.

But when we were creating our decision node, we had to choose from one of seven types. We'll work through them in the following list. In some ways, the name decision node can be misleading; often, we will use these types as *data preparation* nodes to feed into a Decision table:

- **Literal Expressions**: These are simple FEEL expressions, broadly similar to a formula you'd enter in Excel. They return a single value.

- **Decision Tables**: We have covered these in this chapter. They allow us to group rules in a when ... then format.

- **Functions**: This allows us to define reusable logic. We could write a function that takes the parameters of a chocolate bar's weight and the percentage of chocolate, then returns the actual grams of chocolate the bar contains. We'll work through a function example shortly.

- **Invocations**: These are another way of calling external decision models. They overlap with functions but are more useful when working with logic outside of our current Decision Model.

- **Contexts**: These make our decision models simpler. Instead of having lots of individual Literal Expressions, contexts allow us to group them in one place. They also give us options to execute these expressions in order.

Finally, we have two decision node types that return structured data:

- **Lists**: These return a simple collection of values. These can be specific values that don't change, or we can use a FEEL expression to calculate the values within the list. *Figure 4.16* shows our country list, modeled as a List node. The editor will only allow us to enter one column of values:

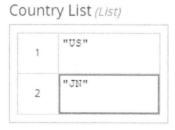

Figure 4.16 – A List Decision Node showing country codes

- **Relations**: These are similar to lists but can group multiple values together, as shown in *Figure 4.17*. Each row in this relation contains useful information about our product. And each column is effectively a list, which is useful if we want to access a list of all our products:

Product Info *(Relation)*

#	Product (string)	Weight in Grams (number)	Vegan Suitable (boolean)
1	"Peanut Crunch"	75	true
2	"Caramel Biscuit"	125	false

Figure 4.17 – Relation Decision Node showing product information

Relations are not Decision Tables

Because of the table format, relations look very similar to Decision Tables. Despite their appearance, they work very differently. Relations return *all* of the information they contain. Decision Tables match the best line(s) and return only that information.

Relations are great for defining information once and reusing it across many decision models. In practice, this table of product information would be pulled from an external system source using an invocation. For now, modeling the information as a relation in one place works well. It also makes it easier to change later as our system evolves.

Play around with the nodes

Most of the nodes we presented in this section are quite easy to understand once you start using them. We encourage you to play around with them in the KIE Decision editor and see the outputs using the Runner. For example, *Figure 4.18* shows the output of our **Product Info** relation node when we run it:

Figure 4.18 – Output from a Relation Decision Node showing product information

We'll use some of these expressions and nodes in our examples to help you understand them better. Since all the nodes are part of the **Object Model Group** (**OMG**) Decision Model standard, there is a lot of information and examples about each of them online. A good place to start is the learn DMN site (which is part of KIE): `https://learn-dmn-in-15-minutes.com/learn/decision-logic`. There is more detailed information on the Drools site (also part of KIE) at `https://www.drools.org/learn/dmn.html`.

Adding nodes to support our Decision Table

Our previous decision table example was simple: one data input node and a table generating an output. Since the power of Decision models comes from combining many nodes together, let's start building an example that links many nodes.

This example will allow us to recommend different chocolate bars depending on which day of the week the customer was born on. This comes from a real-life example and is probably no crazier than some of the business rules that you have been, or will be, asked to model.

We'll start our work based on our previous decision table example, downloadable as `04_First_Decision_Table.dmn` from this book's GitHub site:

1. Open the Decision Model editor, and add the **DayCalc** Decision node.
2. Create an arrow to connect existing **Customer Data Note** to feed data into this new **DayCalc** node.
3. Create another arrow to connect the **DayCalc** node to the existing **Recommended Product** table.
4. Open the **Properties editor** on the **DayCalc** node and set the output to **string**. It should look like *Figure 4.19*:

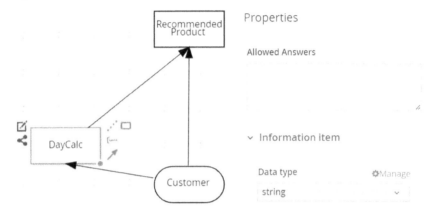

Figure 4.19 – Creating a Function Decision Node

5. Next, edit the **DayCalc** node by clicking on the pen icon next to the node.
6. On the screen that appears, set **Expression type** to **Function**.
7. Edit the parameters of this function by clicking on the **Edit Parameters** box. In the pop-up menu, click on **Add parameter**, as shown in *Figure 4.20*:

Figure 4.20 – Adding parameters to the function

8. Enter a parameter named DOB and give it a data type of **Date**. Click anywhere to exit the whitespace menu.

9. Now that you are back at the node editor, enter day of week (DOB) in the expression box. You've guessed it – this is a FEEL expression that returns the day of the week (for example, Monday or Tuesday) linked to this date. With this edit, your node should look similar to *Figure 4.21*:

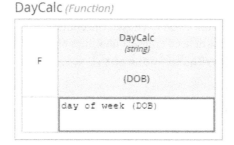

Figure 4.21 – Entering the function

If we have entered our formula correctly (no spelling mistakes), you should see an output in the **Run** panel of **function DayCalc(DOB) - Evaluated with success**.

While it's useful to know that KIE can understand our function, we haven't yet called it by passing in a date and received a response.

Running our function

While we've wired our decision model to make the function available to the decision table, it is helpful to see exactly what is going on. To do this, we're going to add another node to our decision model to allow us to visualize the output:

1. Open our previous example, add another decision node, and call it Customer Birth Day.

2. Link the new node from the DayCalc function. Your model should be similar to *Figure 4.22*:

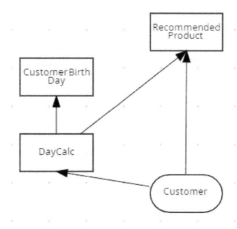

Figure 4.22 – Creating a Decision Node to test the function

3. Open the properties of **Customer Birth Day** to give it a data type of **string**.

4. Edit the **Customer Birthday** decision node, and set **Logic type** to **Context**. Of course, there are many different ways of calling a function, but this is a useful excuse to play with context decision nodes.

5. In the screen that appears once you've chosen the context type, add entries as follows, so it looks like *Figure 4.23*. You will need to insert new lines and select the data type of **string** from the drop-down menus. `DayCalc(Customer.Date of Birth)` and `Day of Week` are literal expressions:

Figure 4.23 – Building a context within the decision node

6. Open the **Run** panel and select a date from the date picker on the **Date of Birth** input field – for example, **2000-01-01**.

7. Immediately, KIE will evaluate the decision model, including the **Customer Birth Day** node we just created. We'll see what day of the week the customer was born on; in this case, it was a Saturday.

> **Tricks of the trade**
>
> Adding an output node so we can see what is going on is a useful tool for debugging (trying to find why something is not working the way we want it to). Since nobody gets things right the first time, we talk more about helpful testing techniques in *Chapter 9*.

The **context** node we used was pretty simple: one calculation and an output line. If needed, we could have added additional lines and have KIE build up the result step by step. Again, it's worth playing with this example in the KIE editor before we move on to build a more sophisticated Decision Table.

A more sophisticated Decision Table

We added a function node to calculate the day of the week our customer was born on. But we still haven't used that day of the week to recommend a suitable product. Let's update our previous example (downloadable as 04_Customer_Birth_Day.dmn) to make this happen:

1. Open the Decision Model, right-click on the **Recommended product** decision node, and choose the edit icon.

2. Add **Input Clauses** (pale blue) so that you have the three input columns, as shown in *Figure 4.24*. You can do this by right-clicking on an existing input column and choosing **Add right**.

3. Double-click on each input clause to set where the data is coming from, as shown in *Figure 4.24*. Customer.Country of Residence and Customer.Number come directly from our data model. DayCalc(Customer.Date of Birth) calls the function (once) that we created and makes the result available to match against our rules.

4. We've resized some columns and dragged and dropped them to re-order them – but this doesn't change the rule's functionality.

5. In the main body of the table, enter the values as shown. Pay attention to the quote marks needed for text values.

6. The - values denote where no match is attempted, and the annotations are just comments to explain what is going on but are otherwise ignored.

RecommendedProduct *(Decision Table)*

F	Customer.Country of Residence *(string)*	DayCalc(Customer.Date of Birth) *(string)*	Customer.Number *(number)*	RecommendedProduct *(string)*	annotation-1
1	-	-	<10000	"Silk Tray"	Only first 10000 custom
2	"SA"	-	-	"Lumpy Fruit and Nut Bar"	
3	"UK"	"Friday"	-	"Crunch Bar"	
4	"US","JN"	-	-	"Peanut Candy"	
5	-	-	-	"Milk Chocolate"	

Figure 4.24 – A more sophisticated decision table

7. Open the **Run** panel to evaluate our model. As expected, **US** customers get recommended **Peanut Candy**. **UK** customers get recommended a **Crunch Bar** – but only if they were born on **Friday**. Otherwise, customers will receive the default suggestion of a **Milk Chocolate** bar. And any person who is in the first 10,000 customers gets recommended our special **Silk Tray** offer.

Note that this decision table is using several different FEEL expressions:

- **Text**: This is surrounded by quotation marks and is a simple FEEL expression. If we didn't include the quotation marks, KIE would think it is an expression or data type and try to evaluate it.

- **Lists**: Like we used to match the US and Japan in one rule.

- The formula to match with the first 10,000 customers where `Customer.Number < 10000`.

- The expression in our input clause – calling a `DayCalc(Customer.Date of Birth)` function and trying to match the result against our rules.

We'll share even more FEEL expressions in *Chapter 9*. This example should have given you a taste of how powerful they can be when combined with Decision Tables to match against different rules. Before then, we need to think again about how we choose which rule to use when more than one rule is a match for our data.

Rule matching and HIT Policies

For the decision table we saw in *Figure 4.23*, a **US**-based customer, with a customer number of less than **10,000** would match with three rules (**Silk Tray**, **Peanut Crunch**, and the default **Milk Chocolate**). But how do we decide which rule we should use? To do that, we need to talk again about **HIT Policies**.

In our previous example, we set the HIT policy to **First** (in the top left corner of the decision table) as it was the easiest to understand. When we match with two rules, **Silk Tray** comes first, so it's the one that is chosen.

That's fine when we have only a couple of rules, but when we have hundreds of rules on a table, it becomes harder to see what is going on. Nudging a rule up or down the decision table could bring big changes to the behavior of the decision model. It also doesn't leverage the full power of the rule engine. For these reasons, the HIT Policy of First is controversial and doesn't form part of the OMG Decision model specification.

A better approach is to write your rules for clear matches against the input parameters and to consider the other matching HIT policies available to you. These HIT policies are as follows:

- **Unique**: This means that your rules have to be written so that only one can match at a time. KIE will automatically analyze your rules and refuse to run if it detects an overlap.

- **Any**: This allows some overlap, but only if all the rules matching have the same output (for example, recommending the same type of product).

- **Priority**: This allows overlapping rules, and uses constrained data types to decide which to apply (based on the order of values in the constraint). For example, we could create a **Product** data type, constrained to the different names of the chocolate bars. If we specified our Decision Table output type as **Product**, KIE could then use the order we list those chocolate bars to decide which rule is most important.

- **Collect**: This allows multiple matches. If we used this policy, we would recommend at least two products to all **US**-based customers (**Silk Tray** and **Peanut Crunch**). There is a second drop-down option under this policy to specify an aggregator: **Min**, **Max**, **Count** (all of which work for text and numerical values), and **Sum** (which works for numbers only).

- **Rule Order** and **Output order**: These also allow and collect multiple rule matches. Those matches are then sorted by the order of the rules (like in **First**), or the order of the outputs (like in **Priority**).

Which HIT Policy works best will depend on the rules you are trying to write. Your focus should be on which gives the easiest and clearest-to-understand rules with the fewest gaps (since you're trying to ensure all scenarios are covered). For now, we suggest you play around with the different HIT Policies to understand them better – paying attention to the **Problems** tabs when KIE complains about the rules being incompatible with the policy.

While writing rules to be **unique** (or any of the more specific HIT Policies) is more difficult initially, it will save you time in the long run. This is because the automatic KIE analysis allows you to identify the gaps now (when it is easy to fix), rather than later on (when you have an annoyed customer on the telephone complaining that no suggestions were made of which candy bar they might like).

A safer Decision Table example

While our Decision model is very powerful, in its current form, it's very dangerous. It recommends milk-based products to lactose-intolerant customers. Even worse, it could be recommending products with nuts to people with severe allergies.

We need to fix this. Our first thought is to update the **Product Recommendation** decision table. It is possible to write our rules to do this but it is also very likely that such an important decision will somehow get lost in all the rules we are writing. If not now, somebody in the future could forget this important rule with potentially fatal consequences.

Far better to *chain* our decision nodes to highlight in our Decision Model how important this health check rule is. *Figure 4.25* is an example of how we could design this:

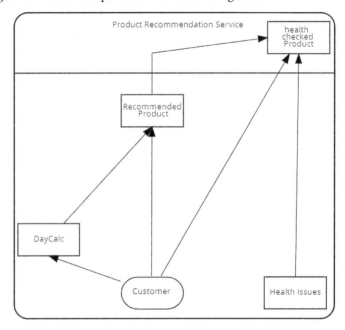

Figure 4.25 – A safer product recommendation service

This model is downloadable as 04_Product_Recommendation-collect.dmn but is simple to recreate yourself with the following changes to our previous decision table example:

1. We removed the **Customer Birth Day** decision node since it was no longer needed for testing, but left the **DayCalc** function for use in our Decision Table.

2. We updated the HIT policy on the **Recommended Product** Decision Policy to **Collect**. It doesn't make a difference for our health checks, but it is better practice than using a HIT policy of **First**. Otherwise, the decision table is unchanged.

3. We make no changes to the **Customer** data type.

4. We've added a new Decision Node of a **List** type, specifying the key health issues we need to look out for. For our example, we specify the lactose intolerant and nut allergy values, as per *Figure 4.26*:

Health Issues *(List)*

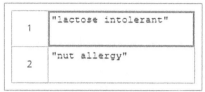

1	"lactose intolerant"
2	"nut allergy"

Figure 4.26 – Health Issues list

5. We added a new Decision node of the **Health Checked** product. While we could have used a small decision table, to keep things simple we make this a literal expression like in *Figure 4.26*. The if Customer.Special Requests in Health Issues then "Potential Health Issue - please check" else Recommended Product expression ensures that any potential health issues get highlighted if they are on the **Health Issues** list. Otherwise, the rule passes through the recommendation from the Decision Table:

health checked Product *(Literal expression)*

health checked Product *(string)*
if Customer.Special Requests in Health Issues then "Potential Health Issue - please check" else Recommended Product

Figure 4.27 – Implementing our heath check in a decision node

6. Finally, we wrap our decision model as a Decision Service to focus people's attention on using the correct **health checked Product** node and not any of the interim calculations.

When we run this decision model, we still make product recommendations as before. However, if there are any potential health issues, they get flagged for human intervention.

This layout is standard practice – we will err on the side of caution with our business rules and allow a real-life person to make the final decision in sensitive cases. Since the person only deals with one or two interesting cases instead of thousands of boring ones, it is still a much better experience for them. It also allows us to focus on writing rules that will apply to the vast majority of cases, so we won't waste too much time on situations that will apply (hopefully) to only a small number of orders.

> **Decision Models as a safety net for AI – neural networks**
>
> Later, when we have hundreds of thousands of orders, we might train a neural network to replace our **Product Recommendation** decision table – as we do in *Chapter 11*. But we would hesitate to trust a neural network to get life or death decisions right (such as nut allergies).
>
> We can't guarantee the output of a neural network in every situation. Combining a rules-based approach (such as the **health checked Product node** with a neural network) gives us a safety net, so we know the important checks will be done exactly as we specify.

Summary

This chapter saw us move from the idea of Decision Models being useful to using Decision Tables and business rules hands-on. Based on a business situation of a chocolate shop, we built a simple product recommendation engine that should give you lots of ideas for your own day-to-day work.

We used many important tools along the way and learned how to model our data using the structured editor, making it clearer what information will be passed in and out of our decision model. We created decision tables, increasing in power and functionality to demonstrate just how scalable a decision-making solution they are. And we looked at the other node types and expressions that help us prepare data for use by decision tables.

Behind these tools, we saw a lot of important concepts – we learned a little bit more about the power of FEEL expressions. We looked at how different HIT policies can make our business rules clearer to understand and avoid gaps. And we saw how to design a decision service to ensure we don't lose sight of mission-critical decisions that might affect people's health.

So far in this book, we've used the KIE sandbox as a tool to write and execute our decision models and business rules. But since we spend much of our working life in Excel, we want to be able to leverage the power of KIE and Drools from within our spreadsheets. We'll look at how we do that in the next chapter.

5

Sharing and Deploying Decision Models Using OpenShift and GitHub

In the previous two chapters, we created decision models and business rules in the KIE Sandbox. While the **Rule runner** screen in the sandbox is great for rapid, iterative development, all the editing is local and we can't share the running decision models with colleagues. Since we're using KIE extended services, models can only be accessed from our laptop. That's not great if we want to collaborate with colleagues or deploy our models into production. We'll remedy that in this chapter by covering the following:

- How deploying our models to the cloud makes them easier to use

- OpenShift as Red Hat's cloud offering

- Important issues on data privacy that you will be glad you started thinking of now

- Saving and sharing your decision models in GitHub, the most widely used collaboration tool

By the end of this chapter, we will have our decision models backed up to a secure cloud location and be able to invite colleagues to collaborate with us on those models. For colleagues who just want to see the result of our work, we'll deploy our decision models to a cloud location where they can run them via a simple web page.

We'll start by looking at a place other than our own laptops where we can run decision models.

How deploying to the cloud makes things easier

If you've ever browsed a website, you've used the cloud. Some computer in a data center received your request and returned the web page you wanted. It doesn't matter if that data center was in Iceland, Ireland, or Indonesia, so long as you have a network connection and clear protocols on how to talk to each other (that's the http and www that you're used to seeing in web links).

Most websites are read-only, or close to it, but what if you could request space in that data center and install an app into it, just like you do on your mobile phone? You'd then communicate with that newly installed app in the data center rather than your phone. That, in very simple terms, is the cloud.

Excel 365, the online version of Office, is an example. You're unaware of the location of the data center that is hosting your document, but you are confident that Microsoft has all of the security checks to keep your information secure. Microsoft specializes in running Office 365 apps in their data centers, so they've gotten pretty good at it and can scale the computers needed up and down to meet demands.

For running Kogito in the cloud and deploying your decision models, Red Hat has an almost-as-slick one-button deployment to host your decision models online. That is based on Red Hat's cloud offering (**OpenShift**) which we'll get up and running soon.

Reality check – why not connect Excel to the local KIE Sandbox?

Technically, it is possible to modify the scripting techniques in this book to communicate between Excel and the KIE Sandbox Extended Services—the local tool you installed in *Chapter 3*.

However, you really don't want to do this for the following reasons:

- The KIE Extended Services' focus is to help your rules development, and they can change from version to version (which would break any Excel sheet connected to it).

- The KIE Extended Services are not available outside of your laptop – which makes it harder for colleagues to use it.

- The KIE Extended Services expect a copy of the DMN decision model sent every time. That's OK from KIE Sandbox in the browser, but we have no easy access to the model from Excel.

In practice, you'll find the one-click deployment so easy to use that hosting your decision models on OpenShift is likely to become your preferred solution. As a bonus, deploying to the cloud automatically gives us a robust, scalable platform to use in production, which is an important aim of this book.

If running decision models locally is vital to you (for example, on a computer on your company premises), take a look at the techniques using *Docker* in *Chapter 10*, which should give you a suitable solution.

OpenShift – Red Hat's piece of the cloud

Red Hat's (IBM) cloud offering is called **OpenShift**. It's full-featured, meaning it can do most of the things the other major cloud vendors such as Google, Amazon, and Microsoft offer. While it is possible to deploy Kogito to these other cloud vendors, we're choosing OpenShift as it offers an easy one-click deployment for Kogito and our decision models.

Being full-featured also means OpenShift has a lot of buttons that we don't need to cover in this book; we're going to ignore those and focus on what you need to deploy your decision models. If you feel the need to learn more, we can recommend *OpenShift for the Absolute Beginner* from Packt at `https://`

`www.packtpub.com/product/openshift-for-the-absolute-beginner-hands-on-video/9781838559090`.

OpenShift has a free layer called the **Developer Sandbox** (not to be confused with the KIE Sandbox). This allows you to try out the deployment with the option to upgrade to a paid-for subscription later. Obviously, the free offering has some limitations, which we will touch on at the end of the section. Broadly speaking, the Developer Sandbox is good enough for developing business rules, but you probably want to upgrade to the full version if you're using it with paying customers.

Let's walk through signing up for the Developer Sandbox, accessing the Sandbox once it is set up, linking the Sandbox to the Developer Sandbox, and deploying our decision models to it.

Signing up for the OpenShift Developer Sandbox

Signing up for the OpenShift Developer Sandbox is a similar process to joining a popular website such as Gmail or Facebook. You go to the website, provide some personal details, verify your email or mobile number, and then you're logged into the site. We'll walk through these steps one by one to get you started:

1. Open the main Developer Sandbox page at `https://developers.redhat.com/developer-sandbox`.

2. While this page has a lot of information, there is a lot here we don't need. Click on the **Start your sandbox for free** button:

Figure 5.1 – Signing up for the OpenShift Sandbox

3. Enter your email to begin the process of setting up your OpenShift account.

    You will be asked for basic details, including a password. When you've filled in all the necessary fields click on the button to **Create My Account.**

4. During the account creation process, you will be asked to confirm your mobile number. That's there to make it more difficult for people to sign up for multiple accounts. You will have to enter the code that gets sent to your mobile.

5. You'll also be prompted to choose a project name during the setup process—this is something you can't change later, so pick one that you'd be happy sharing with your business colleagues.

6. Finally, after confirming your email address by clicking on the link in an email that gets sent to you, you should see the **You're ready to get started!** message:

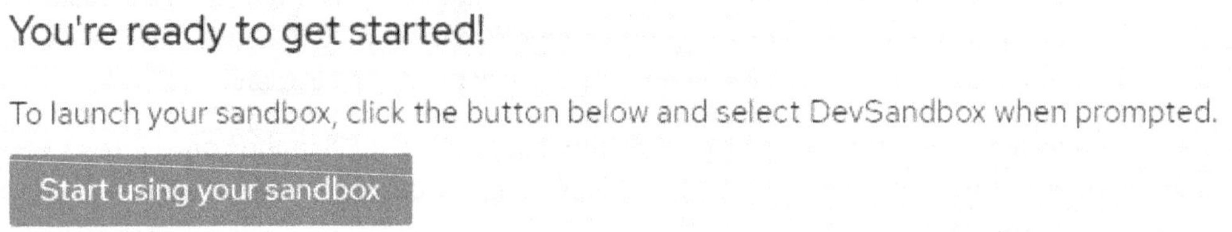

You're ready to get started!

To launch your sandbox, click the button below and select DevSandbox when prompted.

Start using your sandbox

Figure 5.2 – Successful OpenShift sandbox setup

During the signup process, you may see wording in the emails that get sent that you don't quite understand. For example, see the following:

```
Notice: Your Developer Sandbox for Red Hat OpenShift account is
provisioned
```

Sandboxes are a bit like renting an apartment condo. We don't own it, but we're the only ones that can access that piece of the building during the rental period. We expect it to be fully clean with no trace of the previous occupants when we check in, and we expect all the features listed (beds, coffee makers, and so on) to be ready to use. **Provisioned** means that this setup process is complete.

> **A better comparison**
> Since sandboxes are completely torn down and rebuilt after we use them, a better comparison would be German-style rentals where the apartment is stripped back to nearly bare walls, and each person renting must install their own appliances and furniture.

Another reminder in the email is like so:

```
Your account will be active for 30 days. At the end of the active
period, your access will be deactivated and all your data on the
Developer Sandbox will be deleted.
```

Red Hat allows us to use their cloud for free, but they have to draw the line somewhere. 30 days is plenty of time to try out the ideas in this book, and you can sign up again (using the same contact details) for several more 30-day periods.

In general, we'll always have a local copy of our decision models, and we don't store data once the decision model has finished its run, but it's a useful reminder!

Accessing your OpenShift Developer Sandbox

Now that we have our account set up, go to https://developers.redhat.com/developer-sandbox to start using our new cloud environment. The website should remember that you have logged in (but will give you the option to do so if needed), and you may have to click on **Start Using your Sandbox** to view the main OpenShift console like in *Figure 5.3*:

Figure 5.3 – The OpenShift console

There is a lot in this image showing the power of the OpenShift cloud offering. We won't do our normal tour of the screen; instead, we'll take it as confirmation that we have the Developer Sandbox set up correctly. If you're curious, take a look around, but we'll focus on getting two key pieces of information to allow us to link our local KIE Sandbox with this piece of the cloud.

Two vital pieces of link information

Before we leave the OpenShift console, let's make a note of two key pieces of information that we'll need to link to our OpenShift instance later. *Figure 5.4* shows the menu under the project name on the top right of the console. Your project name will be different, but **Copy login command** will be the same.

Figure 5.4 – Copying login details

After you select **Copy login command**, you will be shown a page similar to *Figure 5.5*. There is a lot going on during this process, and it's worth walking through it step by step:

1. Since this is accessing sensitive information, you may be asked to log in again. You'll see a simple screen that reads **Display Token**. Clicking on this link will two pieces of information.

2. Look for the line starting with **Your API token is sha256~_oNI_uw-qyD6A--EI-Qhg1-sddfFezCFZ-gZxLxFZUo**. Note that *your token will be different as it is unique to you and will change daily*.

3. Copy the text starting from **sha256** through to the end of the line.

4. It's probably better to save it to a text file (using Notepad) as we need to copy a second value from this page. We'll use this token instead of a username and password so OpenShift will know it's us when we connect to it from KIE Sandbox.

5. Our second value is the URL (web location) of where to find our OpenShift instance in the cloud. This value is on the next line starting **oc login**. You need to take the text immediately after **server=** through to the end of the line, as highlighted in *Figure 5.5*. Again, your values are unique to you and will be different from the image.

oc login --token= sha256~_oNI_uw-qyD6A--EI-Qhg1-sddfFezCFZ-gZxLxFZUo
server=**https://api.sandbox.x8i5.p1.openshiftapps.com:6443**

Figure 5.5 – Copying server details

6. Save this server URL somewhere—we're about to use it to link to our KIE Sandbox.

Linking KIE Sandbox and your OpenShift instance

If you don't already have it open, go to your local KIE Sandbox at `https://sandbox.kie.org/`. We use the word `local` as up until now, all the decision models have been saved in our web browser on our local laptop.

> **KIE Sandbox is constantly evolving**
> The KIE team has the sandbox under constant development, so it likely the screenshots will differ slightly from what is presented here. The basic concept of providing the token via the settings menu to link the KIE Sandbox to both OpenShift and GitHub will remain the same.

We move to the local cloud as we link KIE Sandbox to our new OpenShift cloud instance:

1. Click on the settings icons on the top right of the KIE Sandbox screen.

2. Click on **OpenShift** in the pop-up screen that appears and you should see the settings screen like in *Figure 5.6*:

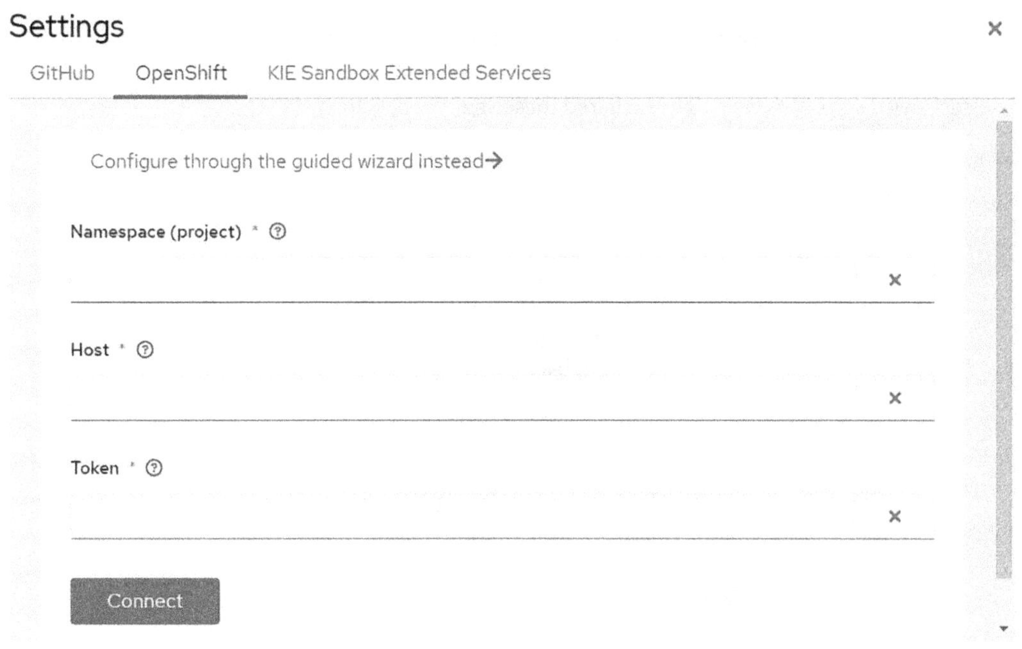

Settings   ✕

GitHub   **OpenShift**   KIE Sandbox Extended Services

Configure through the guided wizard instead→

Namespace (project) * ⑦

_____ ✕

Host * ⑦

_____ ✕

Token * ⑦

_____ ✕

Connect

Figure 5.6 – Entering server details

3.   While it's possible to enter the details directly here, it's easier the first time to click on **Configure through the guided wizard instead**.

The first step of the connection wizard asks for the project name. If you've forgotten what it was, go back to OpenShift; it's on the top right of the screen. Ours is `crt-openshift-dev` yours will be different and must match your OpenShift settings exactly. *Figure 5.7* shows a sample. When this is done, click **Next.**

Figure 5.7 – Connection wizard step 1

4. The second step of the connection wizard is *Figure 5.8* – it asks for the **Host** and **Token** details that we saved earlier. Note the order may be different – Host will start with `https` and Token starts with `sha`. When you have entered these values, click **Next**.

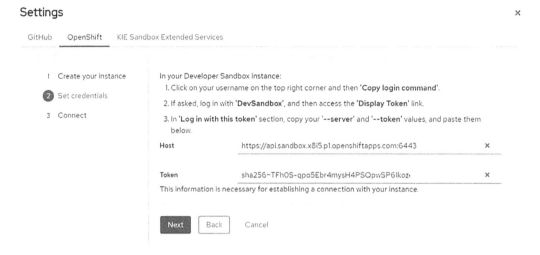

Figure 5.8 – Connection wizard step 2

5. KIE Sandbox will attempt to connect your OpenShift instance and if successful, will show the Connection successfully established. message like in *Figure 5.9*. Click **Save** to complete this step.

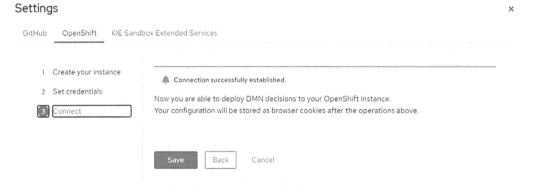

Figure 5.9 – Step 3 of the connection wizard

> **Troubleshooting your connection**
>
> By far, the biggest issue is using the wrong project, host, or token name when trying to set up the connection. Or, you could have the right values but in the wrong place. You could also have most of the values but may be missing the last letter of the token.
>
> Tokens also change every 24 hours, so don't be afraid to go back and check, and of course, always check that your internet connection is working and that your OpenShift instance is running.

Deploying your decision model to OpenShift

Now that we have the connection made, go back to the main decision model editor screen in KIE Sandbox. You may need to click **X** on the top right of the editor.

We're going to deploy the decision model we made in the last chapter to OpenShift. As a reminder, the GitHub page with all the book samples is at `https://github.com/PacktPublishing/AI-and-Business-Rules-for-Excel-Power-Users`, and the specific example you are looking for is at `04_Product_Recommendation-collect.dmn`. If you don't have it already, you will need to download and import it into your local sandbox first:

1. On the top right of the KIE Sandbox screen, click on **Try on OpenShift**, then, like in *Figure 5.10*, select the name of the model we want to deploy (in this case, our **Product Recommendation** sample).

Figure 5.10 – Selecting the decision model to deploy

2. KIE Sandbox will ask for confirmation like in *Figure 5.11*:

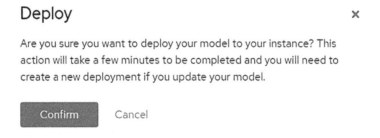

Figure 5.11 – Confirming the deployment

3. There will then be a short *in progress* message like in *Figure 5.12*:

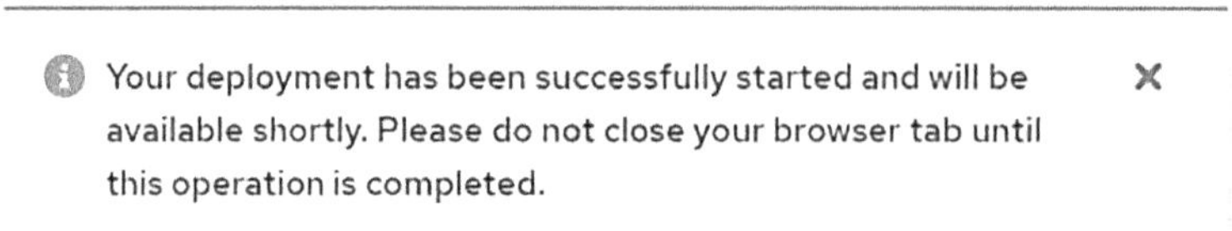

ℹ️ Your deployment has been successfully started and will be   ✕
    available shortly. Please do not close your browser tab until
    this operation is completed.

Figure 5.12 – Deployment in progress

4. When your deployment has been completed, you'll see a message like in *Figure 5.13*:

OpenShift deployments

Connected to 'crt-openshift-dev'
Change...

✅ _04_Product_Recommendation-col...
Created at 20/09/2022, 22:06:41

Figure 5.13 – Deployment successful message

5. If you click on the model name beside the green tick box as you can see in *Figure 5.13* (in this case, **Product Recommendation**), KIE Sandbox will very helpfully open a new web page, pointing to where we have deployed the model on OpenShift, like in *Figure 5.14*:

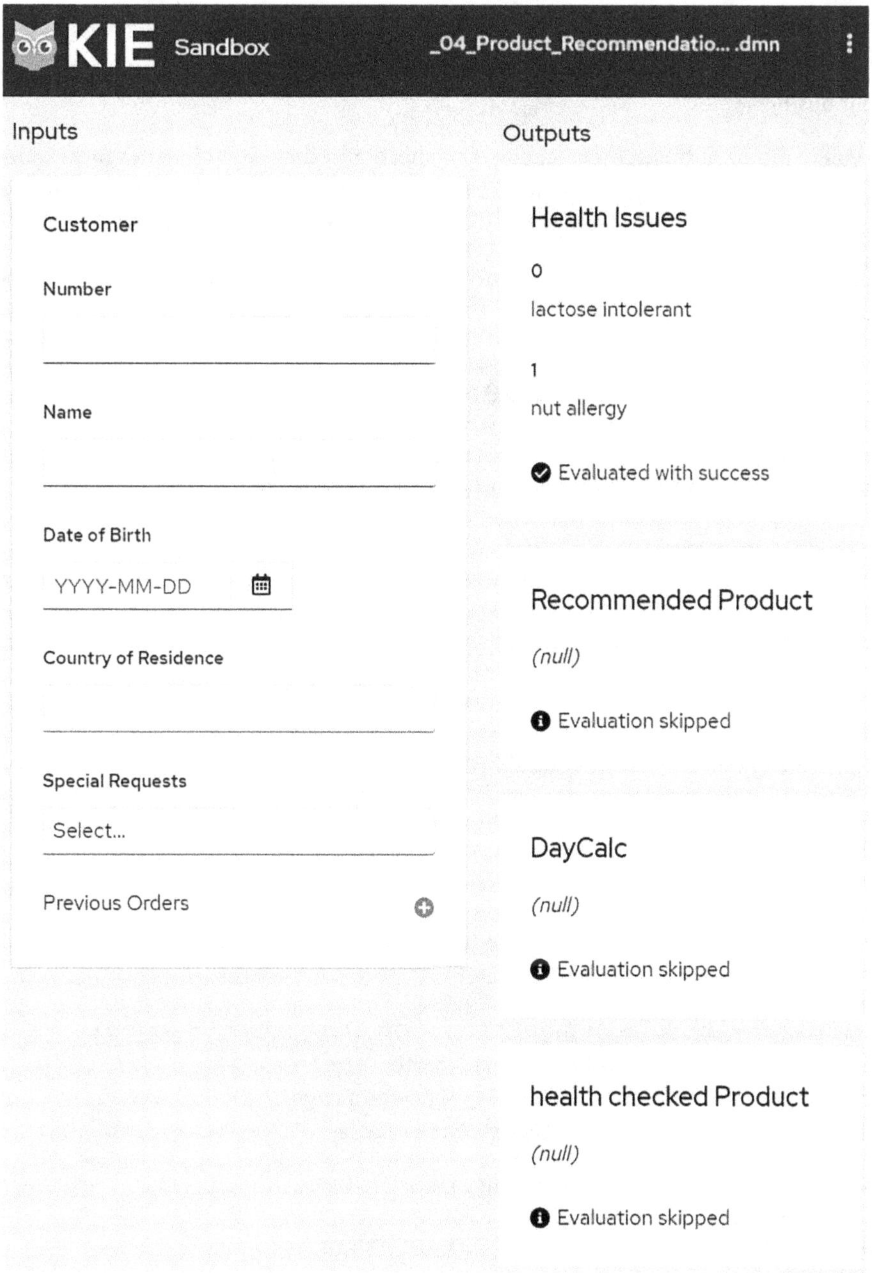

KIE Sandbox   _04_Product_Recommendatio....dmn

Inputs

Customer

Number

_____

Name

_____

Date of Birth

YYYY-MM-DD 📅
_____

Country of Residence

_____

Special Requests

Select...
_____

Previous Orders   ⊕

Outputs

Health Issues

0
lactose intolerant

1
nut allergy

✅ Evaluated with success

Recommended Product

(null)

ℹ Evaluation skipped

DayCalc

(null)

ℹ Evaluation skipped

health checked Product

(null)

ℹ Evaluation skipped

Figure 5.14 – Our deployed model on OpenShift

This screen looks very familiar – it's a version of the input-output screen we had in the KIE sandbox, and it should look familiar; the aim of the sandbox is fast, iterative development with no surprises when you use it after a production deployment like this.

Play around with it; you'll see the inputs and outputs work as expected, but you won't be able to view the model you're using to generate these decisions. You wouldn't want end users to change how you're making your business rules.

No doubt you're proud of this achievement, so go ahead and share it with colleagues. Unlike the sandbox, they can access this page using the same URL as you used. They'll be able to play with this decision model and marvel at you taking your first steps into business rules and AI.

Before we get carried away, we do need to remember that we're still using the Developer Sandbox, and that has certain limitations.

Important notes on the OpenShift Developer Sandbox

The OpenShift Developer Sandbox is great because it is free (you can try before you buy) yet has most of the substantial features of the full-featured cloud offering. However, you need to remember a couple of limitations of the free version:

- Tokens need to be renewed daily. This means you need to (re)link OpenShift and KIE Sandbox using the instructions in the previous section. It's not onerous, but you need to remember to do it, or the sandbox will give you an error.

- The Developer Sandbox needs to be renewed every 30 days, and prior to this renewal, everything within OpenShift data will be deleted. This isn't a problem since you will always have a local copy of your decision model, and you shouldn't be storing any data in your models in the sandbox.

- By default, any model you deploy to OpenShift is public access. This is great for sharing the link with colleagues for them to test out, but you may want to investigate the security and access restrictions in OpenShift to limit who can see your models.

A final point to remember is that if you leave your OpenShift sandbox running, it will be deactivated after 8 hours. You will get an email like this:

```
In accordance with the usage terms of Developer Sandbox, we have
reduced the number of instances of your application to zero (0). You
can restart your application(s) by increasing the number of instances
from the Developer Sandbox User Interface.
```

There are a number of different ways to restart your application. Perhaps the quickest is to do the following:

1. Open the OpenShift web console.

2. At the top right of the screen, there will a set of icons like in *Figure 5.15*:

Figure 5.15 – Command prompt icon in OpenShift

3. Click on >_. This will cause your application to restart; it will also open a panel at the bottom of the screen that looks like a terminal, but that's a side effect and we don't need to type anything into it.

All of these restrictions won't cause an issue during development, but if you do intend to deploy your decision models for real-life business use, it is much better to migrate to the paid-for tier.

Remember the online resources

The KIE Sandbox and Red Hat teams have put a lot of effort into the online resources we mentioned in *Chapter 2*. Now is a good time to go look at those again. There is a particularly good video on linking KIE Sandbox with OpenShift at `https://youtu.be/2zY85TXFNuw` (or search the KIE YouTube channel for *DMN Dev Sandbox Developing and deploying DMN decisions in the cloud*).

Since we've made an important step into deploying our models outside of our own laptops, it's probably a good time to have a conversation about how to treat data.

Taking care of your data

We're glad about the trend of legislation toward increased data privacy. As professionals who work with data, we have been known to curse the regulations sometimes, but in many ways, it's just ensuring what we hope you would seek to do anyway: *be respectful when working with personal data.*

Personal data is anything that could identify a person—a phone number associated with a name, an email (since that will often always include the first name or last name), or an address. For example, if we're talking about a male, under 21, living at 59 Bolton Square, it may be obvious who the person we're talking about is.

Even if you don't live in Europe, you've probably felt the impact of the EU's **General Data Protection Regulation (GDPR)**. For example, if you're US-based, and you're dealing with a client that lives in the EU, the regulation still gives that client protection, with the thread of eye-watering fines to back it up. There are many other local equivalents (California in the US being the most notable).

The regulations are pretty well written and it's easier to start following them from day 1. Up to now, many of your decisions and personal data have been kept internal to your company (in an Excel sheet). The GDPR and data protection regulations still apply, but you'll notice that we've started passing data to external services (just now IBM/Red Hat, and shortly Microsoft). This makes the topic of the GDPR even more important.

The good news is that the approach that this book suggests is likely to make you more GDPR-compliant:

- We talked in the last chapter about not using specific personal information in business rules. Since we should only pass in the information that we need to make a decision, it is far less likely that our system will be impacted by the GDPR.

- IBM and Red Hat have spent a lot of time on security and customer confidentiality and ensuring they are GDPR-compliant. These vendors stake their reputations on keeping data secure to a level that not every smaller company (including yours) will be able to achieve.

- This book advocates more formal techniques for managing your data and making decisions. We're on a journey from having Excel spreadsheets scattered around the organization (a data management nightmare) to storing and processing them in a coherent manner. This approach also makes GDPR compliance easier.

Starting with good habits in managing data will make your life a lot easier later. Another good habit that you will be glad about later is to back up and version control your decision models. Let's look at the built-in integration that KIE Sandbox has with GitHub to allow us to do this.

Saving and sharing your decision models using GitHub

You probably haven't thought about it too much (other than the **Ephemeral** message in KIE Sandbox), but you're currently saving decision models in local storage associated with your web browser. While this is great for getting started, it isn't something we'd recommend for long-term use. What if your laptop gets lost—do you have a backup? How can you share decision models with a colleague? What if you realize you made a mistake and want to revert to the version you had 5 minutes ago? Local storage doesn't easily let you do any of these things.

Luckily, the KIE Sandbox has a link to the best collaboration site available: GitHub. You may remember GitHub from *Chapter 2* when we introduced the KIE and Drools projects, allowing many hundreds of developers to collaborate, share files, and navigate through different versions of their work.

GitHub has a private repository option that you can use for your own project and restrict to just the people that you want to collaborate with. It's important to note that your repository is your space—it's not linked to any Red Hat projects hosted on the same site, but it does mean we need to set up our own space and link it to KIE Sandbox. Let's walk through that now.

Signing up for GitHub and getting your token

To use GitHub, you need to sign up for an account. The site is owned by Microsoft, and logins from their other sites aren't (yet) usable. To get your GitHub login, do the following:

1. Go to the GitHub home screen at `www.github.com`.

2. You'll see a welcome page with a large **Sign up for GitHub** button.

3. Clicking this button will take you to the account sign-up screen in *Figure 5.16*:

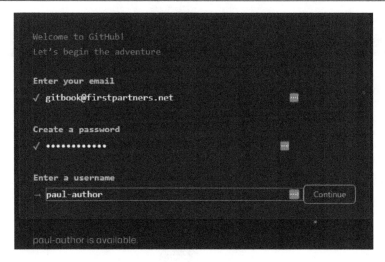

Figure 5.16 – GitHub sign-up screen

4. After entering your details, including a new username and email address, hit the **Create Account** button.

5. You'll get sent a message to verify your email address. Clicking on the link in this email will take you to your personal homepage on GitHub.

A tour of your personal homepage on GitHub

The page you are seeing in *Figure 5.17* is different from the project page that you saw for Kogito/Drools back in *Chapter 2*. It's your personal page on GitHub, with options to explore the multiple projects that you might want to interact with.

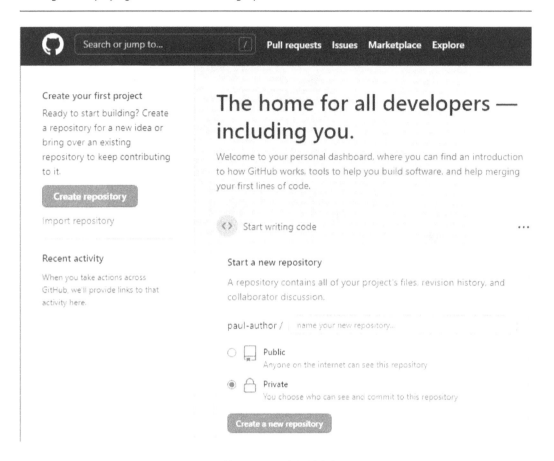

Figure 5.17 – Your personal GitHub home page

There is an option to create a repository here (using the green button at the bottom of this page), a space to store our decision model files, but KIE Sandbox can also do that for us (will see exactly how later in the chapter). Let's focus on the steps we need to link KIE Sandbox with the GitHub repository that we have just created.

To create the link between KIE Sandbox and GitHub, we need a personal token on GitHub. A bit like with OpenShift, this token replaces our username and password so that GitHub knows that KIE Sandbox is authorised to act on our behalf. To create this token, follow these steps:

1. At the top right of GitHub (any screen), click on the profile settings as shown in *Figure 5.18*.

Figure 5.18 – Your GitHub profile settings

2. Search for **Developer settings** (bottom left, end of the list) then highlight **Personal access tokens** like in *Figure 5.19*:

Figure 5.19 – GitHub's Personal access tokens screen

3. Click on the **Generate new token** button and then confirm your GitHub password when requested.

4. The screen in *Figure 5.20* will appear, allowing you to set the permissions associated with this token. The permissions must include the repository scope so that when KIE Sandbox uses the token, it can create a new repository to store models. Note that there are more options, but we've cropped the image to fit on the page.

New personal access token

Personal access tokens function like ordinary OAuth access tokens. They can be used instead of a password for Git over HTTPS, or can be used to authenticate to the API over Basic Authentication.

Note

Note that this is for chapter 5 of the book

What's this token for?

Expiration *

30 days ⬍   The token will expire on Mon, Oct 24 2022

Select scopes

Scopes define the access for personal tokens. Read more about OAuth scopes.

☑ **repo**	Full control of private repositories	
☑ repo:status	Access commit status	
☑ repo_deployment	Access deployment status	
☑ public_repo	Access public repositories	
☑ repo:invite	Access repository invitations	
☑ security_events	Read and write security events	
☐ **workflow**	Update GitHub Action workflows	

Generate token   Cancel

Figure 5.20 – Setting permissions for a new personal access token

Copy the token that appears on the screen (like in *Figure 5.21*) immediately, as it will not be displayed again. We'll need it soon for our first step in the next section, which is adding the token to KIE Sandbox to link it to our GitHub account.

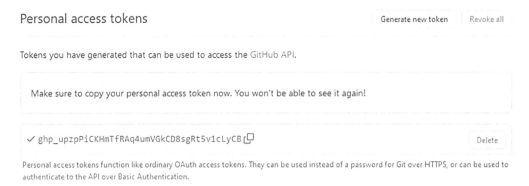

Figure 5.21 – Copy the newly generated personal access token

> **More on GitHub tokens**
>
> We'll just give you enough info on GitHub tokens to create the link with KIE Sandbox, but if you want to know more about GitHub tokens, a good place to start is `https://docs.github.com/en/authentication/keeping-your-account-and-data-secure/creating-a-personal-access-token`.

Using your token to collaborate on KIE Sandbox

Since we have our GitHub account set up and made a note of our unique access token, we want to link KIE Sandbox to it:

1. You need to start by opening KIE Sandbox on the usual page at `https://sandbox.kie.org`.

2. Click on the person icon on the top right to select **Connected Accounts**, then select the option to connect a GitHub account.

3. Paste your GitHub token on this screen. Immediately after pasting the token, you should get a message confirming the connection (like in *Figure 5.22*):

Figure 5.22 – Successfully linking KIE Sandbox and GitHub

4. After you get this success message, close the popup by clicking **x** in the top right-hand corner.

5. Now, if we click on the **Share** menu on the top right of the main KIE Sandbox, you'll see we have additional options like in *Figure 5.23*. Note that we've removed a couple of menu items for space reasons, so you may need to scroll down on your screen to see the option we've highlighted, and of course, your GitHub username will be different.

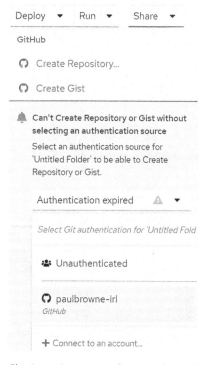

Figure 5.23 – Sharing using our newly created GitHub connection

6.   Scroll down and select the GitHub account that you just connected.

Now that we have KIE Sandbox and GitHub linked, let's use that link to solve some of the problems we saw previously.

GitHub flows for saving and project collaboration

Once KIE Sandbox is linked to GitHub, we will have more options in the **Share** menu on the top right of the screen. Since our concern is local storage, we want to save our decision models somewhere more robust:

1.   On the **Share** menu, we now have the **Create repository** option. Click on this, and you will see an options screen like in *Figure 5.24*:

Figure 5.24 – KIE Sandbox creating a repository for our decision model in GitHub

2.   Enter a repository name and select the option to create privately (we can change this later).

3.   After a few seconds, you'll see a confirmation message that the repository has been created and the link where you can view the files like in *Figure 5.25*:

Figure 5.25 – Repository successfully created in GitHub

Before we go to check out our files saved on GitHub, it's worth taking a minute to note some of the other screen changes now that KIE Sandbox and GitHub are linked. The main changes are highlighted in *Figure 5.26*, *Figure 5.27*, and *Figure 5.28*.

Figure 5.26 – Changes to the KIE Sandbox screen when linked to GitHub, top left

- The word **Repository** replaces ephemeral, indicating our decision models are being saved in GitHub.

- **main** indicates the branch that we are working on. While it is possible to work solely on **main**, branches allow you to work on a parallel track and merge an entire set of changes back to the primary (main) track when you are ready to do so.

- KIE also indicates the username/Git repository name and a green tick to indicate that all is well.

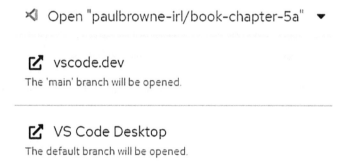

Figure 5.27 – Changes to the KIE Sandbox screen, top right, new options for VS Code

Other options on the screen have appeared as well. On the top right, we have options to open our decision model in Visual Studio Code. We'll cover that in more detail in *Chapter 12*.

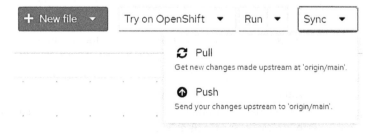

Figure 5.28 – Changes to the KIE Sandbox screen, top right, new options to sync

Also on the top right, there is a new sync menu. Pulling and pushing are standard GitHub concepts that you'll use a lot:

I.   **Pull** is used when you want to take other people's changes and download them to refresh your local copy

II.   **Push** is used when you have made changes locally and you want to send them to GitHub to the main upstream repository

We'll demonstrate these concepts when we go through common workflows in editing and saving your decision models. Now that we've completed our tour of what has changed, let's check how KIE actually saved our repository on GitHub.

4.   Go back to your personal page at GitHub.com. You'll see that KIE has created a private repository like in *Figure 5.29*:

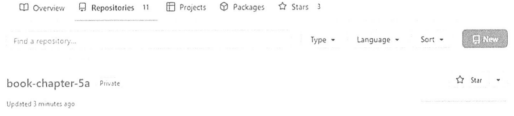

Figure 5.29 – New repository created on GitHub

5.   When you click on the repository, you'll see that it contains all our decision model files (like in *Figure 5.30*):

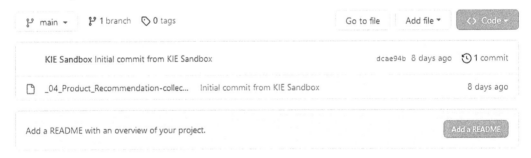

Figure 5.30 – The decision model shared/stored within the repository

6.   If you click on the model's name, you'll see it's a standard XML format, full of nested <**Tags**>; it's just an XML file. If you use Chrome, KIE has a plugin to visualize and edit this XML file as a decision model. However, the functionality is very similar to the KIE Sandbox editor, so while it's useful to install, we won't cover it in detail.

More importantly, now that we have a file securely saved in the GitHub repository, let's invite selected colleagues to collaborate with us on them.

Sharing your repository

Since we set our repository as private, we need to invite our colleagues to collaborate with us:

1. Open your project (not personal) settings page on GitHub. You'll find this under the project name (like on the far right of *Figure 5.31*):

Figure 5.31 – Finding the project settings on GitHub

2. Once you see the project settings screen, click on the collaborator's options, and you'll have the option to invite colleagues like in *Figure 5.32*.

3. Of course, you will need to know their GitHub names. Once you invite them, they will have access to your repository (just this project).

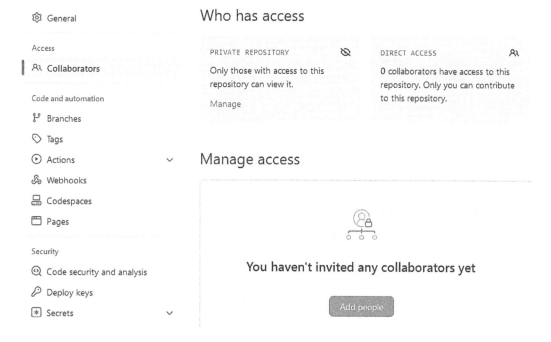

Figure 5.32 – Inviting other people to collaborate on decision models

Now that your colleagues have access, how do they collaborate with you on these decision models? What makes Git and GitHub so powerful is that there are a number of different workflows for you to do this, and which one is most appropriate for you is a matter of personal choice.

> **Git and GitHub**
>
> This book talks about **Git** and **GitHub** as if they were interchangeable, and since the tools we use in this book (KIE Sandbox, and later Visual Studio Code) have the Git protocols embedded in them, you're never likely to use Git tools directly. However, it is useful to know that **Git** is the tool that allows people to collaborate over multiple files on a project, and **GitHub** is the website that helps you find these projects and groups of people.

Different workflows

You may be used to Office 365, where everybody works on a common version of a single file. Word and Excel are quick enough that you see changes in real time, so conflicting changes don't tend to be an issue. Office 365 offers simple versioning; if somebody else makes an edit you don't like, you can roll back to the previous version, or the version from last week that everybody agreed was OK.

While we currently have a single file, we will very quickly progress to multiple interlinked models that we want to collaborate on. That's why Git and GitHub offer you more powerful workflows for collaboration.

One important difference is that while it is possible to edit the files directly on GitHub, most of the time you're working with a local copy. When you're happy that everything is working as it should, it's only then that you push your files up to the main branch on the upstream repository.

There are many ways of using Git, which is what makes it so powerful. If you want to know more, check out the Packt books on Git at `https://www.packt.com/?s=github&post_type=product`.

For now, let us talk through two of the most common Git workflows.

A simple one-person workflow using KIE

Perhaps the easiest way to use Git and KIE is as follows:

1. Link KIE and GitHub as we described. This gives you a local copy of your decision models and a backup copy on the GitHub site.

2. Make your changes to the decision models as before. Like before, these changes are automatically stored locally.

3. At regular intervals, push/commit your local changes to your GitHub repository online.

This is good practice—you will have a backup copy of your work in case you lose your laptop, and it allows you to be braver in your editing since you will have all of your previous versions that you can revert to. It also gets you used to using Git workflows.

However, the true power of Git tools becomes clearer when we collaborate. Here is one simple collaboration workflow that you might use.

A simple collaboration workflow using KIE

We'll assume that you have already linked KIE and GitHub:

1. Invite your colleague to collaborate as per the previous instructions.
2. Both of you will have a local copy (in KIE Sandbox) so you can continue to edit as before.
3. You can continue to push your changes to GitHub, but your colleague may need to create a pull request asking you to inspect their work before accepting or rejecting it onto the main branch.
4. Git will notify you of any conflicts (for example, if both of you edited the same file at the same time) and will give you the opportunity to resolve them.

You'll note that we haven't described either of these workflows in great detail. There are many other ways of using Git and GitHub, but as an industry-standard collaboration tool, it is well worth learning the basics of versioning, main and other branches, repositories, and the concepts of pushing and pulling files. At a minimum, we recommend using the simple one-person workflow to back up your files, and to build your confidence with the GitHub tools.

We'll walk through one final example of using GitHub that isn't really a workflow but is useful when trying out examples as you work through the book.

Importing models directly from GitHub

As a reminder, there are several options to import decision models on the KIE Sandbox homepage. This includes the option like in *Figure 5.33* to import a model directly from GitHub, where the URL is the homepage of the project that you want to use.

Figure 5.33 – Importing a decision model directly from a GitHub repository

This is very useful since GitHub hosts many samples (such as the ones for this book) that you just want to download and play with and don't want to put under full version control.

Summary

In this chapter, we moved from editing our decision models alone to being able to show our work to colleagues and collaborate to develop those models.

We covered OpenShift as Red Hat's cloud offering and deployed our KIE decision models into it. We also covered GitHub as a collaboration site and showed how to use it for common collaborative workflows.

Since we now have a firm basis for building and deploying our decision models with our colleagues, we will move on to linking them to a tool that many of them use: calling our decision models from Excel.

6

Calling Business Rules from Excel Using Power Query

In the previous chapter, we looked at how we could collaborate to share and edit our decision models. We also saw how to deploy them onto the OpenShift cloud so that other people could run them through an automatically generated web interface.

That was very impressive, but our colleagues are still likely to be doing most of their work using Microsoft Excel. How can we link our business rules, AI, and decision models to Excel and make all the tools work together? That's what this chapter covers, including the following:

- Five different ways to link rules, AI, decision models, and Excel – using Power Query, Visual Basic for Applications, Script Lab, Office Scripts, and Power Automate

- Machine-readable web pages using REST and how to link these to our decision service

- Swagger – a more human-friendly link to KIE and Kogito decision services

- Calling the decision service using Power Query with step-by-step examples to build a solution that you can expand on for your own work

By the end of the chapter, you will have learned how Kogito publishes a machine-readable web page, and how we can use Power Query in Excel to link to it.

Prerequisites

Before you start, it is best to have Microsoft Excel installed on your laptop. While the free online version (`https://www.microsoft.com/en-us/microsoft-365/free-office-online-for-the-web`) is getting more and more powerful, some techniques in this chapter (for example, using Power Query) will only fully work in the desktop version.

Fortunately, the Script Lab approach we will describe in the next chapter will work with the online version of Excel. And we will introduce other alternatives (such as Office Scripts and Power Automate) that work outside of Excel – and are compatible with other tools (such as Google Sheets and OpenOffice) that can read and write Excel format files.

Since we will cover so many approaches to linking Excel to our business rules, let's start with an overview of what they are.

Five different ways to link rules, AI, decision models, and Excel

At the end of *Chapter 5*, we saw that KIE and Kogito autogenerate a web page based on our decision model. We'll soon see that there is a machine-readable version of this page that we can link to Excel. That page won't change no matter what technique we use. *Figure 6.1* shows some of the ways we can make this link.

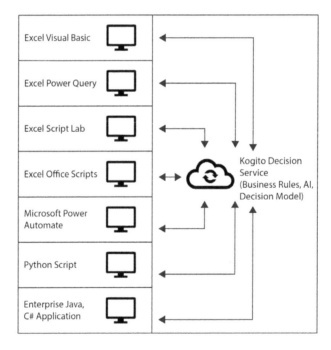

Figure 6.1– Many different ways of linking Excel to our decision service

You may be familiar with some of the techniques listed in this diagram – even if you're not, we'll run through them in the next section. The key point is that no matter which technique you choose, the core Kogito decision service (including your business rules and AI) stays the same. That allows you to choose the technique that works best for you now, knowing that your investment in decision models is still valid even as you evolve toward other tools.

It is highly likely that later in your journey with business rules, you will see colleagues calling them using full enterprise coding languages such as Python, Java, or C#. While this is outside the scope of this book, it does reassure you that Kogito gives you tools to capture, run, and share your business rules in a way that will still be valid in the future.

First, let's introduce the five techniques we will use to link Excel to our decision service as mentioned in *Figure 6.1*. It's worth mentioning that all five techniques are industry-standard with a lot of books and web articles available for each of them. And whichever you choose, they are a good investment of your time. You will use these tools in a lot of other Excel work – not just linking to decision services.

VBA

VBA was game-changing for Excel power users when it was introduced almost 30 years ago. It allows Excel users to record their actions, edit the generated script, and then play it back in an almost enterprise-level programming tool.

While VBA has a huge install base, it is showing its age. If you're using VBA, it's because you have a legacy spreadsheet, or you've been working with it for a long while. Don't worry – we haven't forgotten about you. We cover how to link Excel to decision services in the next chapter.

Script Lab and Office Scripts

If you are starting to automate Excel Spreadsheets today, we'd recommend using a more modern alternative from Microsoft – Script Lab or Office Scripts. Both are based on the same concept of manipulating Excel using code, and Office Scripts have a similar *recorder* to VBA, which allows you to capture actions and then edit the autogenerated script. The difference is that both Script Lab and Office Scripts integrate more easily with modern web technologies than VBA – for example, they use a version of JavaScript that you might already have played with when building web pages.

There is a large degree of crossover between Script Lab and Office Scripts – both use the same JavaScript object model to manipulate Excel. Learning one automatically gives you a head start with the other. This is especially important as Office Scripts are newer, and it is expected that Microsoft will continue to build out its capabilities.

Currently, Script Lab is better if you want to focus on the user of your spreadsheets. It allows you a choice of user interface elements and will run on both the web and desktop. It also allows you to build custom functions that you can call from within your spreadsheet in a format similar to `=myCustomFunction (A1).`

Office Scripts are the better choice for running within Office 365 in the cloud (currently, they can be run but not edited from the desktop version of Excel). They are better for automated flows where a user does not need to be present since they can be called from Power Automate. While slightly less powerful (they don't have as many user interface options), they are slightly easier to learn and do have the script recorder, which is a great help in getting started.

In real life, you're likely to switch back and forth between Script Lab and Office Scripts depending on what you're trying to achieve. We will cover Script Lab in the next chapter, then expand on it using Office Scripts as part of Power Automate flows in *Chapter 8*.

Microsoft Power Automate

Remember back in *Chapter 3* when we said decision models aren't workflows, since they execute all at once? Power Automate *is* workflow-based and allows you to get the computer to do a lot of the repetitive manual steps you may need to do in dealing with Excel and other Microsoft Office documents. Typically, a Power Automate flow will span several different systems, one of which could be calling our decision services for a key business decision, before maybe updating an Excel spreadsheet with the result. We'll go into more detail on this approach in *Chapter 8*.

Power Query

Our final technique is the simplest. Power Query allows you to bring a wide range of data sources into Excel, manipulating it in a way that is repeatable and that allows you to refresh the data later from the original data source. It's a very powerful element of a data analyst's toolkit and one that is well worth learning about in its own right.

Our interest in Power Query is that one of the many data sources it can pull data from is JSON, using a REST API. That is exactly the machine-readable format that Kogito generates from our decision service. Since all our techniques link into the same REST and JSON format, it's worth looking at what we're working with in more detail.

Machine-readable web pages using REST

We've been talking about machine-readable web pages using REST and JSON as a common language.

REST stands for **Representational State Transfer**, which is another way of describing machine-readable web pages. Let's take a look at what that looks like with a simple example, before exploring the Kogito REST API in more detail.

A simple REST example

REST uses a lot of the same infrastructure as browsing the web – so you can open a REST URL such as `https://api.github.com/repos/OfficeDev/office-js` using a web browser, like in *Figure 6.2*. This screenshot was taken using Firefox, as it colors the JSON for us, but Edge and Chrome will give you similar results. Note that a lot more information will be returned – we've edited the image for clarity.

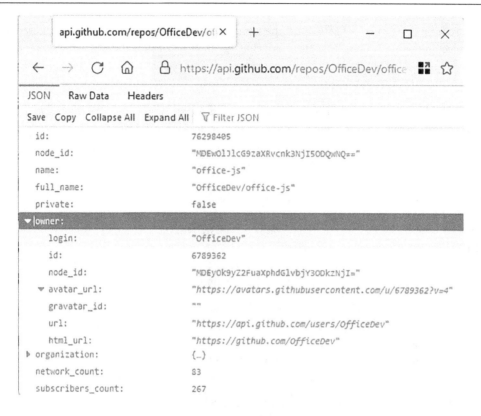

Figure 6.2 – A simple REST call

This REST call gives you information about a project hosted on GitHub. From the URL, you can guess that it contains information about a repo (project), and that project is the Office JavaScript example from the Microsoft team. Looking at the information returned, at the very bottom, we can see the "subscribers count" – the number of people following the project.

While the REST format is mostly used by machines, it's not unfriendly to humans. We have already learned the following:

- REST calls are made over the web using standard transport (the HTTP that you're familiar with). In particular, this is a GET request, where all the information we want to pass in is contained in the URL.

- REST URLs are structured to give a clue about the information that will be returned. From the JSON returned, we get pointers to other URLs (or endpoints) that might be of interest.

- The call returns JSON, a format we first met in *Chapter 4*, which allows us to guess the meaning of a lot of information. In fact, it returns too much information, but we can ignore everything except the field that we were looking for (Subscriber count).

- If we refresh the page, we get almost the same result (unless somebody else has followed the project in the meantime). This gives us a clue that the REST call is *stateless* – the server takes our request, deals with it, then forgets about us. Our next request will be treated as a fresh new inquiry using the information we pass in at that time.

Our simple sample uses the browser to make web requests. As you might guess from our screenshot, REST doesn't really care who or what is calling it, as long as it is a valid request. In this case, *valid* means that the client making the call knows how to "speak" HTTP, that the client is calling the right URL, and that it passes in the information expected to that URL.

More on REST – GET and POST requests

In our previous example, we talked to the server using a GET request – all the information was in the URL. GET is the best option for simple requests – for example, Google uses it for its search queries where you can copy and paste a URL such as `https://www.google.com/search?q=packt+books` into different browsers and get the same response every time.

Our requests are likely to pass in more complex information, which is why will use the POST option. You're likely to have used this option without realizing it, for example, when filling out a form on a web page and then hitting submit. If the web page URL doesn't change or show your data, then the way the information gets transmitted behind the scenes is via a POST call. While they are easy to use (as we'll see shortly), in POST calls, information is more hidden but more powerful.

You've probably guessed that there is a lot more to REST than the just-what-we-need-to-know introduction we've covered here. A good source of information if you want to read more about it is `https://restfulapi.net/`.

Our focus on learning REST is to communicate with our Kogito decision server. Let's look at what that looks like in more detail, starting with Swagger – a tool that makes REST easier.

Swagger – a more human-friendly link to Kogito

While REST is not unfriendly, Kogito helpfully uses a tool called Swagger to make REST pages even easier to understand.

We'll pick up where we left off in *Chapter 5* where we deployed our decision model to the OpenShift cloud (dev sandbox) and shared the web page for our colleagues to admire. It's worth going back to that web page now – remember that it looks similar to *Figure 6.3*.

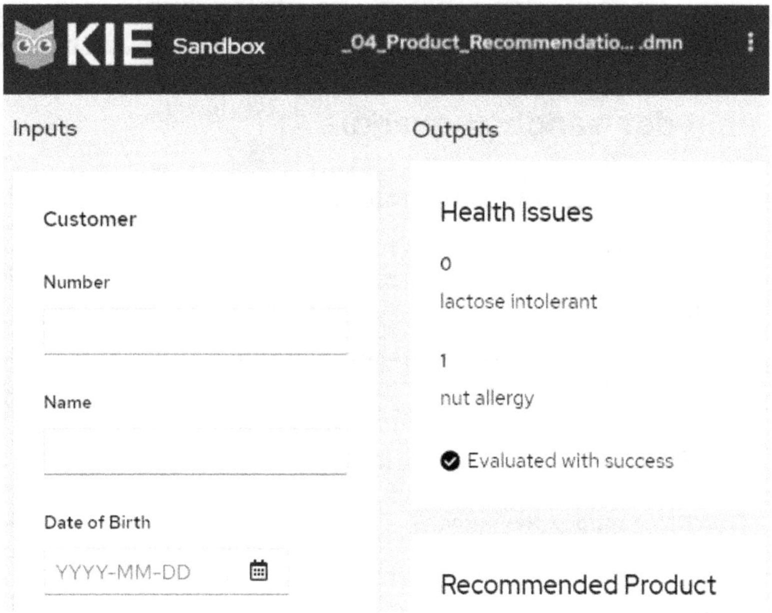

Figure 6.3 – A reminder of what our decision model looks like in the cloud

Remember – you may need to restart/redeploy to OpenShift

As a friendly reminder, the OpenShift dev sandbox times out after 24 hours – you may need to go through the instructions in *Chapter 5* again, to link the KIE sandbox to OpenShift. You may be getting tired of this renew-every-24 hours limitation. We'll fix that in *Chapter 10* when we look at more places we can deploy our decision models.

Getting to the machine-readable version of this page with the Swagger API is pretty simple – click on the dots at the top right of the page (in *Figure 6.3*), then click on the Swagger UI that appears. You'll see the Swagger page giving a summary of the REST interface that Kogito has generated on our behalf, as in *Figure 6.4*.

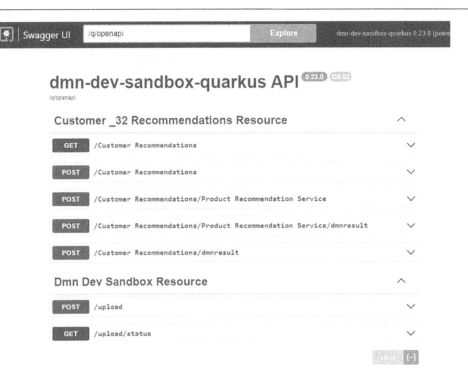

Figure 6.4 – The Swagger summary of the REST API generated for our decision service

Before we look at this screen in detail, think of it like taking the fire escape in your hotel or apartment block. You're still in the same building, you're still using the stairs, but you get to see a lot more of the behind-the-scenes details than you're used to, for example, exposed piping, cables not hidden behind panels, bare concrete, and brick walls. Similarly, here we are seeing a lot of technical details – so we're going to focus on the key points we need to link Excel to our decision service.

We know from the final model we created in *Chapter 4* that **Product Recommendation Service** is the one we want to use – we wrapped our model in this decision model node specifically to highlight that it's the one intended for us to call externally. Before we explore this service further, let's take a quick look at the other endpoints being exposed:

- `GET /{modelname}`: Allows us to download the original decision model
- `POST / Upload` Upload a new model – only really used by the KIE tooling
- `GET / Upload/status`: Allows us to view any errors from uploading the model
- `POST - {modelname}` and the similar `{modelname}/dmnresult`: Allow us to view the results of executing all decision nodes in the full model

There is a second version of **Product Recommendation Service** with a `/dmnResult` tag. This is the same as the main service, but adds information on Info, Warn, and Error messages returned by the KIE when executing the decision model.

Designing a good REST API like this is an art – more information on the thinking and design choices made by the KIE team can be found at `https://blog.kie.org/2020/08/kogito-2840-about-dmn-endpoints-on-kogito.html`.

> **Note on security**
>
> There are a lot of endpoints exposed here that are useful in development, but not in a real-world deployment. Your network admin should allow access only to the endpoints(s) that you need to call.

Exploring Product Recommendation Service

Since we know that **Product Recommendation Service** is the service we need, let's explore it further in the Swagger UI, to see how we can call it from Excel:

1. Starting on the Swagger UI that we can see in *Figure 6.4*, click on the drop-down arrow next to **Product Recommendation Service**.

2. Click on **Try it Out**. The screen should update as in *Figure 6.5*. The JSON content you see on this screen is autogenerated to match exactly what the decision service expects.

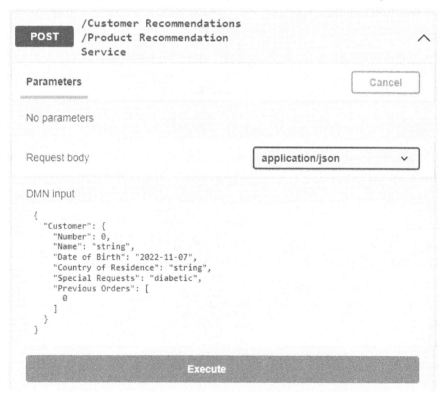

Figure 6.5 – Autogenerated JSON to call our decision service

3. While it is possible to edit this JSON (to pass in a country such as the US or a customer number higher than 20,000), the sample will also run as is. Note that if you edit the JSON, pay attention to formatting, especially the quote marks and commas, or you will get an error when you try the next step.

4. To get the Swagger web page to make the REST call, click on the **Execute** button.

5. The screen will change – further down the screen, you will see the response body generated by the decision service, as in *Figure 6.6*.

Figure 6.6 – Swagger showing our successful REST call

Congratulations! You've just called your first REST API! Not surprisingly, the results are the same as the web page. We'll be spending some time connecting Excel to this REST API – so play around with it, passing in different customer numbers, countries, dates, and so on, and see the returned values change.

Before we prove that we can use multiple clients to call the decision service, we'll take a look at some vital information. This will also help our understanding of what we need to do to make a successful REST call in the samples in this and subsequent chapters.

Some vital information – service endpoint and contents

Just below the text in *Figure 6.6*, Swagger also helpfully lists the command you've just executed in a format that you can copy and paste into a command prompt – such as the following listing:

```
curl -X 'POST' \
  'https://dmn-dev-sandbox-yu88r16qu490-crt-openshift-
    dev.apps.sandbox.x8i5.p1.openshiftapps.com/Customer
    Recommendations/Product Recommendation Service' \
  -H 'accept: application/json' \
  -H 'Content-Type: application/json' \
  -d '{
  "Customer": {
    "Number": 0,
    "Name": "string",
```

```
    "Date of Birth": "2022-10-23",
    "Country of Residence": "string",
    "Special Requests": "diabetic",
    "Previous Orders": [
        0
    ]
  }
}'
```

We're not going to run Curl, but it is important to copy-paste this text into a tool such as Notepad, then save it. This text contains everything we need to make a successful REST call and it is vital for running the samples in this chapter and the next. In particular, we will use the following:

- The web address (or **endpoint**), starting `https://dmn-dev-sandbox` ... (your link will vary slightly). This is the decision model in the cloud that all our examples link to.

- The JSON that we want to send to this web address (it's the part after `-d`, starting with `{"Customer` . . . . It tells us the layout of the messages we need to send.

> **Important – most of the samples in Chapters 6, 7, and 8 will need this information**
>
> Most of the samples in this and the following two chapters will use this endpoint, so it's worth bookmarking the pages leading up to this point. It is good practice to check whether the endpoint is still live (can you see the web page in *Figure 6.3*?) before you try linking to it to Excel.
>
> If you cannot see that web page, remember that the free version of OpenShift stops working after 24 hours. In that case, follow the instructions in *Chapter 5* to relink KIE to OpenShift and redeploy the decision model.

Other desktop REST clients – HTTPie

Since Swagger is a web page, it's not immediately obvious that the Swagger page is separate from the Kogito REST API, and that calls are passing between the two. You can see this more clearly if you use a desktop client such as **HTTPie** to make the call. These steps are not strictly necessary, but are useful to see what is going on in more detail:

1. Download and install HTTPie from `https://httpie.io/download`.

2. Run HTTPie – then click on the **Headers** button as in *Figure 6.7*. These header values will always need us to pass in a call to our Kogito decision service. If you look carefully at the previous curl code listing, you'll notice they are also set there using the `-H` flag.

Figure 6. 7 – Setting the headers in HTTPie

3. Clicking on the main `Body` tag, set the URL of our decision service as in *Figure 6.8* at the top of the screen. This URL is a combination of the OpenShift URL of our deployment and the decision service name. Helpfully, we can just copy-paste it from the curl sample we saw earlier – it looks like a normal (if long) web page request starting with `https`.

4. Beside the box where we entered the URL, we need to set the request type to `POST`.

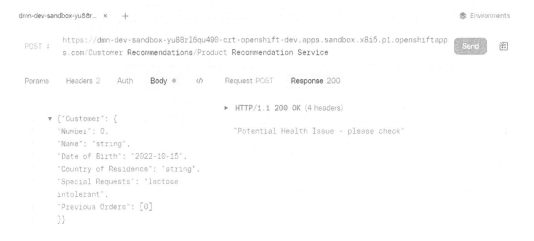

Figure 6.8 – Setting up our REST call in HTTPie

5. We need to specify **Body**, or values, that we send across as part of our request. These JSON values are exactly the same as our previous calls – so copy and paste the JSON we saw in the CURL or Swagger listings.

6. To make the request, click the green **Send** button at the top right of the screen.

7. The result of the REST call is displayed in the main pane. 200 is a standard web code for a successful request, and you'll notice that since we specify a lactose-intolerant customer, we are correctly getting a health warning in response.

> **Later – HTTPie as a debugging tool**
>
> Even if you don't install HTTPie now, keep it in mind for later – it can help us decide whether any issues are being caused by the formulas we write, by the request we send, or by the decision server we call. Knowing where the issue is helps us fix it more quickly.

Since we now know how to make a successful machine-to-machine web request, let's use Excel to make one of those requests in our decision service. Let's start with the easiest way of doing this, using Power Query in Excel.

Calling the decision service using Power Query

We explained earlier that Power Query allows you to connect Excel to a wide range of data sources. We'll focus in the next section on using it to connect to the decision service REST API. But if you are curious about what else it can do, I'd encourage you to check out the Power Query and related Power BI series from Packt: `https://subscription.packtpub.com/expert-reading-lists/power-bi-for-business-intelligence-beginner-to-advanced`.

Connecting Excel via Power Query takes lots of simple steps that we will cover one by one: a simple REST call, passing in parameters, and a more advanced POST call, before combining them to link Excel and our decision service.

A simple Power Query REST example

We're going to work through the most simple Power Query call to an external API possible – the GitHub API we encountered earlier at `https://api.github.com/repos/OfficeDev/office-js`.

This a GET call, with no parameters, which makes it the perfect starting point. The completed example is downloadable from the book's GitHub sample site – `https://github.com/PacktPublishing/Business-Rule-Engines-and-AI-for-Excel-Power-Users` as `06_simple_power_query.xlsx` – but I'd encourage you to work through the following steps as well:

1. In Excel, select the **Data** menu, then **Get Data**. You should see a wide range of data sources, as in *Figure 6.9*.

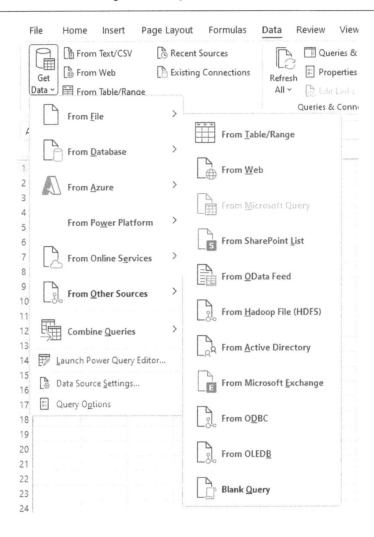

Figure 6.9 – Power Query data source options

2. For this simple sample, we're going to use **From Web**. Later on, we'll use blank queries and write the connection from scratch.

3. In the dialog that opens, enter the URL of our API: `https://api.github.com/repos/OfficeDev/office-js`. You'll see that this dialog gives us only GET options – which is fine for our simple example.

4. Clicking on **OK** will open the Power Query editor.

5. Click on the **Into Table** button on the top left of the screen. This transforms the results into a table that is easier to manipulate in Excel.

6. You'll be able to view the results returned by the call at the center of the screen – as in *Figure 6.10*.

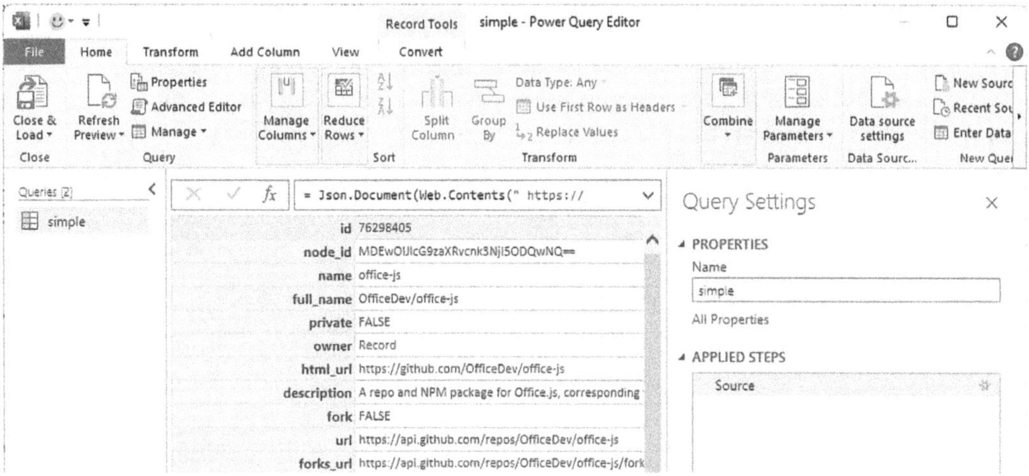

Figure 6.10 – Power Query showing the results of the REST API call

We'll spend a bit of time in the Power Query editor, so it's worth taking a look around this screen:

- The data returned by Power Query is always at the center. Not surprisingly, it looks the same as the data when we made the same call in our web browser.

- Above this is the *formula bar* – similar to Excel spreadsheets. However, these formulas are in the Power Query M language, describing steps to transform the data.

- At the top are various commands that we can apply to this data. We're currently on the **Home** tab, but there are options to transform our data, alter views, and so on.

- Since Power Query makes notes of the steps you apply to this data, it can replay them again when you refresh the data. On the right, you can see **APPLIED STEPS** – steps that you have already made, which will be replayed when you refresh.

- On the left is a list of all the queries in the current Excel spreadsheet. Since this is our first Power Query, only one is listed.

Security checks

Power Query is correctly built with security in mind, so when running this sample, it may ask you a question about how sensitive you consider this data to be, as in *Figure 6.11*.

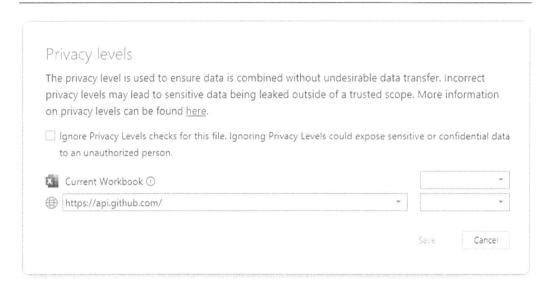

Figure 6.11 – Power Query data sensitivity check

In this case, the data is public, and we are sharing no information in our GET call, so select the public value in the dropdown and click **Save**.

Now that we are able to access JSON data from a REST web source in Excel, let's do something more useful with it.

Using Power Query REST data in Excel

Having the JSON data in Power Query is great, but there is far too much information for us to use. We need to filter and transform this information before returning it to Excel:

1. *Right-click* on our query name on the left-hand side of the screen, and rename it office_js.

2. *Right-click* on the first column of the table in Power Query.

3. In the context menu that appears, select **Text Filters** and **Does Not End With**, as in *Figure 6.12*. Hint: if you do not see this option in the context menu, make sure you carried out *step 5* of the previous example (converting our results into a table).

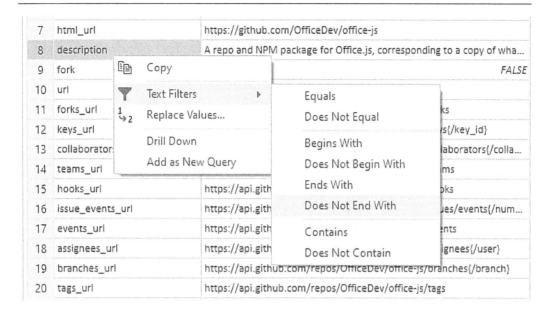

Figure 6.12 – Filter context menu

4. In the filter box, set the _url value (including the underscore). When you click **OK**, you'll see that our data list is now much shorter and an additional step has been added to the **APPLIED STEPS** list.

5. Let's swap rows and columns by selecting **Transform** and then **Transpose** from the menu.

6. Also in the **Transform** menu, select **Use first rows as headers**.

7. While our data is wider than the screen, it is much tidier than before. It will look not unlike *Figure 6.13*:

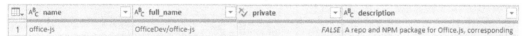

Figure 6.13 – Filter context menu

8. The data is now ready to be returned to Excel. From the **Home** menu, select **Close and Load**.

9. In the dialog box that appears, select a new sheet as the destination within your workbook. It is better to use a new rather than an existing sheet since Excel will complain if data from external sources overlaps. All being well, Excel inserts the information as a table, as in *Figure 6.14*:

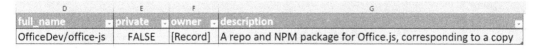

Figure 6.14 – The data loaded as a table in Excel

For some applications, this might be enough. But it's likely that you'll want to use the information elsewhere in your spreadsheet. If you do want to extend the sample, the formula to refer to information in a table like this is =office_js[subscribers_count], where office_js is the name of the table, and subscribers_count is the name of the column we're looking for.

> **Table naming**
>
> In our example, we named our query office_js, so that's the name Excel used when it put the data into the workbook. If the example formula doesn't work, go back and check the name – the spelling and case need to match exactly. In Excel, the **Name Manager** command on the **Formula** menu will allow you to check both of these.

This has been an important first step, to pull information from a REST API into Excel. But it's not going to help unless we can pass parameters to modify our query. Let's try that now.

Passing parameters into Power Query – things we need to know

If you've used Power Query before, or if you have read some of the many articles (I'd recommend the series https://exceloffthegrid.com/power-query-using-parameters/), you'll knowthere are two main approaches to using parameters. Unfortunately, we're not going to be able to use either of them:

- In the Power Query editor, there is a **Manage Parameters** option. However, these parameters are only available within the query editor, and not more widely in Excel. That might be suitable for some cases, but we need a more flexible solution in this chapter.

- Other articles show how to import data (from a table/range) and then cross-reference it in your main query. However, since we're pulling information from across the internet, you risk running into the Power Query formula firewall – you would get a warning as in *Figure 6.15*.

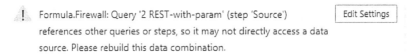

Figure 6.15 – Power Query formula firewall

We won't cover these methods since we can't use them in calling our REST API while passing details from Excel. The method we will use involves some knowledge of the M query language used in Power Query.

The Power Query M language and the advanced editor

If you can use formulas in Excel, you can use the M language and the advanced editor too. Another advantage of these text-based examples is that you should be able to copy-paste the examples, then tweak them so that they work for you.

For the sample in the next section, you have a choice – you can start with a blank Excel workbook and work through it step by step or you can download the completed example from the book's GitHub. The filename is 06_params_power_query.xlsx.

Remember all the transformation steps in the previous example that Power Query captured in the **APPLIED STEPS** pane? These are recorded behind the scenes in the M language, which is a great help in learning it. It's worth looking again at the previous sample using the **Advanced Editor** button on the **Home** tab of the Power Query editor. The M query you see there is very similar to the query we will build in the next section.

> **Power Query M formulas are not Excel formulas**
>
> It's important to remember that M formulas are not Excel formulas. Typically, Excel formulas operate on one or more cells. M formulas apply to a data source or the table of information we get back from that source.

Referencing an Excel named range using M in Power Query

Before we reference a **named range** in Excel, we need to create it! In our example, we have two cells, one above the other, as in *Figure 6.16*.

Figure 6.16 – The range we are going to name in Excel

1. In Excel, we create a named range by selecting **Formula** from the menu, then **Define name**. Make sure that the range you select isn't already part of another named range or external data source.

2. We're going to call the named range SourceUrl – make a note of this, as we'll need to use the same name later. If we forget, we can always check later by using the **Name Manager** command on the **Formula** bar.

3. Power Query doesn't yet know about the named range. We can link it by selecting **Data**, **From Table / Range** to load it into the Power Query editor.

4. A dialog box will appear asking us for the range or table we want to load – in this case, we type SourceUrl as shown in *Figure 6.17*.

Figure 6.17 – Creating our table for use by Power Query

5. Power Query will create a table of this name and open the Power Query editor. The name of the query will be the name we gave in the dialog in *step 4*.

Now that we have the table named and loaded into Power Query, we can reference it in a Power Query M formula. You should already have the Power Query editor open from the previous step. Let's create a query to read information from this table:

1. In the **Queries** pane on the left-hand side of the editor, right-click and select **New Query**, **Other Sources**, then **Blank Query**.

2. The new query that is created will be called Query1 or similar. Rename it by *right-clicking* on it – in the downloadable sample, we called it RestUrl-onestep.

3. Open the advanced editor by clicking **Advanced Editor** on the **Home** menu.

4. The screen that appears is just a bigger version of the formula bar we saw earlier. Replace any text that Excel suggests. Replace it with the following query:

```
let
    // "SourceUrl" with quotes needs to match the named
range on our Excel sheet. You may need to change {1} to
{0} depending on when your first line begins
    pSourceUrl = Excel.CurrentWorkbook()
{[Name="SourceUrl"]}[Content]{1}[Column1]
in
    pSourceUrl
```

5. Make sure the text is exactly as shown. Click **Done** at the bottom right of the screen to save the code and exit the screen.

6. Power Query will run and bring back the parameter you entered on the spreadsheet. We're not going to show a screenshot, since all we've done is shuffle information from one part of Excel to another – but it's a key step!

More importantly, we'll take a look at what just happened in the formula we just entered. All M formulas follow a standard `let  ...  in` format. `let` sets out the steps to obtain data and transform it. `in` displays the data to the user. In this case, `let` has only one line, but there are four key things happening in it:

- `Excel.Currentworkbook` gets the current workbook
- `{ [Name="SourceUrl"] }` gets the range/table of that name from that workbook
- `[Content]` returns the content of that range/table
- Since we only want one value from the entire content, we use the `{1} [Column1]` expression to select the row number and column name that we are looking for

If you wanted to use this example in your own workbook, all you would need to do is copy-paste these lines. It's then simple to update it with the name of the range or table you are using, and the row/column you want from that table.

> **Working step by step will save you time later**
>
> In the downloadable samples, we kept this example as a separate query, even though we later build it into a more complex example. This allows us to check whether anything goes wrong – at least we know we can read the values from the spreadsheet correctly, and see what those values are.

More info on `Excel.Currentworkbook` and other Power Query M formulas is available in the documentation from Microsoft: `https://learn.microsoft.com/en-us/powerquery-m/excel-workbook`.

Since we're going to have to close the Power Query editor to continue to the next step, we'll save it as **Connection Only**. This keeps our query without displaying results in Excel. You can do this in the following ways:

- Select **Close and Load** in the Power Query editor
- Select **Connection Only** in the dialog that appears

We'll come back to parameters again soon in this chapter. But first, we need to figure out how to make a POST request in Power Query since we'll need that to link to our decision service.

Calling our decision service from Excel using Power Query

Earlier in this chapter, we did a simple GET request from Excel using Power Query. But the API we need to link our decision service is more complicated – it needs JSON data passed in via a POST request. Let's build on our Power Query knowledge to do that now, starting with a hardcoded example without parameters.

This example is downloadable as `06_power_query_decision_service.xlsx` and we will work through it step by step:

1. If not already open, open the editor (**Data** | **Get Data** | **Launch power query editor**).

2. Create a new query (in the **Queries** pane on the left-hand side of the editor, right-click and select **new query**, **other sources**, then **blank query**). You should also rename the query to something more meaningful.

3. Open A**dvanced editor** in the **Home** menu and then copy and paste the following text:

```
let
    // the Rest URL we are calling - you will need to
    //update this with the value from your Swagger API
    RestUrl = "https://dmn-dev-sandbox.openshiftapps.com/
Customer Recommendations/Product Recommendation Service",

    // The JSON Values we will pass in to call the
    //decision Service
    Payload = "
{""Customer"": {
  ""Number"": 0,
  ""Name"": ""string"",
  ""Date of Birth"": ""2022-10-15"",
  ""Country of Residence"": ""UK"",
  ""Special Requests"": ""lactose intolerant"",
  ""Previous Orders"": [0]
}}
    ",
  // Do the JSON Call
  Response= Web.Contents(RestUrl, [Content=Text.
ToBinary(Payload),
        Headers=[ #"Content-Type" = "application/json",
#"Accept" = "application/json"]]),
  //Convert the response for display
  JsonResult = Json.Document(Response)

 // display the results
in
  JsonResult
```

4. You will need to update the endpoint listed in the line starting `RestUrl` with the value of the one in your deployment of OpenShift. As a reminder, it's the value we told you to make a note of in the *Some vital information* section – the URL starting ... `https://dmn-dev-sandbox-`.... Pay attention to quotation marks when editing this value in Power Query.

5. When you have completed editing, click on **Done**, then **Refresh Preview** in Power Query. If you have forgotten to refresh your Power Apps key today, or you have entered an incorrect value for `RestUrl`, you will get a `[DataSource.Error] Web.Contents failed to get contents from` ... error. If so, go back to *step 4* and correct this.

6. The first time you use this query, Power Query will ask whether you need to log in to use this service, as in *Figure 6.18*. For all our examples, **Anonymous** access is okay – but if you deployed this service in real life, you would want to review the security and login options. Click on **Connect** to exit this dialog.

Figure 6.18 – Power Query login check

7. Congratulations! We get the expected response from the decision service. A **Potential Heath Issue – please check** message should be displayed in the main area of the Power Query window.

Much of what is happening in this query we can guess – since it is merging the REST calls we saw in Swagger with the Power Query formula format. But it's worth highlighting the key steps we've just taken in this query:

1. Note that each line in the `in` section is separated by a comma. That is how Power Query knows that each line is a separate step. Be careful when editing, as Power Query will complain if you remove it!

2. As we saw (and edited), the line starting `RestUrl = "http://` ..." sets the REST endpoint we want to call. We save it as a variable as it makes it easier to edit later.

3. We create another variable, `Payload`, which is almost exactly the same JSON text as we used before in Swagger. Since this text needs to have quotes in it, we've had to use double quotes so that M doesn't get confused and think that we've finished the line prematurely.

4. The line `Response = ...` uses the `Web.Contents` connector from Power Query to do the POST call. You'll see that this connector allows us to set the headers needed by our decision service.

5. After the call is complete, `JsonResult = Json.Document(Response)` formats the text returned so that Power Query knows we're using a JSON format.

6. The final `in` part of the query specifies which of the variables we want to return as the result of our query.

It's great that we've finally connected Excel to our decision service using Power Query. But while we can edit the query, that's not practical for day-to-day use. It's very easy to break this query when editing by putting a comma or double quote in the wrong place. Let's fix that, using the knowledge of Power Query parameters that we learned earlier.

Calling the decision service using parameters

In this section, we're bringing all the parts together – REST calls and parameters from Excel into Power Query, making a POST call, then bringing the information back to Excel. Since we've already walked through the individual steps, it makes sense to give you a complete downloadable sample at `06_power_query_decision_service.xls` on the book's GitHub sample site. This allows us to highlight the key areas to allow you to extend the approach for your own work.

If you open the example, you'll see the main sheet, and two other worksheet tabs, as in *Figure 6.19*.

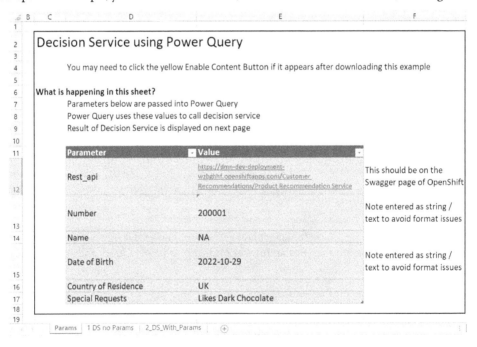

Figure 6.19 – Main sheet and other tabs of our full sample

There are a few key Excel items in this spreadsheet that are worth highlighting:

- The area highlighted in gray is a named range/table called `ParamsTable`. This contains the information that we want to pass to our decision service to get a recommendation on the type of chocolate or candy bar that might be suitable for us.

- In the Params table, we can easily update the `Rest_api` value. It's important that you edit it now to a valid endpoint for your own OpenShift instance; otherwise, this sample won't run. It's the same value as we used for `RestUrl` in the previous example.

- The second worksheet tab, `1 DS no Param`, is the output from the hardcoded REST call in our previous example.

- The third worksheet tab, `2 DS with Params`, gives the output from this example when we run it.

If you open the Power Query editor, you'll see that we've followed our own advice and kept several earlier queries to help with debugging. Please note that the entire formula is still contained in a single query called **2 Param-decision-service**; otherwise, the formula firewall will stop us from mixing internal and external data sources.

Other queries in our sample are not essential but useful to have, for when you evolve this sample to use in your day-to-day work:

- **1 DS No Params** is our earlier hardcoded query. That's useful to confirm our decision service is accepting POST requests but not used in the final query.

- The main example is **2 DS With Params**. Let's open that in Advanced Editor in Power Query and walk through it step by step. The first few lines of the following script get the URL of our decision service from the spreadsheet and put it into a variable:

```
let
    // the Rest URL we are calling - you will need to
    //update this with the value from the Swagger API
    // This example takes it from Excel
    RestUrl = Excel.CurrentWorkbook(){[Name="ParamsTable"]}
[Content]{0}[Value],
```

The next lines are new compared to our previous hardcoded example – we read our parameters from Excel into M variables. This keeps building the JSON string (in the next step) clean and easy to read:

```
    //We set our values into variables and then build the
    //JSON - it means we are less likely to break the
    //Payload formula.
```

```
    pCustomerNumber=Excel.CurrentWorkbook()
{[Name="ParamsTable"]}[Content]{1}[Value],
    pDateOfBirth=Excel.CurrentWorkbook(){[Name="ParamsTable"]}
[Content]{3}[Value],
    pCountryOfResidence=Excel.CurrentWorkbook()
{[Name="ParamsTable"]}[Content]{4}[Value],
    pSpecialRequests=Excel.CurrentWorkbook()
{[Name="ParamsTable"]}[Content]{5}[Value],
```

The following step builds the JSON payload string using the values we have just read. While the triple quote marks " " " look strange, they are needed to get the JSON in the correct format.

In practice, editing this when you build your own decision service is easier than it looks – you'll replace the field name (for example, Number), taking care not to disturb the quotes. And if you do encounter an issue, see the troubleshooting section on how to quickly find and fix errors:

```
// The JSON Values we will pass in to call the decision
//Service
Payload = "

{""Customer"": {
  ""Number"":" & pCustomerNumber &",
  ""Name"": ""Joe Bloggs"",
  ""Date of Birth"": """& pDateOfBirth & """,
  ""Country of Residence"": """& pCountryOfResidence & """,
  ""Special Requests"": """& pSpecialRequests & """,
  ""Previous Orders"": [0]
}}
"

,
```

Our JSON call is almost exactly as before, as is the final in part of the query to display the results:

```
// Do the JSON Call

Response= Web.Contents(RestUrl,
    [
        Content=Text.ToBinary(Payload),
        Headers=[ #"Content-Type" = "application/json",
            #"Accept" = "application/json"]
```

```
        ]
    ),

    //Convert the response for display
    JsonResult = Json.Document(Response)

  // display the results

in
    JsonResult
```

To use this example to call our chocolate shop decision service, no knowledge of Power Query is needed. Close the Power Query editor and return to Excel, then take the following steps:

1. Enter the values in the table on the first screen – make sure you have a valid endpoint. The endpoint would normally be hidden from users, but it makes our sample easier for now.

2. Go to the output tab for our example, **2 DS with Params**.

3. Right-click on the table and click refresh to update the table – there are options available to do this automatically every couple of minutes.

4. The decision service will process the values provided and pass back the recommendation to be shown in the Excel table (as in *Figure 6.20*). As expected for the sample, we recommend **Silk Tray** products to customers who order early, and the more generic **Milk Chocolate**. If you have edited your decision model before and deployed it, your results may vary.

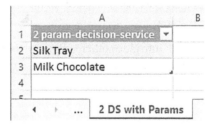

Figure 6.20 – The results of our decision service call in Excel

This might appear to be a simple step, but it is a key milestone as we approach the halfway point of our book. We have been able to take knowledge previously embedded in Excel, deploy it into a decision service, take advantage of business rules and AI, and link that service back to Excel so that most users will still be able to access it.

Before you rush off to expand this example, we want to leave you with some key steps for troubleshooting. Sooner or later, your M formulas will break, and these steps will help you find and fix the problem:

- We've seen already how to break down our query step by step, even if our main query does everything end to end. That lets us check whatever we like if we read our parameters in correctly.

- If we need to see interim values (for example, the JSON Payload that we are generating), we can change the last line of the query to return Payload instead – just remember to change it back.

- We can use comments such as `//` or `/* multiple lines*/` to comment out code we want to skip.

- In this example, we display the values as a table, but in reality, we would manipulate them further in Excel – using the formula `=TableName[column_name]`, which we saw before to extract key values.

If you follow these steps, any problem you may encounter will become much easier to solve. A bigger problem is knowing when you should use Power Query instead of the other approaches we have mentioned.

When to use Power Query

There is a reason why we started with Power Query as the first option for linking Excel with our decision service. It's the closest approach to an Excel formula, and the M query language is very powerful for building out your solution. Even better, all the tools needed are built into Excel – so any user who receives your spreadsheet will be able to use it.

However, the fact that everything is packaged in Excel is also a reason to not use it. Users have full control over your spreadsheet (even if you attempt to lock it down). Most of the time, these changes are well intentioned but clumsy, but there have been instances of fraud by people manipulating Excel spreadsheets to hide what they were doing.

You'll see in the next chapter that we will introduce other scripting-based approaches. Power Query is still likely to be an approach you'll consider, but there may be better options depending on the solution that you're trying to build.

Summary

This chapter bridged the Excel world that you were already familiar with and the world of AI, business rules, and decision services that you learned about in previous chapters. To do this, we did the following:

- Introduced five different ways to link rules, AI, decision models, and Excel.

- We learned about machine-readable web pages using REST and how to link to our decision service using Swagger – a more human-friendly link to Kogito decision services.

- We called our product recommendation decision service using Power Query. The step-by-step examples we gave are a solution that you can expand on for your own work.

Even if you stopped reading this book now, you would already know how to untangle Excel spreadsheets and move business rules into an external decision service.

So what is left to cover in the second half of this book? We'll cover techniques to do this in a better, faster, more flexible, and more scalable way. We'll start with an area we mentioned in this chapter – linking Excel to our decision service using more powerful scripting-based approaches (Visual Basic, Script Lab, or Office Scripts).

Part 3:
Extending Excel, Decision Models, and Business Process Automation into a Complete Enterprise Solution

Even if you stopped reading the book after the previous section, you would have an end-to-end solution to include business rules and AI in Excel. But the tools have so much more power, well worth exploring further to build scalable, robust, and enterprise-level solutions.

This section includes the following chapters:

- *Chapter 7, Using Business Rules in Excel with Visual Basic, Script Lab, and Office Scripts*, offers three alternative script-based methods to give you more choices about how you link Excel with your business rules.

- *Chapter 8, AI and Decision Services within Excel and Power Automate Workflows*, introduces Microsoft's business automation tool and shows how we can use our models to make decisions at key points in a flow.

- *Chapter 9, Advanced Expressions, Decision Models, and Testing*, explores the full power of the expression language built into KIE and introduces the scenario testing tools so we can guarantee our decision models behave as we expect.

Using Business Rules in Excel with Visual Basic, Script Lab, or Office Scripts

In the previous chapter, we said that no matter what technique we use to link Excel to our decision service, the approach is similar. We'll prove that in this chapter. Power Query is a great approach but has limitations. We'll explore linking Excel and decision services using Visual Basic, Script Lab, or Office Scripts – which approach you use is your choice. Along the way, we'll cover the following topics:

- Calling decision services from Excel using Visual Basic for Applications

- Installing Microsoft Script Lab and using it to link Excel with our decision service

- Introduction to Office Scripts and making the link to our decision service using that Excel script online

Why are we covering multiple ways of doing essentially the same thing? We'll explain that in this chapter as well, exploring the strengths and weaknesses of each approach.

Since it has by far the largest install base of all the approaches, a good place to start this chapter is with **Visual Basic for Applications (VBA)**.

Calling decision services using Visual Basic for Applications

There are plenty of good reasons to consider linking Excel and your decision service using VBA. You may have many years of experience in Visual Basic. Or you may have inherited a code base that uses a lot of VBA logic, and your organization isn't ready to migrate away from it. Since this chapter assumes familiarity with Visual Basic, if it's been a while since you used it, take a look at *Appendix A*, for a refresher.

> **Do I really need to know about Visual Basic for Applications?**
>
> The simple answer to that question is no. If this is your first time scripting in Excel, you don't need to know VBA since it is a legacy solution. Unless you or your company already use Visual Basic extensively, please skip to the next section, *Meet Microsoft Script Lab – a modern version of VBA*, to read about a better alternative.

I have a lot of fondness for Visual Basic. It formed an important stepping-stone in my own career and still powers many Excel spreadsheets worldwide. So, it is with the greatest respect that I recommend you *avoid* using VBA wherever possible. Even in this short section, you'll recognize its limitations – security restrictions that you cannot control on users' machines, the ability to run only on desktops/laptops (not in Office 365), and its clumsiness in sending and receiving JSON data over the web. Remember that Visual Basic was born before the internet took off, and its age shows that.

On a positive note, migrating business logic out of VBA and Excel and into Kogito decision services is a good first step to making the situation better. So, if you have one of these many older spreadsheets, or feel this is a route you must take, please read on! We need to start with something that the users of your spreadsheets will encounter – security checks.

Security checks in running Excel macros

I feel compelled to give you a stern warning before you download the first sample for this chapter from the usual GitHub site: `https://github.com/PacktPublishing/AI-and-Business-Rules-for-Excel-Power-Users`.

Immediately after downloading the sample file, `07_Decision_Service_VBA.xlsm`, Windows will give a security warning. This is because Excel files containing VBA from malicious authors have been known to act as a virus.

Compounding the problem is that Excel files are binary files, and the macro can be set to auto-run when you open them. You will not get the chance to inspect them properly like the other book examples, which you can open in a normal text editor before running. Remember the earlier caution we gave about trying to avoid using VBA if possible? The other approaches later in this chapter do not have these security limitations.

> **Security warnings can halt the adoption of your solution**
>
> Keep in mind that any user you distribute your Excel workbook to (including the VBA scripts) will get similar security warnings. From personal experience, these warnings cause friction with users and will interfere with the successful rollout of a VBA-based solution – no matter how good it is.

While I'd like to think you trust me as an author (after all, we've got to this point in the book together), encouraging you to execute VBA files you've downloaded from the internet is a bad idea. So, you might want to skip the download and just read through the text descriptions on the following pages instead.

If you do decide to download from the preceding link, you need to explicitly tell Windows that you trust the Excel sample file. Find where you saved the file, right-click on it, and select **Properties**. Within the dialog box that appears, select **Unblock**, like in *Figure 7.1*.

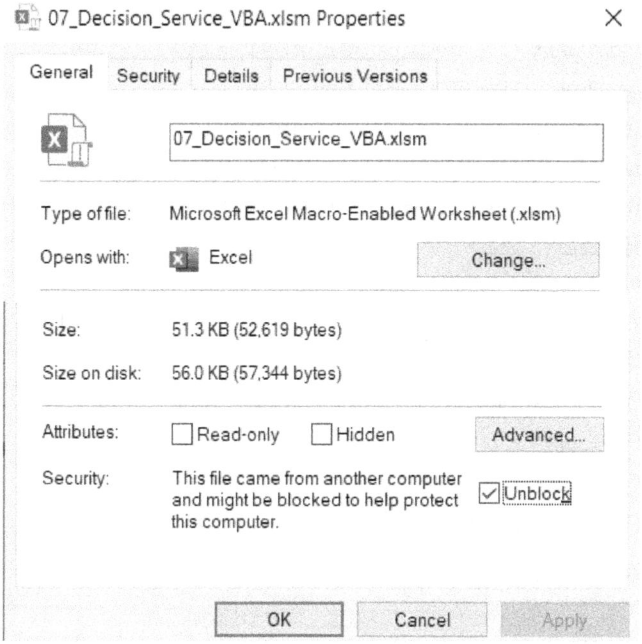

Figure 7.1 – Giving the sample macro permissions to run

Sending JSON calls via VBA to our decision service

Since the Kogito decision service Web API is the same no matter what type of script is trying to call it, it is straightforward to generate a JSON web call to it. Take a look at the following example:

```
Sub DecisionService()

    'Handle to the library that helps VBA call JSON Objects
    Dim ds_request As MSXML2.ServerXMLHTTP60
    Set ds_request = New MSXML2.ServerXMLHTTP60

    'Update this url to match our decision service
    'important - update this as your server key will be
      different
    ds_url = „https://dmn-dev-sandbox-0x11ooc1w216-
```

```
    crt-openshift-dev.apps.sandbox.x8i5.p1
    .openshiftapps.com/Customer%20Recommendations/
    Product%20Recommendation%20Service"

'use the library to setup our REST call
ds_request.Open "POST", ds_url, False
ds_request.setRequestHeader "Accept",
    "application/json"
ds_request.setRequestHeader "Content-Type",
    "application/json"

'build up our body JSON
ds_req_body = "{""Customer"": {" _
    & " ""Number"": 0," _
    & " ""Name"": ""Joe Bloggs "", " _
    & " ""Date of Birth"": ""2022-10-15"", " _
    & " ""Country of Residence"": ""US"", " _
    & " ""Special Requests"": ""None"", " _
    & " ""Previous Orders"": [0] }}"

' send the request
ds_request.send (ds_req_body)
ds_request.waitForResponse

MsgBox (ds_request.getAllResponseHeaders)
MsgBox (ds_request.responseText)
```

You'll notice that even though it is a very different language, much of the approach is similar to the Power Query M example in *Chapter 6*. Let's walk through the key parts step by step:

1. We create the helper object from Microsoft, `MSXML2.ServerXMLHTTP60`, which will carry out the actual JSON call.

2. We capture the URL that is our REST endpoint. This will be different in your deployment – it is the endpoint link from OpenShift that you used in *Chapter 6*. Like before, you may need to check that the decision service is still running and redeploy or restart if needed.

3. We prepare our call to this URL. The type of call (`POST`) and the headers are the same as we used in *Chapter 6*.

4. We need to build a payload of JSON that contains the information we want to pass into the decision service. This is contained in the `ds_req_body` variable. For simplicity, the JSON text is the same every time. But you could manipulate this string to take values from cells in the Excel spreadsheet using standard VBA.

5. The `send` and `waitForResponse` messages make the actual call to the REST page.

6. `getAllResponseHeaders` and `responseText` allow us to show the values passed back to us from the JSON call.

Extending our example

To keep this example simple, we hardcoded the values that we passed. It is trivial to read these values from an Excel cell instead, using an approach like that shown in *Appendix A*. Another shortcut that we took is the previous script only shows the values in a message box. In real life, your solution would probably do something more sophisticated – such as updating the values back into the Excel spreadsheet.

Since Excel is clumsy in dealing with JSON, you're probably going to need some help in parsing the response to extract the values you need. Downloading and importing the widely used VBA-JSON library into your VBA project is a good first step. It's available at `https://github.com/VBA-tools/VBA-JSON/releases`.

The downloadable code sample from the book's GitHub page gives some more lines where it iterates through the individual JSON values returned by our JSON call. But since the JSON will vary from service to service, we highly recommend you add error handling to it to handle all possible situations.

When you write your VBA script, it is very possible that you will make mistakes in the text you are passing over to the REST API. Like in *Chapter 6*, we recommend using a tool such as HTTPie to test the values you are passing in and out to see whether the error is in the REST API or in your VBA code.

You'll see from even this short code sample that VBA suffers from not having native JSON handling. Another shortcoming is that on every machine that you want to run this code, you must manually set the project references. Let's walk through how to fix it.

Fixing project references

If you are getting an error similar to **User-defined type not defined** when trying to run your VBA script, then the most likely cause is that you've forgotten to specify the additional libraries you want to use. This is easy to do but will need to be done on every machine that you wish to run the project. The steps are as follows:

1. In the Visual Basic editor, select **Tools** then **References** to open the references editor, as shown in *Figure 7.2*:

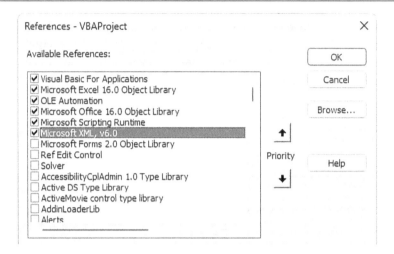

Figure 7.2 – Referencing the libraries our code sample needs

2. Select the two libraries we need – **Microsoft Scripting Runtime** and **Microsoft XML**. You may need to scroll down to find them.

3. Click **OK**, then run the code sample like before. Everything should now work correctly.

Next steps after VBA

The good news is that Kogito exposes the KIE AI, decision services, and business rules via a standard REST web interface. It is agnostic to what technology is used to access that interface. So, most of the more advanced techniques described in this book remain available to you as a VBA developer.

While we encourage you to look at other technology solutions, we recognize that there are good reasons for you to call the decision service using VBA. When done correctly, moving (some) of your decision logic out of Excel and into a Kogito-based decision model is an important first step to untangling what could be a messy legacy code base. Let's take a look at a more modern approach – Microsoft Script Lab.

Meet Microsoft Script Lab – a modern version of VBA

Script Lab is a free Microsoft add-in for Excel, downloadable from the official app store. If you're new to scripting in Excel, here's a rundown of what Script Lab gives you:

- It allows you to automate any boring, repetitive actions in Excel. So, a list of steps gets executed at a simple press of a button.

- It gives you an editor within Excel to write your scripts – with guidance as you type to suggest the keywords you are looking for.

- It gives you a way to save and share your solution with other users.

Microsoft Script Lab is what a modern version of VBA would look like. It leverages familiar web technologies such as HTML and JavaScript and gives many more options for a responsive user interface. Even if you don't know these technologies, you can see the value in investing your time to learn them. Script Lab also runs within Excel, both on your laptop and on web versions of Excel. It comes with a code editor that automatically refreshes, allowing you to have a rapid code-test-update-test cycle to quickly build your solution.

Microsoft has a 1-minute video that is well worth watching as an introduction: `https://www.youtube.com/watch?v=yt6os8zPUKc`.

Like all the tools we introduce in this book, Script Lab gives you a clear path and the next steps to evolve your solutions even further. This could be using Office Scripts (which we will cover later in this chapter, in the *What is Office Scripts?* section), building full add-ins for Excel, or using Script Lab on other Office products, such as Word or Outlook. Since Script Lab's editor uses similar technology to Visual Studio Code, not only is it powerful but it also gives you a head start if you decide to use it as an advanced editor.

One term that you'll see mentioned often in this chapter is **Office.js**. Office.js refers to the way that our scripts communicate with Excel, for example, to get values from a range of cells, or to update the background color of a worksheet. Office.js is used by both Script Lab and Office Scripts, which makes it easier to switch between these two tools. More information is available at `https://developer.microsoft.com/en-us/office`.

> **Where's the recorder?**
>
> If you're familiar with VBA, the biggest thing missing in Script Lab is the recorder – the ability for Excel to capture your actions as a script that you can edit later. The recorder is particularly useful for learning how to manipulate Excel objects such as ranges and worksheets. Thankfully, Office Scripts (see the next section in this chapter) does have this recorder, and the Office.js interface for manipulating ranges and worksheets is similar in both tools.

There's a lot we can do with Script Lab, not just for linking Excel with our decision service. But first, we need to install it, take a tour, and try out a `Hello World` example to get more familiar with it.

Installing Script Lab in Excel

Installing Script Lab on either desktop Excel or Excel 365 online is easy using the Microsoft official store. Our screenshots show the steps on the desktop version. The online installation is very similar:

1. In Excel, click on the **Insert** menu, then on **Get Add-ins**.

2. In the Microsoft Store dialog that appears, search for `script lab`, as in *Figure 7.3*:

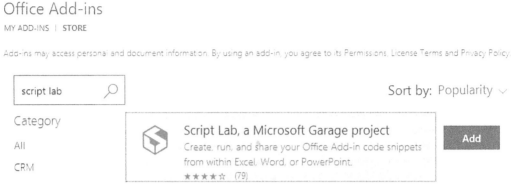

Figure 7.3 – Installing Script Lab through the Office Store

3. Click on **Script Lab** to make sure you have the official plugin from Microsoft.

4. Click on the **Add** button, then accept the terms when requested. Click on **Trust this add-in**, as in *Figure 7.4*:

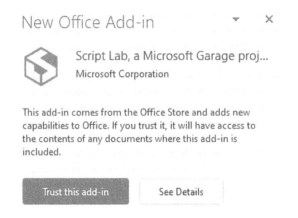

Figure 7.4 – New Office Add-in window

A more trustable model than VBA

The new plugin model that Script Lab uses is designed to be secure and trustable from the ground up. When you clicked the **Trust this add-in** button, you gave it much more limited access than the VBA equivalent. This is good news – when we share our Script Lab solution with users, it's much easier for them to trust and use it.

When you've completed these steps, you should have the **Script Lab** add-in installed. You'll see a new **Script Lab** option on the Excel toolbar, and several icons, such as **Code**, **Run**, and **Help**, on the toolbar, as in *Figure 7.5*:

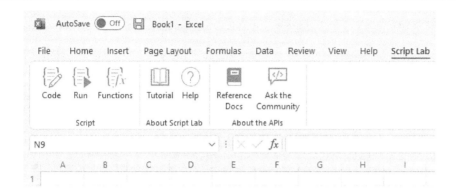

Figure 7.5 – Script Lab toolbar in Excel

Before we write our first script, it's worth looking into the new features we've just added to Excel.

Tour of Script Lab

Now that we have Script Lab installed, let's take a look at its key parts, starting with our new toolbar shown in *Figure 7.5*:

- **Code**: This will open an editor where we can enter our scripts and supporting user interface elements.

- **Run**: This will allow us to run our script. It also gives us a **Run side by side** option – meaning we can make a change in the code pane and see the effect immediately.

- **Functions**: This allows us to create custom functions to augment the built-in functions, similar to functions such as =Sum() that are already built into Excel.

- There are plenty of links to supporting materials provided through the remaining buttons – **Tutorial**, **Help**, **Reference Docs**, and **Ask the Community**.

Click on the **Code** button. It will bring up the main Script Lab editing pane, as shown in *Figure 7.6*:

```
$("#run").click(() => tryCatch(run));

async function run() {
    await Excel.run(async (context) => {
        const sheet = context.workbook.worksheets.getActiveWorksheet();

        console.log("Your code goes here");

        await context.sync();
    });
}
```

Figure 7.6 – Script Lab editor pane

Most of our work with Script Lab is done within this **Code** pane, in particular, the four main tabs:

- **Script**: This is the editor we use to write our scripts – the step-by-step instructions that Excel will follow.

- **HTML**: This allows us to build sophisticated user interfaces, based on standard web and HTML technologies.

- **CSS**: Also known as **Cascading Style Sheets**, this allows us to set the look and feel of our user elements/HTML pages. While we use the standard CSS in our examples, it's good to know that we can tweak it if needed.

- **Libraries**: This allows us to import standard functionality into our Script Lab projects. Typically, we use Office.js, which we mentioned earlier, plus **jQuery** – an industry-standard library for interacting with HTML and web pages.

We'll write scripts using the editor here shortly. But it's worth completing our tour of this screen with some of the additional options on the top row of the Script Lab pane. The visible options on the top row are as follows:

- **Run**: The **Run** option does the same thing as the **Run** button we saw on the main **Script Lab** menu.

- **Delete**: This allows us to delete our current project.

- **Share**: This gives us options to share our projects. The gist options mentioned here are similar to how KIE Sandbox saves projects in GitHub. There is also a **Copy to Clipboard** option, which allows you to copy-paste the entire project in one go.

- **Login / Logout** (of GitHub).

Finally, we can click on the hamburger menu on the top left (three lines stacked on top of each other). This menu has additional options for managing snippets and projects, as shown in *Figure 7.7*:

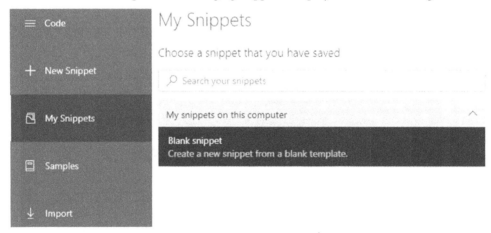

Figure 7.7 – Snippets and samples

These options include creating a blank new snippet and reviewing projects you previously created in **My Snippets**. There are also many well-documented examples under **Samples** that are well worth working through to explore Script Lab further. Finally, we'll use the **Import** option in the next section to quickly bring in the examples that we'll use later in this chapter.

As we finish our tour of Script Lab, it's worth taking a quick look at the Microsoft documentation to learn more. A good starting point is `https://docs.microsoft.com/en-us/office/dev/add-ins/overview/explore-with-script-lab`.

Saving projects in Script Lab

Let's repeat something we mentioned in the previous section: Script Lab projects are not saved in the location that you may expect:

- Unlike in VBA projects, Script Lab projects are not saved as part of the current Excel sheet. This is a good thing as other users cannot modify or break the script. But it does mean that users need to install Script Lab to import the scripts. This is not a big deal but involves a separate step that we'll describe shortly.

- Scripts are not (as you also might expect) saved in the Excel folder on your laptop. This is because they need to work with the Office 365 version of Excel as well. In effect, they run within a web browser that is itself embedded in Excel, so both the online and desktop versions have a similar environment to work within.

- Because of this, Script Lab projects are hosted and saved within the web browser's local storage, not unlike KIE Sandbox. Like KIE Sandbox, there is the option to save the scripts automatically to GitHub using gists. We won't cover saving it in detail since it is so straightforward, using the **Login** and **Share** buttons we encountered previously.

Having the script separate from the Excel spreadsheet gives you more options. It is possible for you to give instructions on how to install Script Lab to all users.

But more likely, you would share the spreadsheet as normal, and then a smaller number of power users would perform the checks using the scripts. For example, a mortgage broker might pass out a loan application form in Excel to all clients, and only run the script on the returned spreadsheets. That allows the broker to keep their business knowledge about which loan to recommend private.

Importing scripts into Script Lab

We previously shared and saved a Script Lab snippet in the book's sample GitHub folder as `07_Script_Lab_Hello_world.yaml`. We're going to use that in the next section, so it's worth importing that script into Script Lab now, as follows:

1. Download and open this script in an editor such as Notepad.

2. You'll see that this text file contains some metadata about the platform it targets (Excel), plus a summary of all the information from the four tabs of the Script Lab editor.

3. Copy all of the text from Notepad (or equivalent). Make sure you don't miss anything at the start or the end.

4. Open the hamburger menu in the top left of Script Lab, then select **Import**.

5. In the dialog box that appears, paste the text you previously copied, then click **Import**.

That's it – you should have the `Hello World` project available to use in your copy of Script Lab.

> **TypeScript or JavaScript?**
>
> You'll notice in the metadata that the script type is listed as TypeScript. This can do everything JavaScript can do, and more. While it's slightly stricter, it's a good habit to use TypeScript as it allows the editor to make more useful suggestions as you write your scripts.

Hello World in Script Lab

At first glance, our script is complicated. But it gets easier to understand when you know that there is a standard format to our script and one place (in the middle) that we edit to create our own scripts:

```
// Register our function to run on Button click
$("#run").click(() => tryCatch(run));
// our hello world function
async function run() {
      await Excel.run(async (context) => {

    // Our main sample starts here
        console.log("Hello World");
    // Our main sample ends here

      await context.sync();
    });
}
/** Default helper for invoking an action and cover
errors. */
async function tryCatch(callback) {
  try {
    await callback();
```

```
    } catch (error) {
        // Note: In a production add-in, you'd want to
        //notify the user through your add-in's UI.
        console.error(error);
    }
 }
```

Let's walk through the key points in this script. In reality, you should only need to edit the script that we highlight in *step 4* to do what you want, with the other lines being a standard template:

1. The first line, starting with $("#run"), uses jQuery to link the button on the HTML page (called **Run**) with the function of the same name.

2. You might recognize function run() as defining the block of code that will be called when the button is clicked (the link we set up in the previous line). The async keyword means don't wait for the function to complete – so Excel doesn't freeze while the function is running.

3. The next line, starting with await Excel.run(..., is standard in Excel scripts. Basically, we pass the next couple of lines of script to the Excel engine, and we then wait for the results.

4. Our code outputs Hello World to the console. There are comments before and after this line to show that this is the main area to edit, if you want to extend the sample later.

5. Because previous lines told us to run multiple items in parallel (the previous line with async), await context.sync forces Excel to pause and have everything catch up.

6. Note the closing brackets match the opening brackets in reverse order. You shouldn't need to edit this section, but be careful to keep these brackets aligned if you do.

7. Finally, there is a try/Catch helper function. This traps any errors, to make sure the user gets an update no matter what happens. You're unlikely to need to edit this.

While we know what should happen from our walk-through, let's run our script anyway:

1. From the main Script Lab toolbar, on the top left of Excel, click **Run**. Select the option to run side by side.

2. The sidebar should update like in *Figure 7.8*. Note the two Script Lab icons, which give us the option of viewing the running project and script editor side by side with live updates between the two:

Figure 7.8 – Running Hello World

3. Click the **Run** button in the main pane. The console should appear at the bottom of the side pane with **Hello World**, like in *Figure 7.9*:

Figure 7.9 – Hello World result

While it's only a `Hello World` example, we've seen the structure of a standard Script Lab project. That structure won't change – which makes our next step, calling our decision service from Script Lab, much easier to write.

Calling our decision service from Script Lab

Since the `Hello World` project follows the standard Script Lab format, and our calls to the decision service are also in a standard format, it is no surprise that we will be familiar with much of the script when we combine the two to call our decision service from Script Lab in Excel.

Rather than repeat a lot of the familiar elements, we suggest you download the sample from the GitHub book site – it's `07_Script_Lab_Decision_Service.yaml`. Like before, open this text in an editor, copy all of it, then open the hamburger menu in the top left of Script Lab, select **Import**, and paste all of the text.

That way, we can focus on the interesting parts in the following walk-through.

There are several elements of the user interface defined in this file. Take a look at the **HTML** tab in Script Lab and you can see the input for `Customer Number`, as in the following extract. The other text fields follow a similar pattern:

```
<div class="ms-TextField">Customer Number
    <input type="number" id="cNumber" value="update me"/>
</div>
```

Together, this and the other HTML elements give a user interface as in *Figure 7.10*. To keep things simple, we haven't included fields for all the information we could possibly pass to our decision service – but it's trivial to add them using the same pattern if you want.

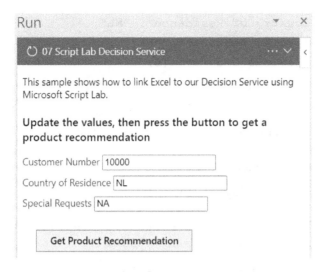

Figure 7.10 – The user interface for our decision service example in Script Lab

Let's walk through the lines in the **Script** tab, and focus on the items that we have changed to link Excel to our decision service using Script Lab:

1. Like the previous example, we have some comments and logging using `console.log` to explain what is going on.

2. We set `url` to point to our decision service. You will need to update this value. It is the same as our Power Query example; we can get it from Swagger UI. It's the link that ends with `Customer Recommendations/Product Recommendation Service`.

3. We need to set headers for our POST call. We define them as a constant as they will always be the same for calling Kogito decision services:

```
const headers = {
  Accept: "application/json",
  "Content-Type": "application/json"
};
```

4. We define a payload, with default values. This generates the exact same JSON as Swagger UI. We will update these default values using a script later:

```
let payload = {
  Customer: {
    Number: 10000,
    Name: "Jane Doe",
    "Date of Birth": "2022 - 10 - 15",
```

```
    "Country of Residence": "NL",
    "Special Requests": "NA",
    "Previous Orders": [0]
  }
};
```

5. We update the user interface with the values from our default payload. `$("#cNumber")` is how jQuery finds the HTML field. `val` sets the value using the payload JSON we defined earlier. We repeat this pattern for all the fields:

```
$("#cNumber").val(payload.Customer.Number);
```

6. As in the `Hello World` example, we link the button to run our main function, `callDecisionService`, when the button is pressed:

```
$("#get-product-recommendation").click(() =>
tryCatch(callDecisionService));
```

7. `callDecisionService` is defined using the same async code that is passed to Excel, as we saw in the previous example:

```
async function callDecisionService() {
    await Excel.run(async (context) => {
```

8. Just in case the values on the user form have changed, we update our JSON payload with them. This is the reverse of *step 5*; we repeat for all the fields. The + symbol forces the value to be converted into a number:

```
payload.Customer.Number = +$("#cNumber").val();
```

9. The call to the decision service using `fetch` is surrounded by logging, so we can see the values we pass into and get back from the service. As part of our call, we use the URL, headers, and JSON payload we set up earlier:

```
const response = await fetch(url, { method:
    "POST", headers: headers, body: JSON.
    stringify(payload) });
const jsonResponse = await response.json();
```

10. Our decision service returns a lot of JSON information that we don't need. We get the specific decision information we want using `let productRecommendation = jsonResponse["decisionResults"][0]["result"];`.

11. Now that we have our product recommendation, the rest of the code just manipulates the spreadsheet to display it. We delete and then recreate the worksheet using `worksheets.delete()` and `worksheets.add()`. We add a header and set its formatting using the `sheet.getRange()` method.

12. Finally, we update the sheet with our product recommendation using a second `sheet.getRange()` method and display the sheet using `sheet.activate();`.

13. A final `await context.sync()` allows the Excel user interface to catch up with our script.

14. Our `tryCatch` helper function to catch and display errors is the same as before.

Not surprisingly, when we run this script, the console shows the values before and after the decision service call, like in *Figure 7.11*. These are interactive if you want to drill down into them.

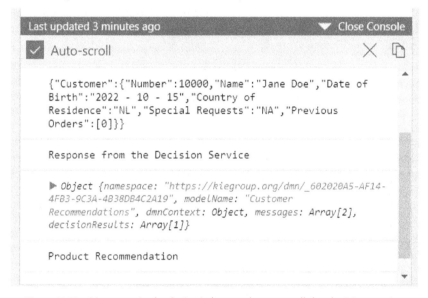

Figure 7.11 – Messages in the Script Lab console as we call the decision service

A new sheet is (re)created, giving our product recommendation, as in *Figure 7.12*:

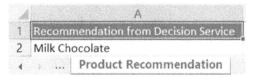

Figure 7.12 – The product recommendation saved by Script Lab in Excel

If for some reason your Kogito decision service has stopped running (or you need to do a daily update of tokens for the dev sandbox), Script Lab will give you a **Failed to Fetch Type** error. Check out the **Decision Service Swagger** page and update the URL in the script if needed.

It's worth downloading and going through the script again. With some small changes, it can be used to call your own decision service. I'd also encourage you to look at the built-in Script Lab examples. They cover most of the ways that you might want to extend your project with even more sophisticated user interface elements.

> **Alternative approach – custom functions in Script Lab**
>
> You may notice, as you work through the examples, an option to create a custom function using Script Lab. At first sight, this appears attractive – it would allow you to build your own bespoke function, then type something such as the following directly in a cell in Excel:
>
> ```
> = callDecisionService (customerNumber, countryOfResidence,
> dateOfBirth ..)
> ```
>
> However, for this approach to work, you need Script Lab installed, the custom function registered, and for the function to be entered into a spreadsheet. If you miss even one of these three steps, your spreadsheet will break.
>
> For most use cases, the Power Query approach we covered in the previous chapter is more robust. It acts in many ways like a custom function, it comes built into Excel, and it doesn't need to be run on first-time use to register it with Excel.

There is a lot more to learn about Script Lab and it can give you very powerful Excel-based solutions. Since it and Office Scripts, which we will cover in the next section, have a lot in common, it is a good investment of your time to go through the Microsoft docs at `https://learn.microsoft.com/en-us/office/dev/add-ins/reference/overview/excel-add-ins-reference-overview`. If you're looking to do a deep-dive into either tool, I would also recommend the following book to fully explore the power of extending Excel using these tools – `https://leanpub.com/buildingofficeaddins`.

What is Office Scripts?

While all Excel users have access to Script Lab, not everybody will have access to Office Scripts – yet. Since we already know it shares the Office.js approach to manipulating Excel through scripts, what is the difference between the two?

- While it is very similar to Script Lab, Office Scripts is slightly easier to use. For example, some of the boilerplate `async` calls and error-handling functions are hidden from us.

- Office Scripts has a recorder to make notes of our actions in Excel and transcribe them into scripts. This is very useful for learning about Office.js in particular.

- Office Scripts comes pre-installed in Office 365 online – although it may need to be enabled by an administrator.

- It is easier to share scripts. While (like in Script Lab) the script sits outside the workbook, by adding a button to the worksheet, anybody who can see the Excel sheet can also see the script.

- Office Scripts is highly integrated with Power Automate – a tool that we'll meet in the next chapter and will allow you to automate a lot of manual steps not just in Excel.

While there are benefits to using Office Scripts, it also has some disadvantages:

- Microsoft is still rolling out Office Scripts, and it is unclear from the roadmap when it will be available to personal (non-commercial) users.

- Office Scripts can only be edited in the web version of Excel. In practice, the editor is good enough (and backed up by the more powerful VS Code online editor) that this is not a major issue. Completed scripts *can* be run on the web and desktop versions of Excel.

- Office Scripts does not have the full set of user interface options that Script Lab does.

In the end, the choice of how to link Excel to your decision service will depend on what else you want to do with the tool. Let's help with making that choice by taking a tour of Office Scripts.

Getting familiar with the Office Scripts environment

To check whether you have Office Scripts available to you, open the online (Excel 365) version. If it has been enabled by an administrator, you should see an **Automate** toolbar option, as in *Figure 7.13*.

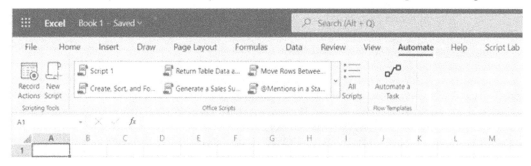

Figure 7.13 – Office Scripts toolbar

Much of the layout of Office Scripts is similar to Script Lab. The toolbar has **New Script** and **Sample Script** Areas. The **Automate a Task** button links to Power Automate (more about this in *Chapter 8*).

The **Record Actions** button works similarly to the tool of the same name in VBA. Clicking on it captures the actions you take in Excel, as a script, in a pane on the right-hand side of the screen. The following script example is of a recording we made while setting some values in our Excel sheet:

```
function main(workbook: ExcelScript.Workbook) {
    let selectedSheet = workbook.getActiveWorksheet();
    // Set range B2 on selectedSheet
```

```
    selectedSheet.getRange("B2").setValue("This is a test");
    // Set fill color to FFFF00 for range B2 on selectedSheet
    selectedSheet.getRange("B2").getFormat().getFill().
  setColor("FFFF00");
  }
```

The pane on the right-hand side of the screen is laid out similarly to Script Lab – with a code editor, an area with the log messages from running code, and several other useful command buttons.

The code editor has a **Save** button. Files are saved in your OneDrive folder under **Documents | Office Scripts**. It's not an automatic save (unlike Script Lab), so make sure you save before running.

The **...** menu in the right-hand panel gives the **Add button** option. Selecting this (unsurprisingly) adds a button to the current workbook that will run the script, as in *Figure 7.14*.

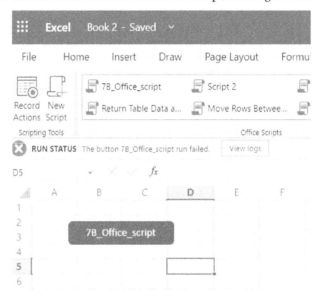

Figure 7.14 – Sharing our script via a button in our workbook

More importantly, creating this button automatically shares our script with people who can view the workbook. This is probably the easiest way to make sure our workbook and script get distributed together. But there are more detailed sharing options available in the **Share** menu option of the **...** menu.

Since much of the layout of Office Scripts is similar to Script Lab, we've kept the descriptions brief. A good starting point to learn more is the Office Scripts documentation at `https://learn.microsoft.com/en-us/office/dev/scripts/`.

Let's prove that the two scripting approaches are similar by modifying our previous Script Lab example to work in Office Scripts.

Calling our decision service from Office Scripts

When I wrote this section, converting the previous example to work in Office Scripts took less than 10 minutes. Rather than repeating the previous steps, we'll show how to import the updated example into Office Scripts, then run through and highlight the changes that we've had to make:

1. Download the full script from the usual GitHub site. The example filename is `07_Office_Script_Decision_Service.txt`. Note the `.txt` extension, as we have given the same example in two different formats.

2. Open the file in an editor such as Notepad and copy all the contents.

3. In the online version of Excel, select the **Automate** menu, then **New Script**, and paste the contents of the file to replace all the previous contents of this window.

4. Save the result.

If you're more familiar with where Office Scripts saves files, it's possible to download the example directly into the OneDrive folder under **Documents | Office Scripts**. Note the format of the file is slightly different – it's the `07_Office_Script_Decision_Service.osts` file that you need. Note the `.osts` extension.

If downloading the example doesn't work, check that you have the right file for the method you are trying to use.

The biggest change in the example is since Office Scripts has no user interface elements, we've removed those from the sample. While the values we pass into the decision service are hardcoded to keep things simple, it would be easy to read these from a cell value instead.

Other key changes in the script worth highlighting are as follows:

- Office Scripts hides a lot of complexity from us. We have a simple `main` method, which always takes `ExcelScript.Workbook` as a parameter so the script can manipulate the current workbook.

- Since the sample uses TypeScript, we need to label the types of objects the script is using – hence, the `workbook` tag in our main method:

```
async function main(workbook: ExcelScript.Workbook) {
```

- Our script set the URL, the headers, the JSON payload, and the URL and carries out the actual REST call using `Fetch` the same as before. We also select the product recommendation from the values returned in the same way.

- The script to (re)create the worksheet and headers and display the product recommendation is broadly the same. Any small differences are due to using a slightly different version of the Office.js API.

- Error handling is built in automatically, so we don't need to write our own function to do this.

The script is well commented and it's worth reading through it before pressing the **Run** button to get it started. After you click on the button, you should get a message saying **Run Succeeded**, and you can view the updated Excel sheet, as in *Figure 7.15*:

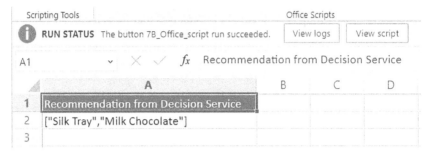

Figure 7.15 – Excel sheet online, updated with decision service results

Since we kept the logging from our previous example, the script output information window gives a lot of information about what just happened, as in *Figure 7.16*. Again, each of these steps is the same as our Script Lab example.

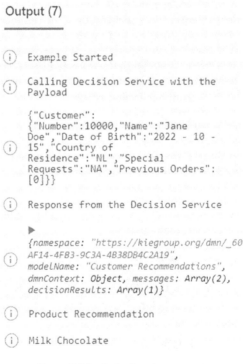

Figure 7.16 – Script logging output

We'll come back to Office Scripts in *Chapter 8*. But for the moment, congratulations! If you ran this example, along with the previous ones, you now have four different ways of linking Excel to your Kogito decision service (and know of two other methods). This now gives you a difficult choice – which method should you use?

Lots of choices – but which one to link with?

There is a good reason why we have mentioned a lot of different approaches to linking Excel to your decision service. There is no one best method – your choice will depend on what else you are trying to achieve with your project. This table might help you decide:

Tool	Advantage	Disadvantage	Use when
Power Query	Built into Excel. Acts as a powerful function.	Users can break it. No UI elements.	Default method to get started.
Visual Basic	Very powerful. Includes UI elements.	Security warnings scare users. Outdated.	Using a legacy code base or team has VBA.
Script Lab	Modern version of Visual Basic based on web technologies.	Needs installing.	Looking for a rich user experience or if Office Scripts is not available.
Functions in Script Lab	Easiest to use – feels like a normal Excel function.	Needs three items aligned to work (Script Lab, the function to be registered, and thefunction to be in the workbook).	Niche – consider Power Query instead.
Office Scripts	Simpler than Script Lab. No installation needed.	Not available to all users. No UI elements.	After you outgrow Power Query – if it is available to you.
Power Automate	External to Excel. Harder for users to break.	More powerful but more complicated.	Need to call the decision service as part of wider workflow.

Table 7.1 – Different methods for linking Excel and your decision service

If you're finding it difficult to choose, here's some good news – any step you take to move your business rules out of Excel and into a decision service such as Kogito is a good one.

Once you've achieved this, it's not as important which method you use to link Excel to your decision service – since that method is likely to evolve over time. No matter what happens, the business rules, now stored in Kogito, are under appropriate version control – so you know they are being well managed.

For example, you may start with legacy Excel sheets using VBA. Migrating to decision services (but keeping VBA) is a quick win, and soon you may convince colleagues to use Script Lab as a modern equivalent. Later, you may decide to automate your entire workflow and call Office Scripts via Power Automate to make it happen.

They're all viable solutions, and all these steps are easy to take as your wider project evolves.

Summary

This chapter was built on our previous knowledge of linking Excel to our decision service using Power Query. We added three other ways of achieving this link – using VBA, using Microsoft Script Lab, and using Office Scripts. For each option, you saw a fully working example that you can extend for your day-to-day work. Just as important, we gave a summary of which linking technique might be the best to use depending on your current project.

You'll notice that while we introduced Power Automate as a tool to link Excel and our decision service, we haven't (yet) covered it in detail. In the next chapter, we complete the set of deep-dive instructions by looking at Power Automate workflows and how we can use our decision service as part of them.

8

Using AI and Decision Services Within Power Automate Workflows

What we've achieved in the two previous chapters is to move business decisions out of Excel and into our Drools decision service hosted in Kogito. That works well, but we still have to trigger the process manually when needed.

In real life, making a decision is likely to be one of many steps that we take to answer a customer's question. Wouldn't it be great to automate this end-to-end work, creating a flow that calls our decision as needed? This chapter shows you how you can in the following topics:

- What is a workflow?

- What is Power Automate, and why use it?

- Calling business rules and decision services from Power Automate

- Implementing our customer service flow in Power Automate

- Alternatives, such as Power Automate Desktop and Kogito business automation

Power Automate is a very user-friendly tool – but also very powerful. Our aim in this chapter is to give you an awareness of Power Automate and how it can help you. We'll show you flows where you link Excel and the decision services as part of a wider process. But there will be many interesting parts of Power Automate that, due to space constraints, we won't be able to explore. Hopefully, we'll leave you with an appetite to learn more – so we will also give you pointers as to the next steps on your learning journey.

Prerequisites

Power Automate is a (mainly) online-hosted tool from Microsoft – so it's not surprising that you're going to need a Microsoft account. There are two main account types:

- You may already have a Microsoft account from the organization you work in or are affiliated with (if you're a student). If you have access to Office.com or Outlook.com, and if you are able to sign in using something such as yourname@companyname.com, then you have a corporate Microsoft account.

- You may have a personal Microsoft account (such as yourname@live.com or yourname@hotmail.com) – or you might have signed up for the free online version of Office (https://www.microsoft.com/en-us/microsoft-365/free-office-online-for-the-web).

Both these accounts should give you access to Power Automate, with most of the standard features enabled. However, since we dive into connecting flows to decision services, this chapter uses some premium features only available on corporate or pay-monthly accounts. Happily, Microsoft gives you a free trial of Power Automate with these features – click on the **Start Free** option at the following link: https://powerautomate.microsoft.com/.

The examples used in this chapter also assume that you have OneDrive running on your machine. While not strictly necessary for running Power Automate, it's probably easier to install it now if you intend to follow the examples.

> **Where are the downloadable samples for this chapter?**
>
> Power Automate is great because it is so visual. Unfortunately, that makes it harder to share samples – there are no easily readable scripts that we can publish on the GitHub site.
>
> While there are ways of sharing Power Automate solutions, due to space in this chapter, we focus on giving you clear, step-by-step instructions that you can follow to link Power Automate and your KIE decision services.

Now that we understand which Microsoft Account we will be using to access Power Automate, let's start by reminding ourselves what a workflow is.

What is a workflow?

Every company follows a workflow, even if those steps might be manual. *Figure 8.1* gives a sample workflow that our chocolate shop might follow in responding to customers:

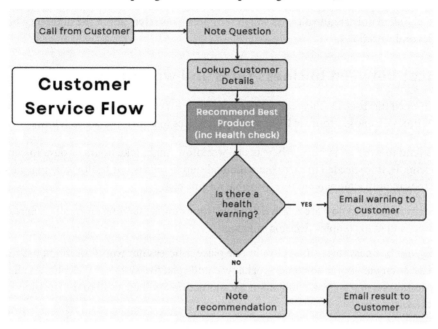

Figure 8.1 – Sample customer service workflow

This workflow is pretty simple – take a customer call, look up previous details, use that knowledge to make a product recommendation, then share that recommendation with the customer. You've probably written or followed workflows that are much more complex, but the basic building blocks remain the same:

- Interaction with external actors – in this case, a call from the customer triggers the start of the workflow, and an email from us to the customer completes it.

- Reading and writing from internal systems – for example, noting the question asked, and looking up the customer details in our system.

- Making a decision – in this case, recommending the best product (including health checks). These steps can be quite complex and (no surprise) are ones that we can hand off to our KIE decision service hosted in Kogito.

- Once we've made a decision, our workflow may branch into different paths – in our example, we send a different type of email with a health warning if needed.

This workflow is deliberately simple, as it's the one we're going to implement in Power Automate during this chapter. But remember the example from *Chapter 1* – triaging patients as they come into a hospital emergency dept? Using the same building blocks, we could map out a workflow to handle and recommend treatment for patients as they arrive.

Since this is a book mainly about rules, it's worth reminding ourselves about the difference between business rules and workflows.

Differences between business rules and workflows

We first mentioned this back in *Chapter 3* – since both business rules and workflows have a graphical format, sometimes people get confused. The main differences to remember are as follows:

- Rules tend to work all at once, whereas our workflow might take hours or days to complete. For example, if we needed to carry out a manual step to review our health warning, we would have to wait until a human became available for this task.

- The steps in the workflow are relatively simple (for example, sending an email), whereas rules are more suited to complex decision-making.

- Ideally, our business rules should live in one place, whereas our workflow might use multiple systems. Even our simple customer workflow could span five systems: a telephone call, saving the question on one system, a lookup of a customer on another, a call to the decision service, and then an email.

Since both rules and workflows focus on different areas, they work very well together. We run our rules at one step in our workflow (the *recommend product* step in *Figure 8.1*). Can you imagine how much more complex our workflow would be if it also described the product recommendation process? Carrying that out as one step within our decision service makes a lot of sense.

The other thing the tools have in common is that both describe business knowledge in a graphical format, and they describe it in a way that we can directly execute – the rule engine or the workflow engine can act directly on the graphical diagram, so we know that what is described is what actually happens. This isn't always the case in other types of systems if developers need to do the translation for us.

> **Workflows instead of scripting**
>
> If you're coming from a programming background, you may think that it would be trivial to write a script to carry out the workflow in *Figure 8.1* – and you'd be right.
>
> But then, as we mentioned in *Chapter 1*, you'd face the problem of knowledge disappearing into code. You would understand the steps being followed, but your non-technical colleagues would not. Using a graphical workflow allows them to review and agree on the process with you.

Now that we've decided that workflow and business rules make a good end-to-end solution, let's meet Power Automate and understand why we should choose it as our workflow tool.

What is (and why) Power Automate?

Microsoft Power Automate (formerly known as **Flow**) is one of the hundreds of workflow offerings on the market – do a search for `Workflow Engine` if you want to look for yourself. So why does this book choose it, especially when Kogito also has a workflow engine built in?

- As a Microsoft product, Power Automate is highly integrated with Office, including Excel. The hosted version is available online, without setup, to most Office users.

- Power Automate is aimed at Excel Power users – a good crossover with the readership of this book. Meanwhile, Kogito's workflow engine is more complex and is targeted at developers. And Power Automate strikes a nice balance – while easy to use, it is still more powerful than consumer-orientated services such as `IFTTT.com`.

- Power Automate follows the **Business Process Model Notation** (**BPMN**) standard, so many of the concepts you learn about in this chapter will be applicable to other graphical workflow engines. We'll see this when we take a quick look at the Kogito workflow engine (jBPM) at the end of this chapter.

So, what is Power Automate? It's a way of taking the workflow (as in *Figure 8.1*), adding the specific actions we want to carry out at each step, and then triggering (or starting) the workflow when specific conditions are true – for example, to start the workflow when we receive an email.

Because it is cloud-based, the workflows will continue to run when your laptop is turned off, even when you go on holiday. So, let's take a look at Power Automate and create our first flow.

Getting started with Power Automate online

Power Automate is linked from several areas of Microsoft Office, but the easiest place to start is the home page at `https://powerautomate.microsoft.com/`. After logging in (or creating a trial account if you need one), you'll be greeted by a home/welcome page with a lot of sample flow templates, and pointers to learning materials on each of them.

It's worth exploring these resources (now or later) – there are a lot of other Power Automate features outside the scope of this chapter. Instead, we'll take a quick look around the screen before starting to build our first flow.

Click on **My flows** on the left-hand side of the home screen. You'll see a screen similar to *Figure 8.2*, although obviously, you may not have any flows listed there (yet). This will be our main area for working with flows, so it's worth taking a look around the screen.

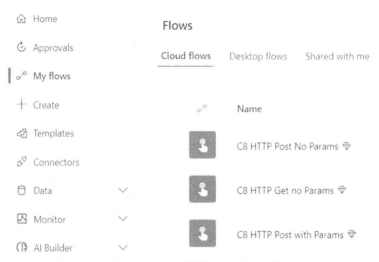

Figure 8.2 – Home screen of Microsoft Power Automate

On the left-hand side is the menu we've already used to navigate between the **Home** and **My flows** screens. It has the option to create a flow, which we'll use shortly, and a **Templates** option, which suggests pre-built solutions – that's well worth exploring in your own time, as it shows just how much you can do with Power Automate.

We won't cover the other options in this chapter, but we'll explain them briefly to encourage you to look at them in your own time:

- **Approvals** are for when you're running flows requiring a signoff, and you're the person nominated to say yes/no.

- **Connectors** allow you to link your flow to many different systems.

- **Data** links you to the underlying Microsoft Dataverse, which will be familiar if you've already used Power Query or Power Apps.

- **Monitor** allows you to see when your flows ran, whether the flow completed successfully, and makes suggestions on how to resolve any problems.

- **AI Builder** links to Microsoft artificial intelligence (AI) tools – the selection here can be very specific. If Microsoft has a pre-built solution for you, then it's well worth using it. But the options to modify them are narrow – in which case, you're better off using other AI approaches in this book or the machine learning techniques we will touch on in *Chapter 11*.

There are some other menu items along the top worth exploring:

- **Cloud flows** are what we're going to create shortly – they run online, regardless of whether your laptop is on or off.

- **Desktop flows** are an extension we'll come to later in the chapter. They are both more powerful (anything you can do on your laptop can be automated with a desktop flow) and more limited (your laptop needs to be turned on, and they are normally triggered by a cloud flow).

- **Shared with me** allows you to collaborate and share flows with your colleagues. Please read the security warnings carefully if/when you do decide to share a flow.

Pay attention to which account you are using (top-right of the screen, not shown in the figure) – especially if you're using a trial Power Automate account, as it can cause problems if you are using the incorrect one.

Now that we've taken a tour of the Power Automate screen, let's dive in and create our first flow.

Our first Power Automate flow

Traditionally, we would start with a **Hello World** example. We're not going to do that since we're starting with the online version of Power Automate. Because flows are hosted in the cloud and intended to run standalone even when you are not there, the user interface options are much more limited. When running in the cloud, even if you could get a message box to pop up, who would see it?

Instead, we're going to start with an example we've already carried out in *Chapter 6* – getting information from an online API. You'll remember this as a simple GET request that returns information about a project hosted in GitHub. Our flow will have three steps:

1. A trigger to start the flow.
2. An HTTP request action to get the information about the GitHub project.
3. A create file action so we can save the results and view them later.

To start building this flow in Power Automate, follow these steps:

1. Click on the **Create** button. You'll be shown a choice of flow types, as in *Figure 8.3*:

Figure 8.3 – Creating a Power Automate flow

2. We're going to pick **Instant cloud flow** since it is the most simple – our flow will start at the touch of a button.

> **What are the other flow types?**
>
> The other flow types are worth exploring later – an **Automated cloud flow** option is started by a trigger such as receiving an email, or a new document being updated to SharePoint. **Scheduled cloud flow** runs every X minutes/hours/days. **Desktop flow** we'll meet later in the chapter, and **Process advisor** makes suggestions to streamline more complex flows.

3. Once we've picked **Instant cloud flow**, we'll then get a choice of different manual triggers, as in *Figure 8.4* (again, worth exploring in your own time). Here, we'll give our flow a name, then choose the **Manually trigger a flow** option, and then click on the **Create** button:

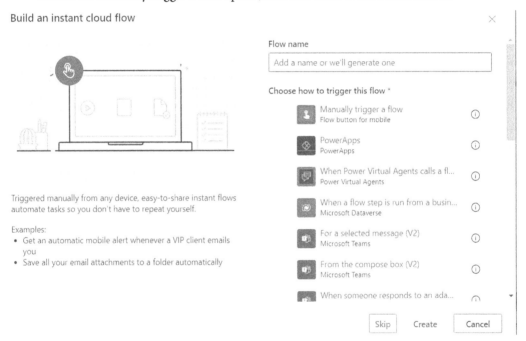

Figure 8.4 – Selecting how to trigger a flow

4. Power Automate will create our flow, and bring us to the main flow editing screen, as in *Figure 8.5*. The first step in our flow (the manual trigger) is already created for us. This screen also gives us options to change the flow name (if we didn't in the previous step), to undo/redo editing steps, to save our flow and flow checker, and test buttons that we'll use later.

Figure 8.5 – The first step in the flow

5.   For the moment, we want to create our next action. Click on the **New step** button. In the **Choose an operation** dialog that appears, type HTTP in the search box to filter our many options, as in *Figure 8.6*. Note that you're likely to have many more options (we simplified this figure) – make sure you select the **HTTP PREMIUM** connection as shown, and not the one for SharePoint, Outlook, or any other product.

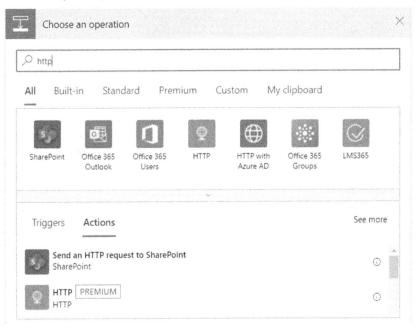

Figure 8.6 – Searching, leading to the second step in the flow – HTTP Connector

---

Keep exploring!

Don't be afraid to take a look at the many other actions that Power Automate offers, and then come back to continue this example later.

6.   Power Automate will create our HTTP action. In *Figure 8.7*, we've already entered the settings for this action – not surprisingly, they are the same as we've used in *Chapter 6* – a GET method and a URI of `https://api.github.com/repos/OfficeDev/office-js`. The other values we can leave blank.

Figure 8.7 – Second step in the flow – HTTP Connector

7.   Even though our flow is now longer, there will still be a **New step** option at the bottom. Click on it, then search for the **Create file** option from **OneDrive**. We won't show the search process this time; if you have the right action, it will have an icon and appearance similar to *Figure 8.8*:

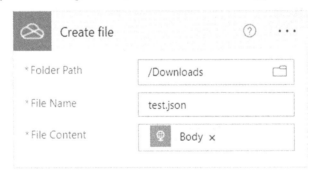

Figure 8.8 – Settings for creating our file

8.   In this action, we select the folder path – clicking on the **Folder Path** field will let you choose a path that already exists in OneDrive. Note, if you've just created a new username for Power Automate, you may need to sign in to OneDrive with this username and password first. We chose a general `Downloads` folder, but any existing folder will do.

9. Enter a name in **File Name** – we chose `test.json`, as that is the format of the data we're going to be saving in it. But for this example, any permitted name will do.

10. By clicking on the **File Content** box, we get the option for dynamic content. Power Automate will suggest values based on previous flow steps – in this case, the **HTTP** action returns **Body** with the response that it has received. Select it, as shown in *Figure 8.8*.

11. Out newly created flow should look like *Figure 8.9*. Click on the **Save** button. Pay attention to any warnings that Power Automate may give you.

Figure 8.9 – Overall flow

12. Click the **Flow checker** button at the top right of the screen. We should have no warnings, but follow the suggestions on how to resolve them if there are any.

13. Now, click on the **Test Flow** button. There will be a series of screens that pop up on the right-hand side. Our only option (due to the type of flow) will be to test manually. Click on **Test**, as in *Figure 8.10*:

Figure 8.10 – Testing our flow

14. The list of permissions needed to run our flow will appear on the right. In this case (as in *Figure 8.11*), we are already signed in to OneDrive, so we have permission to use this account. Since we are using premium features to keep the example simple (the HTTP connection), it is at this point that you will get a warning if you're not using a corporate account or the free Power Automate trial.

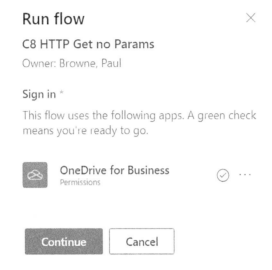

Figure 8.11 – Checking permissions to run our flow

15. After clicking **Continue**, a message will pop up allowing you to go to the **Flow Runs** page. Following that link will show an image similar to *Figure 8.12*. While I hope you also get a **Succeeded** message, clicking on the date of the flow will let you see more details on that particular flow run.

C8 HTTP Get no Params > **Run history**

Start time	Duration	Status
Nov 20, 02:04 PM (9 s...	00:00:02	Succeeded
Nov 20, 02:02 PM (1 ...	00:00:02	Test succeeded

Figure 8.12 – Flow run history

In the flow history, if your flow is getting stuck on the HTTP request, then it is a sign that you've used the wrong URL – check it and try again (but it is also worth checking the URL in a web browser).

What just happened?

Congratulations – if you've got to this part, it looks like your flow has run successfully. To confirm it has, find the `test.json` file in the OneDrive location you specified earlier. If you open it, you'll see the contents of the GET request giving the status of the project from GitHub – we won't show the file, since it should be exactly the same as the web response from *Chapter 6, Figure 6.2*.

At one level, we've just duplicated an example we already carried out in *Chapter 6*. We triggered an action, made a call to a remote web service, and saved the results somewhere.

At another level – it's a big deal! You've just executed your first Power Automate workflow. Okay, that workflow might have only three steps, but you've seen how easy it is to add more. In fact, before we go on to a more realistic example (calling our decision services), we encourage you to explore Power Automate.

A good starting point is clicking on the **...** option beside any of the actions in our flow to explore the additional options it gives you. As shown in *Figure 8.13*, these allow you to copy/paste the action, rename it to something more descriptive, add a note/comment, or delete it. The settings will vary depending on each action, and the peek code allows you to see how Power Automate will save this action – (un)fortunately, the peek code view is read-only.

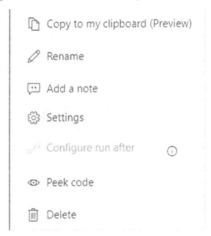

Figure 8.13 – Additional options per step

Our first Power Automate flow was deliberately very simple – nothing that you couldn't already do using a web browser. Let's extend this to a more realistic example.

A Power Automate flow to call our decision service

Our second example flow will call our decision service – so make sure the decision service is up and running, using an updated token if you're hosting it in the OpenShift Developer sandbox. Our example will also demonstrate using variables, and how to save the results in Excel.

Since the steps of adding more actions to the flow are the same as in our earlier example, we're not going to go into as much detail. We will show the flow we're aiming for, and the settings for each step of the flow. Where anything else is different, we will highlight it. One of the differences is that we will need to prepare a table in Excel to output our results.

Preparing our Excel output table

Our Excel output table is pretty simple, but it will automatically get picked up by some of the actions in Power Automate – so let's walk through creating it step by step:

1. Start by opening Excel and creating a new spreadsheet.

2. Create two headers, **ID** and **JSON**.

3. Select the cells **A1:B2** – then **Insert tables**. Click on **My table has headers** and then click **OK** to create the table.

4. Using the **Table Design** menu, give the table a name, as in *Figure 8.14*:

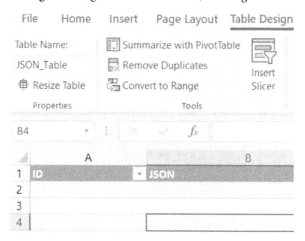

Figure 8.14 – Spreadsheet with table to capture our output

5. Save it in OneDrive with a name that you'll remember (such as Output.xls). If you have OneDrive running on your machine, you can just save it into your OneDrive folder; otherwise, upload it to OneDrive on the web.

Creating our flow to call the decision service

The flow we're going to create to call our decision service will look like *Figure 8.15*:

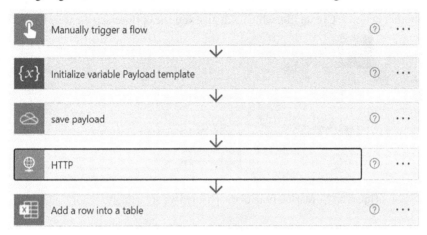

Figure 8.15 – Flow to call the decision service

Let's walk through creating it step by step:

1. The manual trigger action is the same as the previous action.

2. Create an **Initialize variable** action, as in *Figure 8.16*:

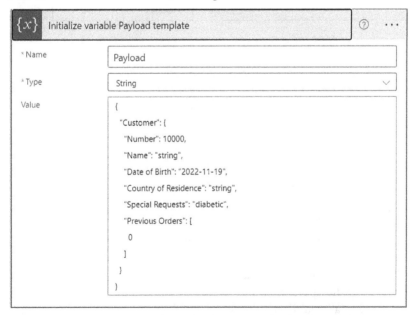

Figure 8.16 – Setting the payload to pass to the decision service

3. In this step, **Name** is `Payload`, **Type** is `String`, and **Value** is the JSON that we're going to pass to the decision service. This JSON is exactly the same payload we used in *Chapter 6* and *Chapter 7*, so it may be better to copy from there so you get the spelling exactly right.

4. Add another action – **Create file**, which will give you the options screen as in *Figure 8.17*:

Figure 8.17 – Making note of the payload we are going to send

5. This is the same OneDrive action we used in our previous example – but this time, we are doing it before the HTTP call (make sure you save the `Payload` variable). This will prove useful in future examples where we're dynamically building the JSON, and it's useful to check what we're sending to the decision service.

6. We update our HTTP call, as in *Figure 8.18* – note that we've removed some blank fields:

Figure 8.18 – Settings for the HTTP call

7. Note from *Figure 8.18* that our **Method** type is now POST. **URI** is the endpoint of our decision service (make sure that spaces are converted to %20 and that the decision service is running). Our headers are set as required by the POST method, and **Body** is the `Payload` variable that we defined earlier in our flow.

8. In the advanced settings of the **HTTP** action, check that we are using no authentication.

9. In the settings of **Excel Online (Business)**, add a row to a table; it should look like *Figure 8.19*. Make sure you're using the Excel Business connector, as there is a simpler Excel connector with a lot fewer options:

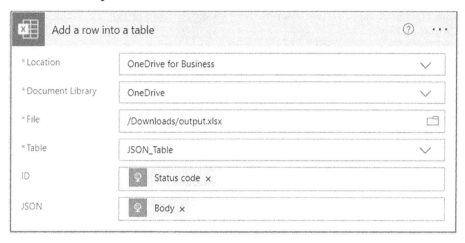

Figure 8.19 – Adding a row to the table

10. In this action, as per *Figure 8.19*, select **Location** as **OneDrive for Business**. Choose the **Document Library** option of **OneDrive**. The folder icon on the **File** line should allow us to select the output.xlsx file we created earlier.

11. Power Automate will auto-detect the tables in this Excel document, which will help us select a **Table** option of **JSON_Table** – the name we added earlier.

12. From the table, Power Automate will auto-detect the two columns in it – **ID** and **JSON**. We set them to be updated with the Status code and Body response from our HTTP call (using the dynamic content option).

Running our updated example

We then save, test, and run our flow, and our output table will get updated, as in *Figure 8.20*:

	A	B
1	ID	JSON
2		200 ["Silk Tray","Milk Chocolate"]
3		200 ["Silk Tray","Milk Chocolate"]
4		200 ["Silk Tray","Milk Chocolate"]
5		200 Milk Chocolate

Figure 8.20 – Results of the call in the table

As expected, our flow has run, called the decision service, and then appended the results to our Excel table. Play around with the values when setting the `Payload` variable in *step 2* of the Power Automated flow we have just created to confirm that the service behaves as expected.

While this is a much more useful flow, the values are still hardcoded, and there are still a couple of steps missing compared to the customer service flow we sketched out in *Figure 8.1* at the start of the chapter. Let's fix that now.

Modeling our customer service flow in Power Automate

Since the customer service flow gathers information, let's start by taking a look at Microsoft Forms.

Introduction to Microsoft Forms

Microsoft Forms is a free offering that forms (excuse the pun) part of Office online. You may have used it already, or similar offerings such as Google Forms or SurveyMonkey. Forms is available at `https://forms.office.com/`. It's easiest to use the same Microsoft account that you're hosting for your Power Automate flow, as it will help in linking them later.

On this page, click **New Flow** to create a new form. We'll edit it step by step:

1. The form will initially be untitled – click to give it a name.
2. Click **Add New** to add your first (text) question. Let's call it `Email`.
3. Click **Add New** again to add another text question. Let's call it `Customer Number`.
4. Click on the **...** options beside this question, select restrictions, and choose **Number**.
5. Click **Add New** to add a choice question. Add the options of US, UK, NL, JN, and UK.
6. On the screen, click on the **...** options beside this question. Select the option to make it a dropdown.
7. At the top right, click on **Preview**. Our form should now look something like *Figure 8.21*:

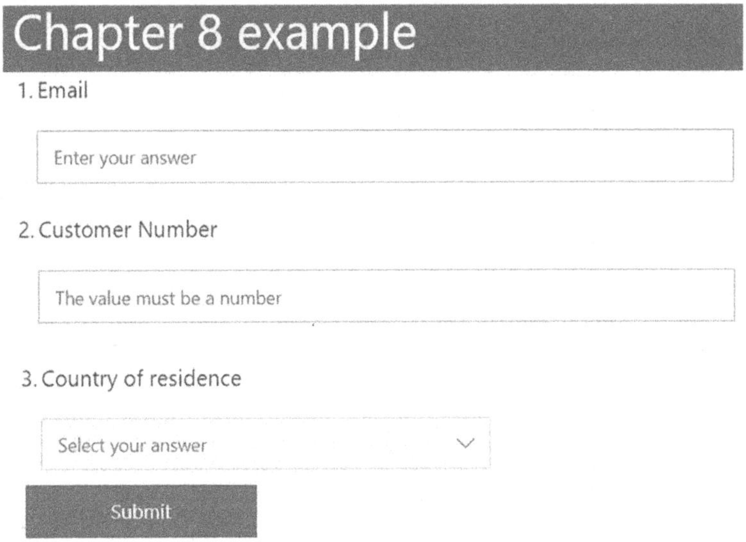

Chapter 8 example

1. Email

    Enter your answer

2. Customer Number

    The value must be a number

3. Country of residence

    Select your answer   ∨

    Submit

Figure 8.21 – Setting up a form to gather information

8.   At the top right of the screen is a **Send** button. This provides a sharable link similar to `https://forms.office.com/r/ETQ900ed1q7T` (yours will be different). Make a note of this link, as we'll need it to trigger our Power Automate flow later.

Note that we're not adding a date of birth or the other inputs to our decision service, as we can add these later. For the moment, we want to keep the example simple.

If you've used Forms before, you know that it will automatically capture the responses for you. We want to do something more dynamic, so let's add a Power Automate flow to our form.

Updating our Power Automate flow

The flow we are aiming to create, mimicking the customer service flow at the start of the chapter, is in *Figure 8.22*. This flow has the same steps as earlier, but mapped to Power Automate actions:

Figure 8.22 – The flow we will build

The flow is an evolution of the steps we took in our previous example. But since our trigger at the start of the flow is different, we'll need to delete the manual flow trigger.

To delete to trigger on the previous flow, click on **…** at the edge of the existing trigger (the first step, **Manually trigger a flow**). Choose **Delete**. That frees up the slot to add an alternative trigger.

Let's walk through the other steps to update the flow:

1. Our first step is to add an alternative trigger. Search for the Forms trigger, **When a new response is submitted**, as in *Figure 8.23*:

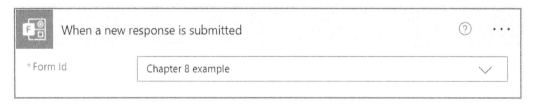

Figure 8.23 – Trigger to start the flow

2. The dropdown gives us a choice of forms to trigger our flow – select the form we created in the previous section.

3. Add another action immediately after this trigger – **Get response details**. Form Id should be the same form, and **Response Id** can be obtained via the dynamic content popup – it should look like *Figure 8.24*:

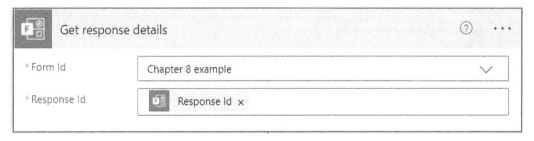

Figure 8.24 – Getting a handle to the form information

If we forget this step, the form IDs don't pop up as suggestions when we try to select values.

4. Add another new action immediately after this step – **Initialize variable** – as in *Figure 8.25*:

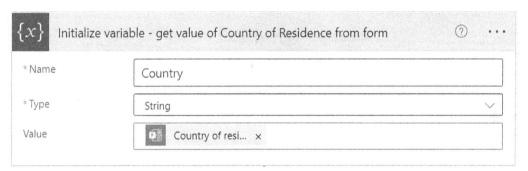

Figure 8.25 – Getting country of residence from the form

5. We name the variable Country, and set its type to String. The value we set (using the **Dynamic Content** popup) is **Country of residence** for our form.

6. Note, we've renamed the name of this (and other actions) to make things clearer – you don't have to do this, but you'll be glad later that you did!

7. We update the step where we initialize our payload, as in *Figure 8.26*. It's renamed Payload_template. Note that the value is also slightly different – with a __cor__ marker in the Country of residence field – we'll find and replace this step later. There is nothing special about this value – it's just some text that is easy to understand, yet unlikely to occur naturally in the file (to prevent accidental matches).

Figure 8.26 – Setting the payload template

8. Add a new **Initialize variable** action. This now defines the Payload variable, of the String type, as in *Figure 8.27*:

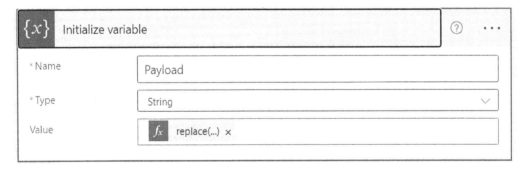

Figure 8.27 – Updating the payload template with our values

9. You notice that the value is set by some dynamic content that we haven't come across before. *Figure 8.28* shows this in detail. We need to select the expression, so enter replace(variables('Payload_template'), '__cor__', variables('Country')) in **Expression** and then click **Update**.

With this flow, this function will find the `__cor__` value in our `payload` template and replace it with the value from our form.

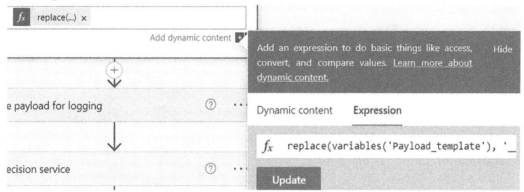

Figure 8.28 – Close up of the dynamic expression

10. The next step, saving our payload before we send it, allows us to spot any errors. It's similar to our previous example, as in *Figure 8.29*.

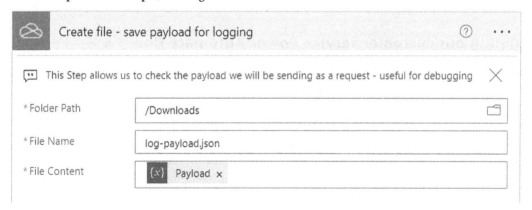

Figure 8.29 – Saving the generated payload

11. The following steps (to do the actual HTTP call and to save the returned value in Excel) remain the same as our previous flow – you can confirm this by looking at *Figure 8.18* and *Figure 8.19*.

12. We add a new step at the end of the flow – **Send an email**. Make sure you use the **Outlook V2** action as there are other connectors available. The **To** box uses the `Email` address provided on the form (find it via the dynamic content value). **Body** can have whatever text you want, and include the `HTTP Body` value, as we will want to email the result to the person who provided the data – as shown in *Figure 8.30*:

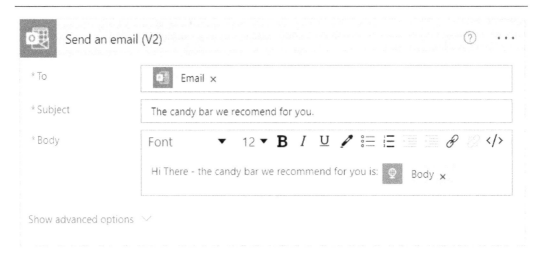

Figure 8.30 – Action to email our product recommendation

You'll notice that to keep things short, we've only used the email address and the Country value from the form. But repeating *steps 5* to *8* allows us to add other form values to our call to the decision service.

Running our customer service Power Automate flow

Starting our flow is even easier than our previous examples – go to the form, using the shareable link we made a note of earlier (our link was https://forms.office.com/r/ETQ900ed1q7T, but yours will be slightly different). Enter some values in the form and click **Submit**. The flow should automatically run, and an email should be sent with the recommendation from the decision service.

If you go back to your flow and click **Test**, you'll see that you now have another option to run your flow, as in *Figure 8.31*:

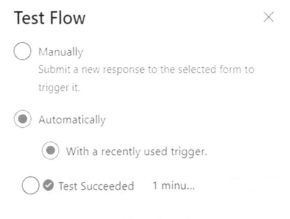

Figure 8.31 – Additional test flow options

The new option allows you to replay the form submission you just made – not only does it save you time but it also guarantees that you will be testing with the same values on each run.

Before we leave flow in this chapter, it's worth noting the **Flow runs** page, which allows you to see the results of each Power Automate step. It also gives you an idea of how long each step should take to complete. If your flow stalls for several seconds on `Http Request`, it is likely that the `url` value is out of date and you may need to refresh the values.

Suggestions to expand this example

Our examples were very clear, but if you've decided to add the other values from our form into the decision service call, you'll notice that the example gets tedious very quickly – creating multiple variables that you only use once, and multiple find/replace steps.

You're likely to evolve these steps further in your own flows – and it may be worth considering the following approaches:

- Combine some steps. For example, use the form value directly in the replace function, without creating a variable first.

- Use the `concat` expression to build our JSON payload all in one go – with all the variables and the fragments of the JSON expression in one line.

- Use an external script (such as **JavaScript** or **Office Scripts**) to build our JSON payload.

- Calculate the JSON as an expression in Excel, then read the value back before passing the JSON to the decision service. This has the advantage of being the easiest to review and update.

> **Why don't we call the decision service in a flow via Office Scripts?**
>
> We just mentioned that Power Automate flows can call Office Scripts. So why not use the techniques from *Chapter 7* to call our decision service via those scripts?
>
> The reason is that the security model restricts what scripts can do in a flow. This doesn't stop us from using Office scripts to manipulate data (e.g., to create the payload). But the only way to make an external call is via the `HTTP` action, as we used in our examples.

In our flow, we send the same email message, relying on the message coming back from the decision service to highlight any health warnings. In reality, you would probably add a test to your flow and a branching action to send a different email depending on the product recommendation result.

We won't cover these techniques in detail, but you can explore them to build on the key steps that we've shown in this chapter. If you are looking to explore Power Automate, this book by Packt author *Aaron Guilemette* is a good place to start: `https://www.packtpub.com/product/workflow-automation-with-microsoft-power-automate/`

Other workflows – Kogito Business Automation and Power Automate Desktop

This chapter focused on Power Automate for a reason, since it is the most (Power) user-friendly workflow tool. But there are two other workflow tools you are likely to encounter – Power Automate Desktop and the workflow that comes with Kogito Business Automation.

Power Automate Desktop

You (briefly) saw the Desktop version of Power Automate, as it was an option when we were creating a new cloud flow in *Figure 8.3*. If you created a desktop flow, you would have been prompted to install the desktop tool (although it comes pre-installed in Windows 11; consult the Power Automate Desktop documentation for more details). You would have been presented with an opening screen as in *Figure 8.32*:

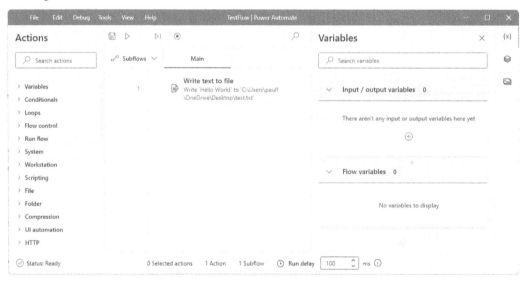

Figure 8.32 – Power Automate Desktop

Many of the concepts for using Power Automate Desktop are similar to using the cloud version. Power Automate Desktop also has an HTTP connector, which is available to all users without any premium restrictions. While that gives you additional options to link your flows to the decision service, it does come with a few trade-offs:

- The actions in Desktop flows are very wide-ranging – pretty much anything that is possible using your laptop can be carried out from a Desktop flow.

- Desktop flows only run when the user is logged in (even if the machine is locked). Cloud flows run (and can be triggered) all the time.

- Desktop flows essentially run as a sub-flow of cloud flows. They can be triggered manually for testing.

- Linking cloud and Desktop flows is a premium feature not available to all users, which may limit how you can use it day to day.

It is well worth exploring Power Automate Desktop to see how you might use it in your day-to-day work. But we'll finish the chapter with a quick a look a workflow that you're unlikely to use just yet – the Kogito business automation.

A quick look at Kogito business automation

Way back in *Chapter 3*, we glimpsed the option to create a workflow in *Figure 3.1*. At the time, we focused on creating a decision service, but it might be worth going back to that screen and creating the sample workflow, as in *Figure 8.33*:

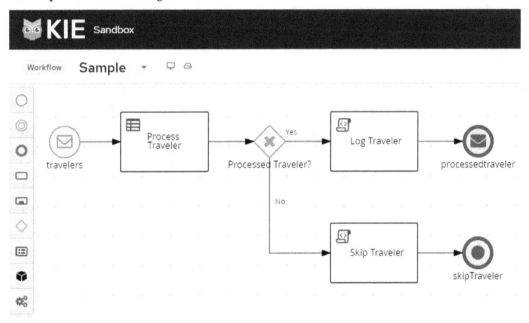

Figure 8.33 – Kogito business automation sample

Since this workflow example is graphical, it is very easy to follow that it is dealing with business traveler reservations. Even better, since it is part of Kogito, the **Process Traveler** step integrates business rules seamlessly into the workflow. As you'd expect, the Kogito tooling follows industry standards – so you can use Kogito to develop process services using BPMN.

However, while a Kogito workflow is business user-friendly, the tooling is not (yet) as standalone as the business rules and decision services. For example, there are more limited options to execute a Kogito workflow process in the KIE sandbox.

There are many situations where we would recommend using Kogito workflow business automation (for example, if you're a Java developer, or you're working with a team who have the skills to support it). But as an Excel Power user looking for a tool that is highly integrated into Microsoft Office, Power Automate is likely to be a better choice for beginners.

Summary

We set expectations at the start of the chapter for how, although we would introduce Power Automate, we would focus on how to link Excel into decision services as part of a complete end-to-end flow.

What we covered in this chapter was workflows, and why we use Power Automate as the workflow tool for this book. We then moved on to how to call business rules and decision services from Power Automate. Finally, we built our full customer services flow in Power Automate, and looked at other workflow tools such as Power Automate Desktop and Kogito business automation.

This chapter was the third (out of three) covering the Microsoft tools to link Excel to our decision service – not just using Power Automate, but other options such as Power Query, VBA, and Script Lab/Office Scripts. Given the power of all these tools, they are well worth exploring further.

Now that we have linked Excel to our decision service, our attention in the next chapters focuses on doing more with it. We start by exploring the FEEL expression language to write more powerful rules and using testing to make sure the rules actually do what we want them to.

Advanced Expressions, Decision Models, and Testing

If you listened to our encouragement after *Chapters 3* and *4*, you may have tried building your own decision models. Hopefully, you then explored the different ways of linking your model to Excel in *Chapters 6*, *7*, and *8* and found the one that works best for you. But as your models become more complex, you may find that things don't work as smoothly as you'd like.

This chapter aims to fix that – we'll explain some more features of the FEEL expression language to make your business rules more expressive. We'll cover ways to structure your decision models to reduce their complexity. We'll introduce testing, and why it is always better for you to break your rules before anybody else. Along the way, we'll give you glimpses of editing tools outside of the KIE sandbox that show you how powerful the tools within the KIE ecosystem are.

The chapter will cover the following main topics:

- Prerequisites and pre-reading
- DMN and FEEL expressions – extending what you already know
- Dynamic lists, contexts, and relations
- Can you use Power FX expressions in decision models?
- More on building and editing decision models
- Common decision patterns to help build your models
- Testing and breaking your rules (before somebody else does)

Prerequisites and pre-reading

As you'd expect from a more advanced chapter, it helps if you've read the previous parts of the book! Much of what we will cover builds on *Chapters 3* and *4*. While we do a quick refresher, you'll need access to the KIE sandbox with the extended services running, as described in *Chapter 3*.

We've previously recommended additional reading around **Decision Models and Nocation** (**DMN**) and the FEEL language. Rather than covering every single function, in this chapter, we'll focus on areas that might not come naturally to an Excel Power User (such as lists). We'll assume that you have taken a quick look at the following documentation:

- `https://kiegroup.github.io/dmn-feel-handbook/`

- `https://learn-dmn-in-15-minutes.com/`

- `https://www.drools.org/learn/documentation.html` – select the latest Drools Documentation and User Guide

Like all the previous chapters, the examples are downloadable from the book's GitHub site at `https://github.com/PacktPublishing/AI-and-Business-Rules-for-Excel-Power-Users`.

You don't need to have learned this reference material inside out – it is okay to know that it is there when you need to reach in and use a particular function from the toolkit. Let's start by reminding ourselves of what we already know.

DMN and FEEL expressions – extending what you know

As we worked through *Chapters 3* and *4*, we covered many of the key points of the FEEL expression language:

- We saw that **FEEL** allows you to write boxed expressions (like what you type into the Excel formula box). There are many different places that you can use FEEL expressions – from decision nodes to lists to decision tables.

- One sort of FEEL expression was text and string manipulation – we used it to create a `Hello [your name]` example. If you've read the reference docs, you'll have seen that most text functions in Excel have an equivalent in FEEL. This includes converting strings into uppercase or lowercase, extracting text from the beginning, middle, or end of the text, replacing values, testing whether the text starts or ends with specific values, as well as splitting or combining text.

- We used variables as placeholders for different values. Looking at the reference docs, you can see that the functions available to manipulate Booleans and numbers are very similar to Excel. We'll cover date and time handling in a bit more detail as while the concepts are familiar, the format of the functions is slightly different.

> **Three types of Boolean values?**
>
> You would expect Boolean values to evaluate to either `True` or `False`. However, FEEL allows a third value, `Null` (or *empty*), where no value has explicitly been assigned.

- Custom data types allow us to build containers to hold our data, using the basic building blocks (such as text, number, and Boolean). We also looked at constraints on data, to limit the values that can be used.

- Lists may have looked familiar (since they are like a range of cells). We'll introduce more advanced functions to manipulate them that stretch this concept. We'll also cover functions to test ranges (think of a list but with sequential values – for example, [1..10])

- Related to lists are **contexts** (also known as **maps** or **relations**), which are like a list of key-value pairs – more on those soon, since while they are easy to use, the idea may be new to you as an Excel Power User.

- We saw if... then expressions for branching and will soon introduce loops to act on list data.

- We covered previously all the different node types in DMN (text, decision nodes, including decision tables, input data, and functions), and will return to **invocation** to better organize your decision models.

Before we (re)start, there are a couple of FEEL language basics worth remembering:

- FEEL is designed to be **side effect-free** – evaluating an expression shouldn't change the values passed into that expression. This is different from (for example) Visual Basic code, which might update the value or color of a cell in Excel.

- FEEL is designed to be human-readable, even allowing spaces in variable and function names. If you've used another computer language (such as JavaScript), you may find this strange.

- Because of this, it's worth remembering that FEEL will evaluate any text not in quotes as a variable name. "Friday" (with quotes) will match that exact text, while Friday (no quotes) will make KIE complain if there is no variable defined with that name. Both (with or without quotes) are **FEEL literals** – an expression that KIE can evaluate to a value.

We'll start exploring the FEEL language with lists – a very powerful but easy-to-use concept. But since lists work slightly differently than Excel, it's worth looking at a few more in-depth examples.

Dynamic lists, contexts, and relations

You might remember in *Chapter 4* that we graphically created **List** using a decision node of the List type. Look at *Figure 4.25* if you want to refresh your memory – it was a great way to clearly show the health issues we were looking for. But lists are much more dynamic than that. We already said that we could use FEEL expressions anywhere – and that includes within lists. For example, the list in *Figure 9.1* is a valid syntax. This example can be downloaded from the sample site (https://github.com/PacktPublishing/AI-and-Business-Rules-for-Excel-Power-Users) as c-09-dynamic-lists.dmn.

Figure 9.1 – Generating our list values dynamically

We've manipulated the figure so we can show the main diagram, our list values, and the input/output in one picture. You will have to press the **Edit** node and **Run** button on the screen to view similar results.

> **Date and time functions in FEEL**
>
> As you'd expect, the FEEL reference lists many functions for date and time handling. We used the `now()` function in this example, and most date functions behave like their equivalents in Excel.
>
> The FEEL guide gives a good overview of dates – even if it is split across several sections of the guide. One thing worth highlighting is the `.` syntax – for example, the expression `(2023,12,20).day` function will return `20` with similar options for `.year`, `.month`, and so on.
>
> You'll notice that support for international dates is not as extensive as in Excel – for example, it is always listed in year/month/day order – `date("2023-12-20")` is December 20, 2023. Notice how we created the same date but using a string instead of numbers. There are also similar constructor options for **time**, **date and time**, and **duration**.

Let's look at the example in *Figure 9.1* from left to right:

- We have a very simple decision model – just one input called **Some Input**. This feeds the value into a decision node of the `list` type (we've called it `Dynamic List`).

- Our list has four values. The first of these is static text. The second is today's date. The third is our input value, converted into uppercase. And the final item is a number that we calculate.

- On the right-hand side are the inputs and outputs. We pass in a simple value (`hello`) and get a list of four values back – we can tell it's List as they are numbered **0-3**. While this is common for scripting languages, it is different from Excel, which starts counting rows at 1.

It's worth downloading the example and playing around with it to explore it further.

> **Conversion functions**
>
> You'll notice our example uses a `string()` function to convert both the current date into a string and **Some Input** passed into a string – FEEL doesn't convert values automatically in the way Excel does.
>
> There are equivalent functions for converting into numbers and dates, with more information on how to use them in the FEEL reference guide.

While the items in this list are generated dynamically, it will always have the same four items in the same order. We can do something more, well, dynamic with lists. Take a look at *Figure 9.2*, also downloadable as `09 Step by Step Context.dmn`.

Figure 9.2 – A more dynamic list

The decision model for this sample is again simple – an input node feeding into the decision node – so we haven't shown it. We do edit the properties of the **Some Input** node to specify that only numbers are allowed, which means we don't have to convert in our functions. If you are trying to create this example yourself, it is worth noting that each of the boxes in the right-hand column of the table is a **literal expression**, and that the names should be consistent. For example the name *Some Input* has a space in it, so all expressions referring to it should also have that space.

We set the decision node to the Context type. While we'll see another way to use contexts later in this chapter, this example allows us to specify step-by-step instructions, manipulating the list(s) at each step. Each step is a literal expression:

1. We create BaseList using the FEEL syntax rather than a graphical format – [30,10,20].

2. We create another list, AddedList, combining BaseList with the number we passed in as **Some Input**.

3. We create a third list, SortedList, and sort our list in it. Note how the sort() function takes named parameters and allows us to specify how we want to sort, which makes it very powerful.

4. Our final line specifies the value we want to return, (SortedList). Changing this value will allow us to view the other lists we've created. Clearing this cell (right-click to get the menu option to do this) will return all three lists we have created.

In the example shown in *Figure 9.2*, we pass in a value of 25, which gets added to the list and sorted, giving an output list of [10,20,25,30]. Note the syntax using the square brackets and commas, which allows you to write a list expression in a very compact form.

More on manipulating lists using FEEL expressions

Now that you've seen the basics of lists and their syntax, the rest of the functions should make a lot more sense. We'll do a quick run-through – most likely, you just need to know that these functions exist. When you need to use them in detail, you can then find out the exact parameters using the FEEL guide we mentioned earlier:

*   We've seen the sort and append functions in the example. reverse and remove are the opposite of these.

*   Max, Mean, Min, Sum, and Count work pretty much as you'd expect.

*   distinct values() removes duplicates from a list – for example, distinct values(["One", "One", "Two"]) will return a shorter list with no duplicates, ["One", "Two"].

*   index of () returns where the item can be found in the list. For example, index of(["One", "Two", "Three","Four"], "Four") will return the number 4. contains is similar but returns true or false depending on whether the list contains the value or not.

Lists can also contain lists – while this is a simple concept, any example we could give would get complicated very quickly! We'll just mention that flatten() will combine all the sublists into one big list. concatenate() is similar but gives you slightly more control over the order of the list that is created. sublist() allows you to chop up this list into shorter lists again.

One item that you may have picked up from our example in *Chapter 4* is that our custom data types can contain lists. Our `tCustomer` data type contained a list of previous orders. Just to show you the power of lists, the opposite is also true – we could have a list of customers, with each customer being represented by the `tCustomer` custom type.

Lambda functions

One powerful feature recently added to Excel is **Lambda functions**. Basically, these are functions that we can pass around, not unlike the way we do with a variable or cell reference.

Similar functions already exist in FEEL expressions. We saw an example of a Lambda function in *Figure 9.2* – the `sort()` command took a named parameter, `precedes`, which was defined as `function(x,y) x<y`. While the sort order we defined in this case, was simple, it does show how much we could customize the sort algorithm.

There are three other list functions that operate in a similar way – remember that these are applied to the list as a whole. For the following examples, we'll create `mylist`, a list of numbers – `[1,2,3,4,5]`:

- `for i in mylist return i * 2` will return `[2,4,6,8,10]`
- `some i in mylist satisfies i > 4` will return `true` as there is one value of 5 meeting the condition
- `every i in mylist satisfies i > 4` will return `false` since only one (and not all) of the list elements meet the condition

Lists are a basic building block of the FEEL expression language and many of the functions associated with relations and contexts will return a list. We'll look at those soon, but first, we'll take a look at ranges, which appear similar to lists, even if they address a slightly different problem.

Ranges instead of sequential lists

In our previous example, we could have defined our list as `[1..5]` – that will still contain the same 5 numbers and is slightly shorter to type. This range syntax is shorter for longer number sequences such as `[1..100]`.

Despite the similarity in syntax, ranges cannot always be dropped in to replace lists. In practice, you will use ranges in a different way – more like Venn diagrams, where you are interested in the overlap between ranges. For example, `overlaps( [1..5], [3..8] )` returns `true` as both ranges have 3, 4, and 5 in common.

There are several related functions to test whether a range is before (`before()`) or after (`after()`) another, whether one range completely includes (`includes()`) another, or whether the start of one range matches the start or end of another range.

When reading range examples, pay attention to the two different types of brackets. `(1..10)` is equivalent to `[2..9]` – the rounded bracket syntax excludes the given number from the range, while the square bracket includes them. Both ranges contain 2, 3, 4, 5, 6, 7, 8, and 9.

Ranges and lists are good but can contain values without meaning. Let's look at relations and contexts, which address this issue.

Relations – tables of information

Take a look at the relation in *Figure 9.3*, which we'll build into the *Bill of Materials* example in the *Graphical contexts* section later in this chapter.

Product Details *(Relation)*

#	Name (string)	Weight (number)	Grams of Cocoa (number)	Grams of Sugar (number)	Grams Milk (number)
1	"Silk Tray"	400	150	150	90
2	"Crunch"	75	10	60	5

Figure 9.3 – Relation showing the ingredients for our different products

Even without us explaining, you can guess that this table of values shows the ingredients that go into our products. It is much more expressive and structured than a simple list.

Building this relation in the KIE sandbox is simple – we create a decision node of the `Relation` type, then add as many rows and columns as needed. It's also helpful to set the data type of each column. When creating this table, we set each box as a literal value – any FEEL expression is valid (not just the static values shown here). And while we kept this example simple, it is possible to nest other expressions within the boxed expressions (for example, to return a **list** of allergens contained in each product).

This relation table is downloadable as part of the `09 Bill of Materials.dmn` example at the book's sample site.

Now that we have our values defined as a relation table, how do we refer to them? The syntax is straightforward, and the following FEEL expressions refer to the table in *Figure 9.3*:

- `Product Details.Name` returns a list, with the values from the Name column, [Silk Tray, Crunch].

- `Product Details[1]` returns the first row of the table as a **context** (more on that in the next section) – a set of key-value pairs, for example, {`Name : "Silk Tray", Weight : 400, Grams of Cocoa: 150 }`.

- `Product[Name = "Crunch"].Weight` gives the value of a single box in the table – in this case, 75.

- `Product.Weight[2]` is an alternative syntax using line numbers. In this case, it also refers to the weight of the Crunch bar (so it returns the same value – 75).

- `Product[Weight>25].Name` is an example of **filtering** – a more sophisticated selection that will return a list of [`"Silk Tray", "Crunch"`] since both have weights greater than this.

Two common data patterns

It is likely that this data on products will be used across many different decision models. A common pattern is to define the relation table once, then include it in the models that need it – more on that in the *Linking decision models* section.

Another common data pattern is to read these values from an external database or Excel file. Our `Invocation` node can also read pretty much any data source. But because it uses Java code to do so, it is outside the scope of this book. More details are available in the KIE documentation at `https://docs.kogito.kie.org/latest/html_single/#_kie_extended_functions`.

Relations are ideal for largely static data that doesn't change very often. If we want a simple table-like layout, but with the dynamic nature of lists, we need to look at **contexts**.

Dynamic contexts

We've already seen that our `Product Details[1]` expression in the previous line returned a context – in that case, a line from the table of {`Name : "Silk Tray", Weight : 400, Grams of Cocoa: 150 }`. Note the syntax we can use to create contexts in FEEL expressions:

- Curly brackets to open and close

- Commas to separate out items

- Contents are a set of `key:value` pairs

If you've programmed before, you may have come across contexts under the name of *map* or *dictionary* – both are maybe more descriptive suggesting that once we know the key, we can use it to look up the value associated with it.

For example, if we stored the preceding context in the `myContext` variable, the `get value( myContext, "Weight" )` expression would return a value of 400.

What makes contexts more powerful is that it is easy to add values. For example, `context put (myContext, "Raising Agent", 1)` would add that item to our ingredient list.

While the full list of context functions is well documented in the FEEL handbook, it is worth highlighting `context.merge()`, which allows us to combine contexts, and `context.get entries ()`, which returns a list of all the values in context.

There are several other graphical ways of creating contexts that are worth exploring.

Graphical contexts

Graphical contexts allow us to define contexts in a more visual format, which is useful for less experienced colleagues to understand what our models do. Remember we came across the other use of contexts in *Figure 9.2*. In that example, we used a FEEL expression context to generate values step by step, with a `result` statement to pass back only the final value.

If we delete or clear that final `result` statement, all of the generated values will be returned as a set of `key:value` pairs. We'll demonstrate this with an example that we'll build out in the rest of this chapter – the Bill of Materials decision model. This is shown in *Figure 9.4* and can be downloaded as `09 Bill of Materials.dmn` from the book's GitHub repository.

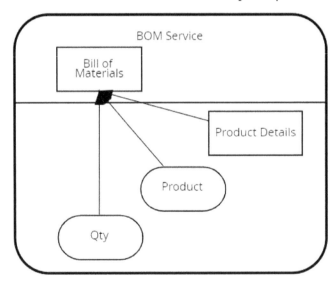

Figure 9.4 – Our Bill of Materials decision service

This decision model has two inputs: `Qty` (Number) and `Product` (String). The third node, `Product Details`, we saw earlier – it's a decision node of the `Relation` type, holding information on the ingredients for each product.

All three of these feed into a decision node of the Context type, which is shown in detail in *Figure 9.5*.

Bill of Materials *(Context)*

#	Bill of Materials *(Any)*	
1	Name *(string)*	`Product`
2	Grams of Cocoa in Product *(number)*	`Product Details[Name = Product].Grams of Cocoa`
3	Grams of Cocoa in Order *(number)*	`Qty*Grams of Cocoa in Product`
	<result>	*Select expression*

Figure 9.5 – A graphical context

Creating this context is similar to before – we added multiple lines with a key of the first column, and a literal expression to give the value. Like before, each line can build on the previous one – so we specify the product names, then use the product name to look up the value in the relation or table containing all the product details. Finally, we multiply the quantity (that we input) by the grams of cocoa needed to calculate the amount of cocoa we're going to need to manufacture this order.

Note that no result is specified – so when this is run, *all* the values will get returned, not just a single result. The result will be in key-value pairs – Name : Some-product-name.

We can prove this by running this model in the KIE sandbox, where we'll get the result as in *Figure 9.6*:

Figure 9.6 – Output from our context

Here, we have input a quantity of Silk Tray – this is quite a heavy product, with a lot of chocolate in it so it's not surprising that it will take 18.75 kg of cocoa to manufacture it in total. The KIE sandbox displays the context in a clear `key:value` format – compare this to our list in *Figure 9.1*, which has a similar format but has numbers instead of keys beside each of the values.

> **More reading on FEEL functions**
>
> This may be a surprise for a book that focuses on KIE from Red Hat and IBM – but I would also suggest looking at the FEEL guides from other vendors such as Oracle, Trisotech, and Camunda.
>
> Since FEEL is a standard, most of what they say is applicable to KIE – and each explains the concepts from a slightly different angle. It's a good way of helping you if you get stuck in any area.

This section focused on highlighting the difference between FEEL and Excel functions, walking through some areas that Excel users might find tricky to understand. The best way of learning is to dive in and try to model some decisions that apply to your organization.

Before we leave functions, we'll look at another expression language – Power FX.

> **Using Power FX expressions in decision models**
>
> **Power FX** is a low-code expression language from Microsoft that is not too far from what FEEL tries to achieve. Roughly speaking, if you could take the formula you were already using in Excel, and remove the references to cells so that they were no longer tied to a spreadsheet, you would end up with something close to the Power FX language. This means that you can use Power FX in Power Apps to build mobile applications and, increasingly, the syntax will feature in Power Automate and other Microsoft platforms. More details on the language are at `https://learn.microsoft.com/en-us/power-platform/power-fx/overview`.
>
> Power FX goes further than FEEL – whereas FEEL is written to have no side effects, Power FX is quite happy to have an impact (for example, to update a cell value or to change the color of a range). Power FX also integrates with a wider range of systems than FEEL, which is focused on decision models.
>
> Using Power FX expressions is currently an experimental feature in KIE – as described by the team in the following post: `https://blog.kie.org/2022/03/using-javascript-and-power-fx-with-dmn.html`.

So far in this chapter, we've focused on expression languages that we can use in our models. Let's take a wider look at some more advanced features for designing and building our decision models.

More on building and editing decision models

In previous chapters, we looked at building decision models and extended this knowledge by exploring the FEEL expression language. This section is going to extend our knowledge of decision models by looking at best practices.

Before we get into more heavyweight decision models, it's worth looking at the keyboard shortcuts available to you in the KIE Sandbox editor – we're highlighting the most useful ones in the table:

Key	What it does
Esc	Unselect the current selection
Delete/backspace	Delete the current selection
Ctrl + C	Copy
Ctrl + V	Paste
Ctrl + X	Cut
Ctrl + Z	Undo the last edit
Shift + Ctrl Z	Redo the last edit
Shift + Up arrow (or another arrow)	Slowly move the selection up (or in another direction)
Ctrl + Up arrow (or another arrow)	Quickly move the selection up (or in another direction)
Alt (hold) and drag the mouse	Pan
Ctrl (hold) and drag the mouse	Zoom
Shift + /	Show the full list of keyboard shortcuts

Table 9.1 – Keyboard shortcuts in the KIE sandbox

As well as these keyboard shortcuts, there are several other editing approaches that are useful to know:

- While the KIE Sandbox editor is very good, sometimes it does get out of sync (especially if your laptop hibernates). Refreshing the web page (and trusting that the model is saved to local browser storage) will resolve many issues.

- Working in the sandbox in the browser is great, but it can be confusing to switch between tabs for editing and tabs for reading documentation. Having a second browser installed on your PC and having one for each purpose is a simple trick to reduce confusion.

- It's trivial compared to other advice, but it is possible to bend the arrows in the diagram to make your diagrams neater and easier for other people to understand.

- The DMN standards treat both the graphical and XML versions of the decision model equally. It is possible to edit the XML of the model directly (for example, using the VS Code editor, which we'll introduce later in the chapter). While this is very powerful (for example, to copy-paste across decision models), it's very easy to break things. So, make sure you have saved a backup copy (to GitHub) first.

While we've focused up to now on the elements of the decision models, let's talk about stylish decision models – using common patterns to make it easier for users to understand your model.

Common decision patterns

If you've created lots of spreadsheets, you probably found that you repeat common patterns again and again. This might be presenting instructions or top-level figures on the first tab of your spreadsheet. It might be a hidden (or locked) sheet containing the complex formula. Or it might be a pivot table displayed beside a graph so that people can see a quick overview or drill into the detail.

We don't repeat these patterns out of laziness, although saving time is a good thing. We will repeat these patterns because they work and because familiar patterns are easier for people to understand. Programmers call repeatable solutions like these **design patterns**, and actively look to apply the patterns they've used previously as part of the problem-solving process.

In decision models, there are also repeatable patterns you will find yourself using again and again. Perhaps the most important is calling one decision model from another – since that allows us to break down our model into reusable and, more importantly, testable chunks. We'll dedicate sections later in the chapter to those two concepts.

Before that, you may notice that you have already (accidentally) created the patterns we're about to mention in your own models. But, since patterns aim to give a common language between and across teams, I'm using the pattern names as used by Denis Gagne of Trisotech and Matteo Mortari of the KIE team:

- **Scoring** – we build a value based on a combination of rules – adding or subtracting points depending on different rules matching. Exams are a classic scoring system, but credit ratings used by banks or airline passenger screening (for additional security checks) are similar examples.

- **Classification** can be based on these scores – for example, an exam score based on a pure percentage, where A grades have more than 85% mark. This might be more subtle with the classification changing so only the top 10 people get this grade. Or classification can be done on multiple values – like our product recommendation service in *Chapter 4*, which considers the country of residence.

- **Ranking** – real-life product recommendation services don't suggest a single value. For example, Amazon suggests up to 10 products (out of millions) that it thinks you are most likely to buy. You can mimic this by sorting based on a score, perhaps modified by different classification rules.

A final pattern is more of a framing of the problem – what question is the model trying to answer? Done correctly, it will make it much easier to both understand and design decision services.

The key takeaway from this section is that other people will have encountered very similar problems to you, even if they work in a different area or industry. Be on the lookout for common patterns that you can reuse – a good starting point is Gange and Mortari's presentation on the topic. The SlideShare link is `https://www.slideshare.net/dgagne/introduction-to-some-dmn-patterns-and-their-value`, with a YouTube video linked from the post on the KIE blog.

Another pattern – linking decision models together

A common pattern in Excel, decision services, and most computer languages is to break larger solutions down into reusable pieces. A bit like Lego building blocks, it makes them easier to understand and reuse. And as you'll see shortly, it makes them easier to test. But if we break the solution into many pieces, how do we link them together? Let's work through an example.

We've tried to make the examples in this book as realistic as possible. But if we show an example complicated enough to break into smaller modules, the mechanism for one decision model to call another will just get hidden in the complexity. So, we'll go in the other direction – the simplest possible example to link models together.

We'll start with *Figure 9.7*, also downloadable as `09-a-SimpleModel.dmn`.

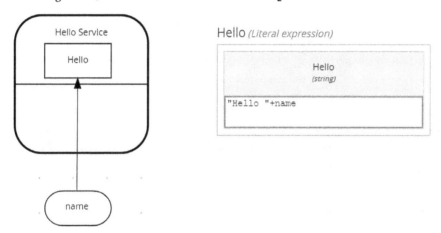

Figure 9.7 – Hello World service

This is a slightly updated version of the *Hello world* sample from *Figure 3.19* in *Chapter 3*. It takes a name as input, then says hello to that person.

In *Figure 9.7*, we put the decision model and the decision node side by side to make it clearer – but there is no major change other than wrapping the node in a decision service. It's also worth noting that the input node (`Name`) is of the `String` type. We also set the properties of the decision service to let KIE know it returns a type of `String` – which helps other people include and reuse this model.

> **A reminder about folders**
>
> Since we can only import models if they are in the same folder within KIE, it is helpful if the KIE sandbox is connected to GitHub – look at *Chapter 5* if you need a reminder on how to do this. You'll get asked what folder name to use – we used `c09` as the name for the folder, but more importantly, both models that we want to link must be saved in it.

Once you have created this model (or uploaded it into the sandbox), make sure it is synced to GitHub using the instructions we gave in *Chapter 5*. We named it 09-a-ImportModel.dmn. Now, it's time to create a second model that will reference our Hello service:

1. Click **New file** and select **Decision** – it will create a blank folder within the same folder.

2. Click on the **Included Models** tab – for the moment, it will show **No external models have been included**.

3. Click **Include model** at the top right of the screen. You'll see a list of models in the folder, as in *Figure 9.8*. If you don't see the other models listed, go back and check that the KIE sandbox is linked to GitHub correctly – both models need to be in the same folder.

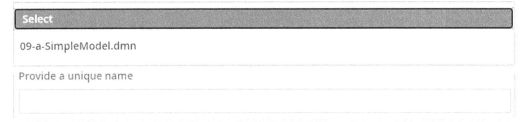

Figure 9.8 – Including another model

4. Select 09-a-ImportModel.dmn and give it a name. It's better to keep it short (we called it simple), as we'll be using that name often. Click on the **Include** button to confirm.

5. If our included model had custom data types, they will appear (read-only) in the **Data Types** tab. The **Decision Navigator** tab in our model will also show the components we have just included, as in *Figure 9.9*. If Decision Navigator isn't already open, you can view it by pressing the map icon at the top right of the screen.

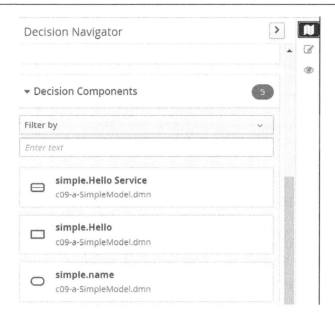

Figure 9.9 – Included components in Decision Navigator

While it is possible to use all these components, the decision service is the one that is intended to be referenced outside of the model. Now that we've included our model, we can invoke it whenever we want. We're going to build out the second of the two models we want to link, as in *Figure 9.10*.

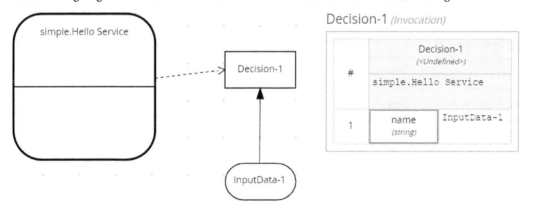

Figure 9.10 – Included components

While this second model is available to download as `09-a-ImportModel.dmn` from the book's GitHub site, it's still simple to set up. From left to right in *Figure 9.10*, we see the following:

1. We dragged and dropped `simple.Hello Service` from Decision Navigator.

2. We created a decision node and kept the default name, `Decision-1`.

3. We linked from the Hello service to the decision node. This direction is important; fortunately, the sandbox editor won't let you link in the other direction.

4. We created a new input node (leaving the default name of `InputData-1`) and set its type to `String`. We connected the input node to the decision node.

5. Editing the decision node, we set its type to `Invocation`.

6. Editing the `Invocation` node, it's important we get the names exactly right. The function name we set is `Simple.Hello Service` – exactly the same spelling and case as the node we included from the other model.

7. The editor will have a line to enter the parameters we want to pass – change the first parameter name from `p-1` to `name`. Again, this must exactly match the input node from our included model. Take a look at Decision Navigator to make sure you get the spelling right. We set the type of this parameter to `String` – again, to match the value our included model expects.

8. We set the value we want to pass as a parameter; click on **Select Expression**, set it to **Literal Expression**, and include the value of our input node (`Input-Node-1`). The type of the parameter (`String`) must match the type the included service is expecting.

9. In the KIE sandbox, double-check that no problems are highlighted. Then, click on **Run** and **As Form**. As shown in *Figure 9.11*, when we enter the name of `Peter`, we get `Hello Peter` in return.

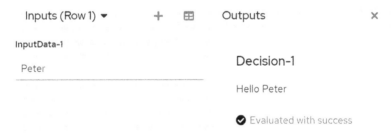

Figure 9.11 – The result of calling out the external model

Small example, big implications

This is a trivial example – we'd never split such a simple example as Hello World. But your models are going to become very complex very quickly and it's good to know that you can split the models into reusable components.

Linking the Bill of Materials example

Since this is such a simple example, we've included a second more sophisticated example, where we reuse the Bill of Materials service that we created in *Figure 9.4*. That example is available to download at 09-Call-BOM. The steps to import and the mapping to our decision model are similar to the hello world example. However, we want to pass over multiple parameters, which we can do by adding an additional line to our invocation table, as in *Figure 9.12*.

DecisionInvocation *(Invocation)*

#	DecisionInvocation *(<Undefined>)*	
	bom.BOM Service	
1	Qty *(number)*	InQty
2	Product *(string)*	"Silk Tray"

Figure 9.12 – Invoking our Bill of Materials service

We'll return to importing and invoking models in *Chapter 11* – when we use a similar mechanism to use and import Machine Learning models to work alongside our business rules.

Now that we know that we can split and recombine our models, the question becomes where to split our models. That is a judgment call since you need to trade off the convenience of being able to see everything on one page against the simplicity of having lots of smaller, easier-to-understand models. But two useful guidelines are as follows:

- Model how people think about the existing business – the more your models follow existing department, team, and process boundaries, the easier it is for colleagues to understand them.

- Model at a level that makes it easy to test. If your model is too big, it will be very unwieldy to test. If your models are too small, you will get tired of writing many trivial tests that add little value.

Since testing is so important, KIE gives you several options on how to build and run them automatically – we look at them in the next section.

Testing and breaking your rules (before somebody else does)

If you are like me, it's always a relief to get a spreadsheet, program, or decision model working. And sometimes, we're reluctant to push our new creation too hard in case it breaks. But whether we look for errors or not, any hidden errors are still there and will come back to bite us later

Even worse, errors get more expensive to fix the longer you ignore them. What is trivial to change now (while the model is fresh in your mind) could take you several hours to track down in a couple of months (when you have worked on several other projects in the meantime). And it could get very expensive if the problem is seen by real customers or end users– we could end up giving away a lot of free chocolate and hurt the reputation of our business.

Even more depressing is that fixing this error could cause other things to break. For example, we might update our bill of materials, and then find out that another decision model relies on it and is now behaving incorrectly. But there are ways to fix this – often known as Agile, Scrum, or test-driven development.

Agile, Scrum, and test-driven development

Happily, enough people have run into these problems for many years before us. So, there is a set of best practices and tooling to help us fix them. Broadly speaking, the solution is as follows:

- To write our tests little by little, so they are easy to write. The focus of each is testing a single part. That way, we're not tempted to leave them until the end and then maybe not write them at all. This approach is called **unit testing** and it's much easier than the end-to-end testing that you may have been involved with before (although there is still a place for that approach).

- To write our tests in a standard way, so while each unit test is simple, together they become a safety net that highlights whether we've accidentally broken another part of our solution.

- To write our tests first, so that they become a contract for what we are trying to develop, and we know we have built everything we said we would.

- To run those tests automatically, so they become part of a game – do our tests pass or not? If we get a green light, great! If not, because each test is so simple, it's easy to find and fix the problem (and run again, to see whether we get the green light).

- To write the tests using similar tools to the ones we used to build our solution, but to organize our tests a bit like scaffolding on a building. That way, it is clear what is the supporting testing framework, with the building (or core solution) being untouched.

- To make these tests fun and easy to write, so they become part of the documentation. With good tests, a colleague looking at your decision model now has a working example of how to (re)use it.

These bullet points are a philosophy and approach to building solutions. You may have been part of a project that follows these principles, often called **Agile**, **Scrum**, or **test-driven development**.

Implemented correctly, the small upfront investment in writing tests will pay itself back tens or hundreds of times over. Even better, projects with tests are much less stressful to work on since you get notified of problems early when you have time to fix them without much fuss.

Health warning – calling a project agile doesn't make it agile

There is a temptation for some managers to label a project *Agile* as an excuse to not do the hard work of project planning. But if you don't invest in the tests, you will run into serious issues later (often when the original project managers have left). If you have had this experience, please keep an open mind for the next section – real test-first projects address a lot of the common pain points in developing technology solutions.

There is a lot of information available on Agile, Scrum, and test-driven development. We'll focus in the next section on the tools the KIE project provides to support this approach. We'll cover one tool built into the KIE sandbox and one more advanced approach that you might want to implement in Excel. Finally, we'll preview some of the advanced testing features available in Business Central (which we cover in more detail in *Chapter 10*) and Visual Studio Code (which we introduce in *Appendix B* and *Chapter 12*).

Run ... as Table

You may have noticed when you were running previous examples in the KIE sandbox using the **Run ... as Form** option, that there was a second option (**Run ... as Table**). Let's look at that now, since it's a good step into the testing approach:

1. We have the Bill of Materials option open in the KIE sandbox (downloaded model: 09 Bill of Materials.dmn).

2. In the sandbox, select **Run ... as Table**. A screen like *Figure 9.13* will appear. Note that we've removed some columns for clarity and added some test values to show more clearly how the table runner works.

#	Qty (number)	Product (string)	Bill of Materials (Any)		
0			Grams of Cocoa in Product	Grams of Cocoa in Order	Name
1	125	Silk Tray	150	18750	Silk Tray
2	10	Crunch	10	100	Crunch
3	-10	Crunch	10	-100	Crunch

Figure 9.13 – KIE sandbox table runner

3. Each line of this table is equivalent to using **Run ... as Form** as we tested our models with up until now. If we put the two values on the left (`Qty` and `Product`) as inputs, on the right, we can state the three outputs we expect (`Grams of Cocoa in Product`, `Grams of Cocoa in PD: Please apply P-code style Order`, and confirmation of the product name).

4. The convenience here is that we can see multiple different orders at once, which allows us to quickly check for anything going wrong.

While the table runner is a useful improvement, there are a couple of areas where it falls short of the test-first approach. The most important is that it does not flag where a test fails. For example, the third value in *Figure 9.13* is a negative value, giving a spurious result. But it would be very easy to miss this – even if you spotted this first time you looked at the image, could you guarantee to see the problem if this was one of the hundreds of output tables you needed to check?

Fortunately, KIE does give tools to fix this problem. We'll cover those tools later in this chapter – but since they are not (yet) embedded into the KIE sandbox, it's worthwhile discussing an Excel-based solution to this problem.

Test cases using Excel

If you look at *Figure 9.14*, you'll see we've evolved our table runner in Excel to solve the problem of rogue tests being missed. While it has the same values as *Figure 9.13*, it's immediately obvious when there is a problem, as it gets highlighted in red.

	A	B	C	D	E	F	G
1	Given		Expect		Actual		Flag
2	Qty	Product	Cocoa in Product	Cocoa in BOM	Cocoa in Product	Cocoa in BOM	
3	125	Silk Tray	18750	150	18750	150	OK
4	10	Silk Tray	10	100	10	100	OK
5	-10	Crunch	0	0	Error!	Error!	Error instead of 0

Figure 9.14 – A test scenario in Excel

This is a very simple idea, with four main groups of columns:

- **Given** are the values we are passing in
- **Expected** are the values we think should be returned by the decision service
- **Actual** are the values that came back in reality
- **Flag** is the column to check whether the **Expected** and **Actual** values matched

We won't give a working example of running test cases in Excel since once you've grasped the key idea, the implementation is straightforward. You can set up this test spreadsheet, linking Excel with your decision service, using the approach you learned in *Chapters 6* and *7*.

The other details, such as conditional formatting, will be up to you, and the layout will be closely linked to the decision service that you have built.

It's worth highlighting that testing in Excel is a completely feasible approach. The scenario simulation approach we discuss in the next section is better again – but it does depend on tools that you may need support in setting up. You might find the next section hard, but achievable. As you work your way through it, know that you always have a backup plan for testing in Excel.

Scenario testing and simulation

Testing in the Excel approach is good, but it is even better to write tests using similar tools to the one we built our model with. That way, our tests sit near our decision models and much more likely to be used and updated. *Figure 9.15* gives a sample of KIE's Scenario Simulation tool, which takes this approach.

#	Scenario description	GIVEN		EXPECT	
		Product	Qty	Bill of Materials	Product Details
		value	value	value	value
1	Silk Tray	"Silk Tray"	125	18750	150
2	Crunch	"Crunch"	10	100	10
3	Crunch	"Crunch"	-10	0	0

Figure 9.15 – KIE Scenario Simulation editor

Figure 9.15 is very similar in approach to the Excel test scenario in *Figure 9.14*. It has the same inputs (**GIVEN**) and expected outputs (**EXPECT**). When we run the scenario simulation, it highlights any variances between expected and actual.

While this is a real screenshot from KIE, at the time of writing, the Scenario Simulation tool is not yet available in the sandbox. It is worth double checking, as the product roadmap is constantly evolving and may have changed by the time you read this. Instead, this Scenario Simulation tool is available in both of the advanced KIE decision modeling tools:

- **Business Central**, the older decision modeling tool from the KIE team, still has more features than the sandbox. As you'll see in *Chapter 10*, Business Central is very accessible to business users. There are a couple of setup steps that most Excel Power users will be able to follow, but some will need support.

- **VS Code**, part of the toolkit aimed at developers rather than Business users. While many Excel users will be able to use it, not every reader of this book will want to take advantage of the power that it gives.

One key aim of this book is to give you a good foundation and clear next steps to explore further. VS Code from Microsoft is certainly one of these areas.

What is VS Code and why use it to test?

You can use VS Code not just for writing decision models but also for a wide range of areas such as ML, web development, data science, and more traditional programming. To encourage you to take this next step, we'll introduce VS Code in the following section, and explain (in *Appendix B*) how to use it to get started writing decision models and scenario tests. That Appendix uses the online version of VS Code with no installation, to get you up and running more quickly.

VS Code is a free-to-use text editor and coding tool from Microsoft, with extensions that can handle pretty much any development project. In some of our earlier examples, we opened some files in a simple text editor such as Notepad. VS Code gives you a similar editor, but with the ability to have multiple text-like files open at once – look at the tabs across the top of the screen in *Figure 9.16*.

Figure 9.16 – Scenario simulation editor in VS Code

Even better, VS Code gives you code coloring and syntax highlighting, which might appear to be simple decoration, but do make the file a lot easier to read. On the left of the screenshot, you'll also see that VS Code gives you a Windows Explorer-like view of all the files in your solution – including the decision model, scenario simulations (which can be seen in the main panel of the screenshot) as well as supporting files such as text, XML, and documentation in the .md markdown format.

The dark gray bar on the left of the screenshot hints at the power available in VS Code. The icons change depending on the plugins we have installed – in this case, we have added the DMN extension from the KIE team. Other icons on this bar allow you to interact with GitHub repositories (in a more powerful way than we can do in the KIE sandbox), deploy items to Azure, and run individual files in your project.

What is even more impressive is that while there is a Desktop version of VS Code, this screenshot was taken using VS Code running within the web browser (which automatically sets up the Azure cloud-hosted Codespaces to do the heavy lifting).

The final section of the screen (the bottom right) contains a lot of text. If you've used a terminal before (either on Linux, macOS, or Windows), this should be familiar. But since commands are typed rather than menus and mouse clicks, it may be intimidating to some readers who are seeing it for the first time. It is for that reason that we cover setting up and using scenario simulations and testing in VS Code in *Appendix B*, outside the main flow of this book.

Since the instructions in *Appendix B* are given on a step-by-step basis, most users should be able to follow them. As VS Code is such a powerful tool that you will use across many different projects, I would highly recommend you dive in and give it a go – with the bonus of making the Scenario Simulation tools available to your project.

Summary and further reading

We've linked to a lot of additional resources throughout this chapter. The KIE project blog has some very useful posts and videos about using test scenarios that are well worth spending time on. And if you want to explore DMN in more detail, an excellent next step is reading *DMN Method and Style* by Bruce Silver.

But we're not finished yet on these topics in this book. *Chapter 10* (where we cover installing Docker and Business Central) gives us another way to run our scenario testing editor. This is just as well, as the Machine Learning we cover in *Chapter 11* needs testing, even more than the rules-based AI that we've covered to date. Finally, in *Chapter 12*, we introduce the DRL format, a more advanced rule-writing format that works well alongside the graphical DMN notation that we learned more about in this chapter.

This chapter aimed to give you a more advanced understanding of both decision models and the FEEL expression language embedded into them. Since more advanced models are more likely to break, we covered patterns to make your models more understandable, and techniques to link many simple models together. We learned about the importance of a test-first approach, and the tools that KIE provides to support it. Finally, we saw a glimpse of the advanced tooling in KIE as part of VS Code, as a way of encouraging you to explore more beyond the sandbox.

Beyond the Sandbox might have been a good title for the next chapter – we continue to explore more ways to host both your decision editor and running models. Since that uses Docker, it gives us additional options to run both on-premises and in the cloud, building on the first glimpse of Azure that we saw with VS Code and Codespaces in this chapter. We'll also look at Business Central as another way of running your scenario tests.

Part 4:
Next Steps in AI, Machine Learning, and Rule Engines

The final section of the book aims to leave you with a good platform to learn more about AI, machine learning, and rule engines.

This section includes the following chapters:

- *Chapter 10, Scaling Rules in Business Central with Docker and the Cloud*, demonstrates the power of the KIE and Kogito decision-making tools, leveraging containers to increase our deployment options and editing capability.

- *Chapter 11, Rule-Based AI and Machine Learning AI – Combining the Best of Both*, introduces the other main part of AI and shows how we can use the tools in KIE and Azure ML Studio to deploy both machine learning and rule-based decision models alongside each other.

- *Chapter 12, What Next? A Look inside Neural Networks, Enterprise Projects, Advanced Rules, and the Rule Engine*, expands on the previous chapters and looks at key areas for future learning with practical first steps in neural networks, enterprise Java projects, and ethical, explainable AI.

10

Scaling Rules in Business Central with Docker and the Cloud

In the previous chapter, we got our first glimpse of the **Scenario Simulation tool** as a device for testing complex decision models. The instructions we introduced in *Appendix B* might also have sparked your interest in exploring advanced techniques in VS Code. But since that technical approach isn't for everybody, you could still be looking for another advanced way to test your models.

Happily, **Business Central** provides the same Scenario Simulation tool in a more user-friendly package. This chapter shows you how to set up the Business Central editor and explores some of the additional rule editing techniques that it provides. In particular, we look at it as an enterprise-level collaboration tool for sharing and editing decision models.

Since we are going to use **Docker containers** to run Business Central, we will also solve another problem we encountered in *Chapter 5*. While we already know how to host our decision models locally (on our laptop) or in the cloud (with RedHat OpenShift), your IT department may want something in between: hosting the decision services on the company network. We will explore containers as a way of enabling this and other deployment options.

Specifically, we will cover the following:

- Comparing Business Central and KIE Sandbox to edit our models
- Images, containers, Docker, and getting help
- Installing Docker on your laptop
- Running Docker and a tour of Docker Desktop
- Running the Business Central rule editor in Docker

- The KIE Server in Docker and Azure
- Roundup of Decision Model deployment options

By the end of this chapter, you should be confident that you and your colleagues will be able to deploy a scalable enterprise-level rules editor *and* create a scalable enterprise-level server to host the business rules you write. This will give you many additional areas to explore beyond what we cover in the book.

> **Two different ways to read this chapter – hands-on, or simply to know it can be done**
>
> While it is useful to know the hands-on techniques, the main purpose of this chapter is to signpost future steps. This gives you an alternative way to read this chapter; try to understand what is possible, knowing that a more technical colleague will carry out the deployment.
>
> Either way, it's great to know that Kogito supports a range of deployment options. The information shared in this chapter will help you convince your colleagues that KIE, Kogito, and Drools is a scalable stack for solving the business and IT problems you face.

Prerequisites

The step-by-step instructions in this chapter are simple. The only thing you need is a laptop powerful enough to run Docker. Most modern laptops will meet this requirement. More info can be found at `https://docs.docker.com/desktop/install/windows-install/`.

If your laptop isn't powerful enough, ask your colleagues whether there is another computer on the network that can host the container. The entire point of Docker is that it gives you multiple deployment options. Since Business Central is web based, you will be able to access it remotely.

Comparing business central and the KIE sandbox

Business Central, as a web-based editor for your decision models, sounds a lot like KIE Sandbox. And you'd be right – if you know your way around KIE Sandbox, there is much in Business Central that will be familiar. But it's a bit like comparing a family car with the latest Formula 1 model. Both are cars with four wheels and an engine, but one is much easier to drive and better for a trip to the supermarket. The other offers a lot more performance but needs the support of a team of mechanics to operate effectively. Some key differences in the features are as follows:

- KIE Sandbox is designed to be easy to use, with no setup, making it ideal for a book like this one. Business Central may be easy to start but still needs about 15–20 minutes of preparation to set up before you can write your first business rule.

- Business Central has a lot more features than KIE Sandbox, which focuses on the core functionality of decision modeling. The core decision model editor and DMN implementation are exactly the same but there are additional features (for example, the Scenario Simulation tool) only available in Business Central.

- The Sandbox is designed for an individual user with some team features, whereas Business Central assumes many people will be working together on the project. Many of its advanced features assume that there is a *mechanic* on your team that knows Java (for example, to set up data types).

- Both the KIE sandbox and Business Central use Git as the mechanism to store models, so it is possible to fashion a workflow where both editors work on the same decision model. However, as you'd expect from Business Central, it gives a much more powerful implementation, which can be intimidating for new users.

In this chapter, we focus on the scenario testing tool, since that is a compelling reason for you to explore Business Central. We also use Business Central to demonstrate some of the more advanced features in *Chapter 12*. Our aim is to give you a good start and to suggest additional paths to explore.

But first, we'll need to get Business Central up and running, and to do that we'll need containers.

Containers, Docker, and getting help

We were introduced to **containers** in *Chapter 2* as the quickest way for readers to get tools and examples running. Even more importantly, containers help all readers run the examples consistently, which means the instructions in the book match what you're seeing happen on your laptop.

The process is simple; we install our container software of choice (Docker) and then use the Docker tools to download the images containing the software and examples we want.

Many Excel power users will be comfortable with installing software. Even if this is something you're doing for the first time, the step-by-step instructions in this section are very easy for you to follow. Before we start, let's remember that not everything you tried in Excel worked the first time. What did you do to fix it?

1. You checked your typing and spelling – this is the biggest cause of error messages.

2. You read the error message carefully – chances are it is suggesting something you can do to fix it.

3. If you were following a guide or book, you went back over the instructions to see whether there was a step that you missed.

4. You copied and pasted the error message (or key parts of it) into a search engine. Most of the time, there will be people who have encountered the same problem and will know how to fix it. At the very least, there will be suggestions on how to move closer to a solution.

5. After trying all these steps, you asked a colleague or friend. You shared the steps you have tried to show that you value their time and that you are genuinely seeking their expertise.

The first part of our step-by-step instructions can be summed up as *install Docker Desktop on your computer*. There is a very supportive and active Docker community to help you do this. And because Docker is a corporate standard, there may be people near you who can help. *Appendix C* has some good starting points, in particular the *Preparing your computer for Docker* section.

Most readers will not need help as they work through the instructions to install Docker in the next section, but it's good to know additional detail is there if needed.

Installing Docker

Knowing that we have all this support, let's walk through installing Docker on a laptop, step by step. The instructions in this chapter are in two clear parts:

1. Install Docker to host containers.

2. Download an image with the samples you want to run in this container.

Make sure the first part is running before you start the second – it makes it much easier to ask for help if you know exactly which part is causing the problem.

Preparing your Docker Hub account

You will be asked later for the details of your (free to register) Docker Hub account. Go to `docker.com` and click on **Sign In** in the top right-hand corner of the web page. You then have the option of creating an account. Make a note of your username and password for later.

Downloading and installing the Docker software

Docker Desktop is quite a straightforward download and install:

1. To get started, go to `https://www.docker.com/products/docker-desktop/` and pick the appropriate installer for your system (for example, Windows, Linux, or Mac).

2. Open the Docker installer that you downloaded in the previous step.

3. Click **Yes** for **Do you want to allow Docker Desktop to make changes to your PC**. If you are asked for an admin username and password at this point, see the notes in *Appendix C*.

4. Click **OK** in the next step – configuration. Note that your version number is likely to be higher (more recent) than shown in this screenshot:

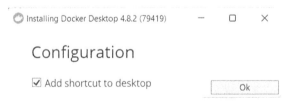

Figure 10.1 – Installing Docker

5. Be patient while the installer downloads and unpacks the files. If all is well, you will get the **Installation succeeded** message – click **OK** and proceed to the next section (a tour of Docker Desktop).

At this point, you should have Docker Desktop successfully installed – let's take a tour of it.

> **Checking your Docker installation**
>
> At this point, it is worth checking that everything in Docker is running correctly. I highly recommend that you work through the Docker **Run a Sample Container** guide. More information (including videos) on how to do this is at https://docs.docker.com/get-started/.
>
> We cover similar material in the *Running a simple Hello World image in Docker* section. It is much better to catch any problems with the Docker installation now because once we start running images and containers within it, it can be confusing where any problems originate (Docker or the image).
>
> *Appendix C* makes suggestions that could help solve any issues, and the Docker documentation has extensive troubleshooting suggestions.

Running Docker and a tour of Docker Desktop

As we congratulate ourselves on successfully installing Docker, let's take a tour of Docker Desktop and run a sample image to ensure that everything is working as it should:

1. Start Docker Desktop. There should be a Docker icon on your desktop, so double-click it. It can also be started via the Windows **Start** menu (a similar icon should be available there).

2. Accept the Docker service/license agreement.

3. Wait while Docker Desktop (and background services) starts – the wait message is shown in *Figure 10.2*:

Figure 10.2 – Docker Desktop starting

4. When Docker has started, you should see the home screen, as shown in *Figure 10.3*. If you don't see this exact screen, try clicking on **Containers** in the top-left corner:

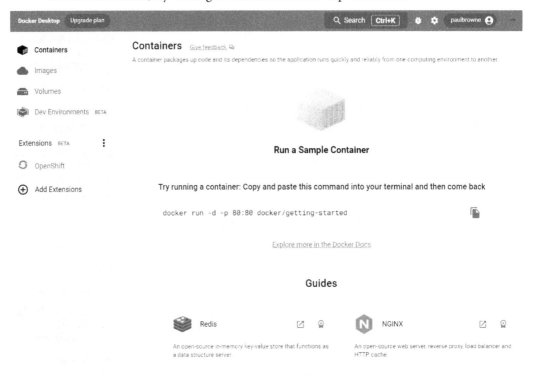

Figure 10.3 – Docker Desktop home screen

5. If your screen is showing the green Docker whale icon (in the bottom-left corner) then congratulations, both Docker Desktop and the background engine (services) are running correctly.

While this isn't a book about Docker, you'll be spending some time on this screen to run examples. It's worth taking a few moments to look around:

- The area at the bottom center of the screen is **Featured Images**, showing the range of containers that can be run within Docker. There are many other sources of images (notably Docker Hub and Quay from Red Hat) – we'll use them to run the sample shortly.

- The **Images** (tab) is the list of available images that you can run. Images are read-only and never change. There are not likely to be many images on your computer at the moment; we'll show you how to download some later in the chapter.

- The **Container** tab (on the top left) also allows you to return to the home page. Containers are your working copy of an image. They will change as you interact with them. This tab also shows the containers that you are running and allows you to stop and restart them and see message logs from running containers.

- **Volumes** are like disks where containers can store their information. In general, Docker will manage them automatically for us.

- The other tabs on the left (**Dev Environments** and **Extensions**) are more advanced functionality. We won't need them for running samples in the book.

Across the top right of the screen, there are some more interesting buttons:

- **Upgrade**, **Troubleshoot**, and **Debug** hint at the more advanced power of Docker. We won't use these buttons much.

- **Account** allows you to sign in using the username and password you created on docker.com earlier. It is a good idea to sign into Docker Desktop now – it will help when we download the Docker images in the next section.

Shutting down the KIE Extended Services

Since we're about to run our first Docker image, now is a good time to remind you to shut down the KIE Extended Services. If you forget, you will get a Port already in use error, since both KIE services and (some of) the Docker images attempt to do similar things and get in each other's way.

First time use of Docker Desktop

Docker Desktop is a great tool for managing our sample images once we have downloaded them. But it currently gives you no way to download these images. To do that, you need to use the **console** (also known as a **terminal** or **command prompt**). In general, we just need to the console only once, because after the image has been downloaded, we can manage it in Docker Desktop.

As an Excel power user, you should have no fear of the console. It allows us to type text commands, just like typing formulas in Excel. Just like in Excel, it is very important to get the spelling right (it's the number one source of mistakes). And just like in Excel, it is important to hit the *Enter* (or *Return*) key so the computer knows that you have finished typing and it can begin working.

To open the console in Windows, press *Windows Key + R*, then type cmd (and click **OK**). You should see a black-and-white window similar to *Figure 10.4*:

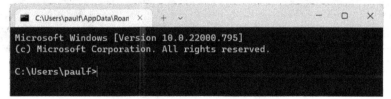

Figure 10.4 – Console on Windows

On a Mac, press *Cmd + Space* to open Spotlight, then type Terminal to search for it.

Note that your screen will be slightly different from this screenshot – paulf is my Windows username, but yours will be different. But the same ideas of typing, pressing *Enter*, and having the computer start working are the same.

The good news is, in the next sections, once we use the commands in the console to download our sample images, the images automatically appear in Docker Desktop. After that, we'll use Docker Desktop to manage them.

Running a simple Hello World image in Docker

Now that we've downloaded Docker, we want to test a simple image. That way, we know Docker is running correctly and if something breaks, we know where to start looking to fix it.

Traditionally, the first example is to get the computer to say Hello World to you. Docker makes this easy. To run the Docker Hello World example, follow these steps:

1. Open the command prompt by pressing press *Windows Key + R*, then type cmd. Mac users, see the note in the preceding section on opening Terminal.

2. In the console, type docker run hello-world, paying special attention to the spelling.

3. Make sure you press the *Enter* key to run the command. You will get the message shown in *Figure 10.5*:

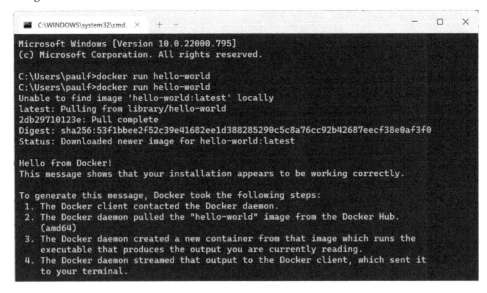

Figure 10.5 – Docker Hello World

4. In *Figure 10.5*, we can see the command we typed (docker run hello-world) and then the text generated by Docker once we pressed the *Enter* key. Since it could not find the image locally, it automatically downloaded the latest version from the **Docker Hub** and ran it.

5. If you see `Hello from Docker` about half way down the text output from Docker, then congratulations – you have just run your first image in a Docker container!

> **Containers hide the hard stuff**
>
> In this sample, we've skipped over the complexity of what Docker does for us – that's why we're using Docker. But if you read the text after `Hello from Docker`, you'll get a hint of the steps happening behind the scenes that you don't have to worry about.

This example might be a bit underwhelming – we've spent a lot of time doing setup, and all we've achieved so far is a `Hello World` message. But now that we have Docker up and running, we can take advantage of what it can do – download images and try out Business Central as a more advanced Business Central rule editor.

Running the Business Central rule editor in Docker

Since we've set up Docker, let's use it to run the first of the images provided by the KIE team. It's as simple as running our Hello World example. And while there is a bit of careful typing needed in *step 2*, we only need to do it once because after that, it's set up in Docker Desktop:

1. Open Command Prompt by pressing press *Windows Key + R*, then type cmd.

2. In the console, type `docker run -p 8080:8080 -p 8001:8001 -d --name business-central quay.io/kiegroup/business-central-workbench-showcase:latest`, paying special attention to the spelling.

3. Docker will spend several minutes downloading and extracting the necessary layers, as shown in *Figure 10.6*:

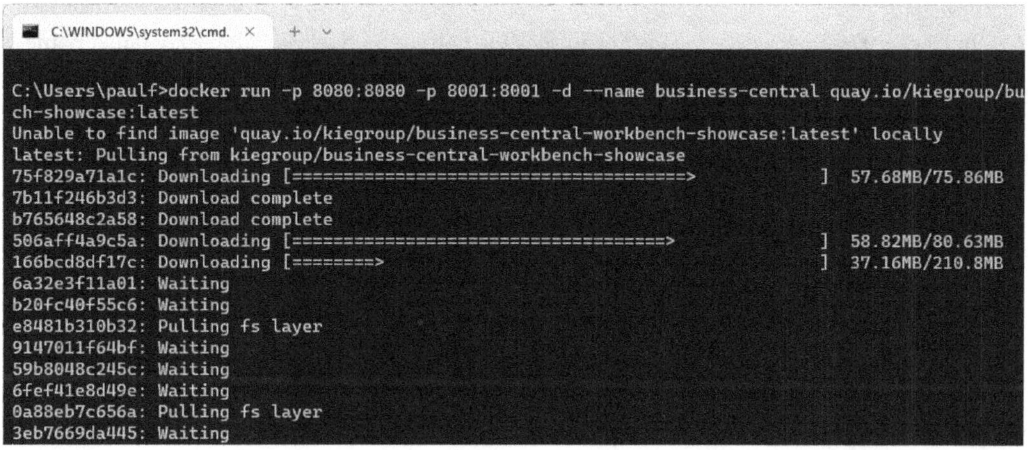

Figure 10.6 – Docker downloading the layers in the Business Central image

4. After Command Prompt has finished updating, take a look at the Docker Desktop **Containers** tab. It should show Business Central running in a container, as shown in *Figure 10.7*:

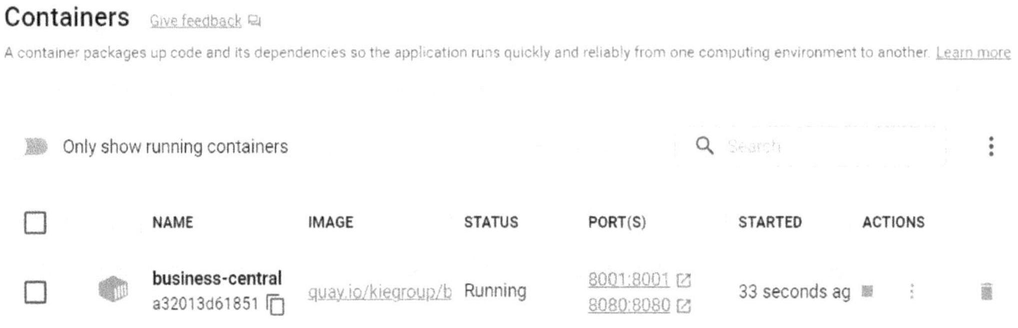

Containers Give feedback 💬

A container packages up code and its dependencies so the application runs quickly and reliably from one computing environment to another. Learn more

🔘 Only show running containers   🔍 Search   ⋮

	NAME	IMAGE	STATUS	PORT(S)	STARTED	ACTIONS
☐	**business-central** a32013d61851 🗐	quay.io/kiegroup/b	Running	8001:8001 ☑ 8080:8080 ☑	33 seconds ag ■	⋮ 🗑

Figure 10.7 – Docker running our Business Central image

5. The values in *Figure 10.7* match what we specified in our startup command. `docker run` asked Docker to run a container using the latest image from `quay.io/kiegroup/business-central-workbench-showcase`, downloading it if needed. We specified the ports using `-p 8080:8080 -p 8001:8001`; otherwise, we wouldn't be able to talk to it in the next step and we gave it a `--name` value of `business-central`, to make it easier to spot in Docker Desktop.

Docker ports

Docker is great as it runs images in their own isolated containers. That's great for security, but it does mean that if we don't specify a port using the `-p` flag, we have no opening to communicate between our laptop and the secure container.

---

6. In Docker Desktop, we encourage to you click the buttons on the line with the container name to explore more. Our container is already running, so we don't need to click the button to start or stop it.

7. It's also useful to click on the container name, **Business Central**. This gives us additional information from the Business Central logs, as shown in *Figure 10.8*. Much of what is shown is technical, but it is a useful source of suggestions if things aren't behaving as you'd expect.

Figure 10.8 – Business Central startup messages in the logs

With one (almost simple) command, you got Business Central up and running. From here, you can start and stop the image using Docker Desktop without using the text-based console again. And since the image has been downloaded, it will be much quicker to start next time.

Opening the Business Central rule editor

The focus of this chapter has been getting the software up and running. To congratulate ourselves on getting this far, let's treat ourselves by looking into the Business Central rule editor image we've just downloaded. With the Business Central container still running in Docker, follow these steps:

1. Open the following URL in your favorite browser: `http://localhost:8080/business-central`.

2. It can take a couple of moments to load the first time, and then you should see the login screen, as shown in *Figure 10.9*. Trust us, Business Central speeds up after the first use.

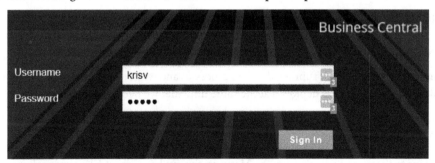

Figure 10.9 – Login screen for Business Central, running in Docker on our laptop

3. The standard **username** is `krisv` and **password** is `krisv`. Click **Sign In** to step through to the initial welcome screen.

> **A bigger team – multiple roles in Business Central**
>
> The web page for this image (`https://quay.io/repository/kiegroup/business-central-workbench-showcase?tab=info`) gives an idea of the team-based nature of Business Central, listing several other roles. The username we suggested is the most useful for a first look.
>
> Note that we're using the showcase image with these roles already defined. There are other more secure images on RedHat's Quay.io site that are intended for production deployment.

The welcome screen shown in *Figure 10.10* hints at the power of Business Central, aimed at full enterprise users.

Figure 10.10 – Business Central welcome screen

While we won't explore all the features of Business Central, it's useful to know its power. From left to right, the options are as follows:

- **Design** which is roughly equivalent to the KIE Sandbox (but with more features), and that we'll explore further in a minute.

- **Deploy** gives us many more targets to deploy our models into than just KIE Sandbox. It also gives us options to configure those environments (for example, for development, testing, staging, or real-life production use).

- **Manage** allows us to track running decision processes and workflows. Remember, we may have multiple decision models deployed at the same time that we need to keep an eye on.

- **Track** gives people who are listed as approvers in the deployment processes the ability to see what requests are waiting for them.

Similar options to these are available from the **Menu** on the top left of most KIE screens. But we want to create a project, so if you click on **Design**, you will see a list of your spaces, as shown in *Figure 10.11*:

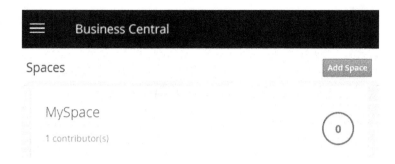

Figure 10.11 – Spaces in Business Central

Think of a **space** like a solution – in our chocolate examples in the previous chapters we included all of the decision models (for sales and marketing, and for production) in one folder. But in reality, using Business Central, each of those different departments would have its own space.

Clicking into a space shows that it can contain multiple **projects**, as shown in *Figure 10.12*, each comparable to a folder in KIE Sandbox. While these levels or nested folders for organizing our decision models and other assets might be confusing when we first open Business Central, for large projects, you'll appreciate the structure that they give.

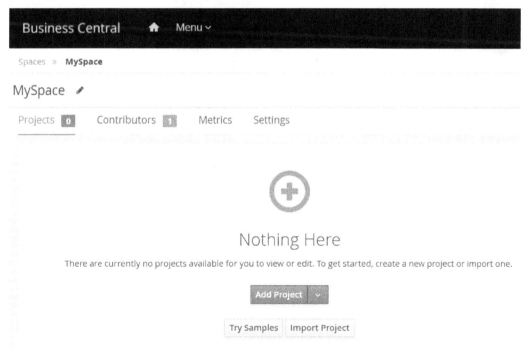

Figure 10.12 – Projects within a space

Now that we've taken a quick look at some of the first screens in Business Central, let's do something useful with it. In particular, let's run the Scenario Simulation tool to test out the model we created in *Chapter 9*.

Scenario Simulation and testing in Business Central

While we have the spaces screen open, let's create a new project. While we'd normally create an empty project, for this exercise, we're going to use an existing sample and add our model to it. That way you have additional assets to explore after you complete this exercise:

1. On the **MySpace** screen (as shown in *Figure 10.12*), click on **Try Sample**.

2. On the selection screen that appears, select the **Traffic Violation project,** then click on **OK** in the top right-hand corner of the screen.

3. This will set up a project similar to *Figure 10.13* – this example shows how much of a fine a driver should pay for various driving issues.

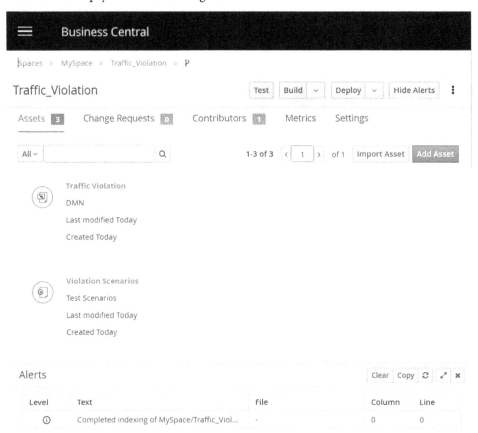

Figure 10.13 – Example project with a decision model and test scenarios

It's worth taking some time to look through this traffic ticket example. It's a clear example of a decision model and a test scenario that are pretty helpful to examine in detail.

Also shown in *Figure 10.13* are some clear examples of the Enterprise features of Business Central. The breadcrumbs show the route you took through the project hierarchy to get here (**Traffic_Violation**). The screen also shows the integration with Maven (**main**), the option to run all the test scenarios in this project, the options to build and deploy the model onto the KIE Server, the options to track change requests and contributors, as well as the fine-grained settings; these are all sophisticated Enterprise-level features.

Setting up our test scenarios

Since we want to show that we can edit DMN models created in KIE Sandbox, we're going to import the model we created in *Chapter 9*, which can be downloaded as `09 Bill of Materials. dmn` from the book's GitHub site at `https://github.com/PacktPublishing/AI-and-Business-Rules-for-Excel-Power-Users`.

To add our existing model to this project in Business Central, go back to the main project screen (the one we showed in *Figure 10.13*) then take the following steps:

1. Click on **Import Asset**, then fill out the values as shown in *Figure 10.14*, then click **OK**. Like in the KIE sandbox, it's good to pick a simple but clear asset name – in this case, we use **bom** – since we'll need it later when creating a test scenario.

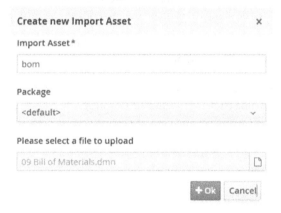

Figure 10.15 – Importing our Bill of Materials decision model in Business Central

2.   Business Central will import the decision model and display it as shown in *Figure 10.16*:

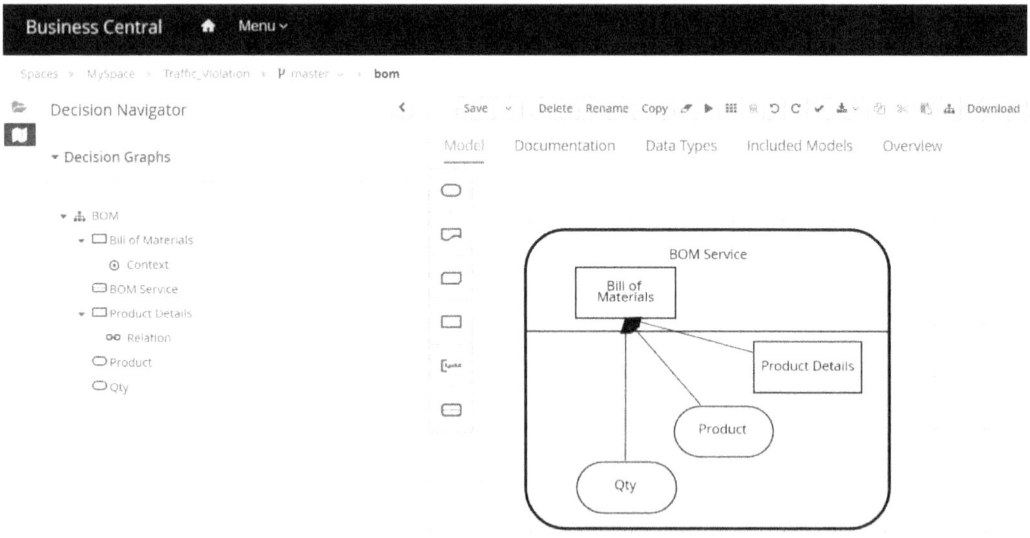

Figure 10.16 – Decision model editor in Business Central

A lot should be familiar in our Decision Model editor; it works in exactly the same way as KIE Sandbox. And you'll see additional Enterprise-level features to help you collaborate with colleagues, such as versioning, automatic layouts, the ability to validate the model, and the save with comments option.

Since our focus is on the Scenario Simulation tool, let's create a new test Scenario Simulation. Click on **Traffic_Violation** to return to our main project list:

1.   From the main project screen (the one shown in *Figure 10.13*), instead of **Import Asset**, this time, pick **Add Asset**. The dialog shown in *Figure 10.17* will give us a wide range of possible assets:

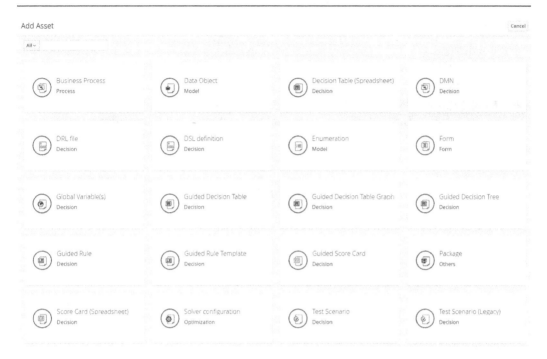

Figure 10.17 – Possible assets we can add to the project

2. We won't go through the full range of assets, although many of them are more powerful versions of items you've come across in the KIE sandbox. We'll cover some of the others in *Chapter 12*. But for the moment, we want to focus on creating a new **Test Scenario** option, so we'll select that option, making sure *not* to pick the (Legacy) option.

3. A **Create new Test Scenario** box will appear, as shown in *Figure 10.18*. We've given the test a suitable name, selected the default package, selected **DMN** as **Source type** (since we're testing a decision model), and chosen the decision model that we just imported (bom.dmn):

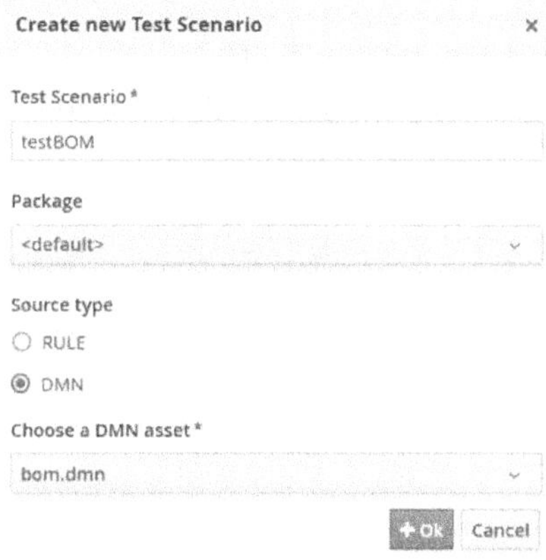

Figure 10.18 – Creating a new test scenario

4.   After clicking **OK**, Business Central will auto-generate a test scenario based on the values it can detect in our BOM decision model. We show this in *Figure 10.19*. But note that we've already populated some test values on the screen and deleted some suggested columns to make it clearer how things work.

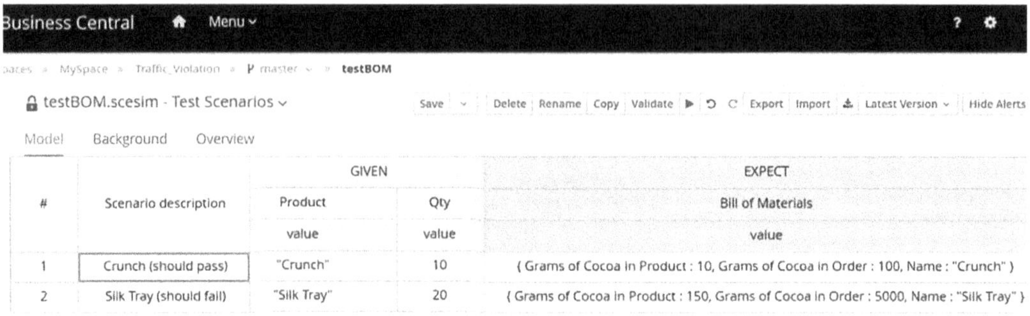

#	Scenario description	GIVEN		EXPECT
		Product	Qty	Bill of Materials
		value	value	value
1	Crunch (should pass)	"Crunch"	10	{ Grams of Cocoa in Product : 10, Grams of Cocoa in Order : 100, Name : "Crunch" }
2	Silk Tray (should fail)	"Silk Tray"	20	{ Grams of Cocoa in Product : 150, Grams of Cocoa in Order : 5000, Name : "Silk Tray" }

Figure 10.19 – Test values in our Scenario Simulation editor

This format is familiar; it's the same scenario testing tool we saw in *Chapter 9*:

- Each line is a separate scenario that we want to try out, and we can give each line a name in the **Scenario description** column.

- We pass in the **GIVEN** columns in the middle of the values during each scenario. The scenario testing tool has recognized our model's inputs (**Product** and **Qty**) and automatically set them up for us.

- The columns under the **EXPECT** heading are the values that should come back from that test run. We've tidied up some of the columns suggested and are using the FEEL syntax to represent the key-value pairs we expect back. For example, the first scenario should return this:

```
{ Grams of Cocoa in Product : 10, Grams of Cocoa in Order :
100, Name : "Crunch" }
```

- This syntax is very compact (so it works well in a book example). But you could also use the Test Tools editor (as shown in *Figure 20*) to create multiple columns and test for a single value in each of them.

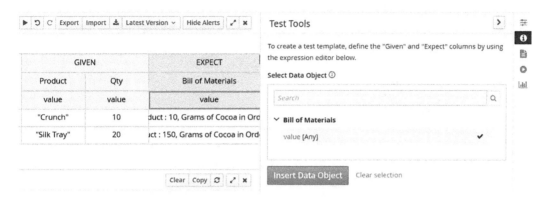

Figure 10.20 – The Test Tools values editor

Running our test scenarios

If you look carefully at the values in our scenarios, the second scenario has been set up to fail. Let's run our tests and check whether it picks up the error:

1. In the scenario simulation, click on **Save** and then click on the **Play** button (triangle).

2. As expected, when we run our scenarios we get an error in our test report (our circle will be red). Back on the Scenario Simulation screen (as shown in *Figure 10.21*), the value causing the error will be highlighted in red.

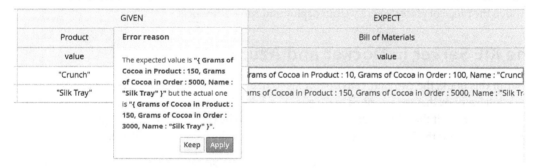

Figure 10.21 – Results of our scenario test run

3. If we mouse over the red cell, it will give more details of the expected values and what was actually returned.

4. In this case, we know the expected answer should have been 3,000 g of Cocoa. The editor suggests this as a fix – we can accept this suggestion by hitting the **Apply** button.

5. If we now press the **play** button on the scenario tests again, they will now pass, as shown in *Figure 10.22*:

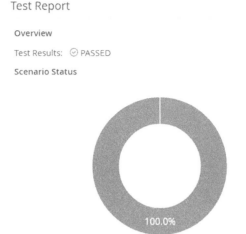

Test Report

Overview

Test Results: ⊘ PASSED

Scenario Status

100.0%

Figure 10.22 – Successful test run

It's great to finish the section on Scenario Simulation with passing tests. While we only added two scenarios, you can see how setting up multiple scenarios and getting Business Central to highlight any failures could become a very useful safety net. It's even better to run these tests automatically so you've no excuse for missing something that gets accidentally broken. The build tools we cover in *Appendix B* are a useful step in this direction.

In this section, we used Docker to support editing our decision models. But we can also use Docker to widen the range of places where we can deploy and run our models.

The KIE Server in Docker and Azure

So far in this book, the two main environments to deploy and execute our rules in have been the OpenShift Sandbox that we described in *Chapter 5* and the KIE Extended Services that we introduced in *Chapter 3*. Even if the KIE Sandbox web page appears to be running the rules, a quick look at the logs shows that it is the KIE Extended Services that is doing the heavy lifting of executing the rules.

This split between the **editor** where we write our rules and the **server** where we run our rules is very powerful. It means we can choose the editor that works best for us (KIE Sandbox, VS Code, or Business Central). And we can then choose the best server environment to deploy our rules.

We'll see in the next section that Docker containers give us an enormous choice of options for where we can deploy our rules, so much choice that we can't cover every option! But we will give you places where you can learn more. We'll focus on replacing the KIE Extended Services with its Docker-based equivalent, then on deploying the more heavyweight KIE Execution Server, and finally we give you pointers on deploying into the Azure cloud (to build on what you know about deploying to the OpenShift equivalent).

Replacing the KIE Extended Services

Let's start with the most simple example: replacing the KIE Extended Services with its Docker equivalent. While this example shows how easy it is to do, most of the time, the KIE Extended Services will work just fine. The exception may be if you have an IT department that's focused on security and that would prefer if you ran a secured container rather than a less controllable .exe file.

Running a Docker image for the KIE Server is similar to what we did to run Business Central:

1. Open Command Prompt by pressing press *Windows Key + R*, then type cmd.

2. In the console, type docker pull -p 21345:21345 --name kie-services quay.io/kie-tools/kie-sandbox-extended-services-image:0.25.0, paying special attention to the spelling.

3. After the image has been downloaded and has started, open Docker Desktop. Click on the **kie-services** container name to view the logs. You'll see a message, as shown in *Figure 10.23*, that confirms the extended services are now running in the container.

Figure 10.23 – The KIE Extended Services running in Docker

4. Now we can open KIE Sandbox at sandbox.kie.org and it will recognize we have a local server running.

5. Sandbox may complain that we are running the wrong version. If so, make a note of the version number and repeat *step 2*, replacing the version number (25) with the one that it expects.

Building you own server

> Unlike Excel, KIE is an open source project, so you have the option of building a server to meet your exact needs. While this is an advanced technical topic, the instructions in *Appendix B* come very close to doing this. You may find if you run the samples that come with the project that you've accidentally built the equivalent of the KIE Extended Services.

Running the KIE Extended Services in Docker is a useful demo, but useful only in limited circumstances as it's intended to support local deployment only. Let's move on to a more heavyweight example – running the full KIE Server in Docker.

Running the KIE Server in Docker

Why do we want our own full KIE Server, if we've already got several good options for running rules? For the following reasons:

- Business Central needs a separate server to deploy the rules into. It doesn't have the easy deployment to OpenShift that is built into KIE Sandbox.

- Your IT department may prefer to have your core business rules running on a server on site, not in the cloud (and certainly not on your laptop!).

- Finally, you may have convinced your colleagues to buy into the rules-based approach to AI. At that point, the KIE Server becomes a repository of much of your business knowledge, with many systems calling on it to make key decisions. You will want more control over where this repository is stored.

Fortunately, **Docker Compose** gives us a way to run multiple Docker images including the KIE Server.

Running Business Central and the KIE Server – Docker Compose

Docker Compose is a tool that was automatically installed when you installed Docker Desktop. It allows us to start and stop multiple Docker containers at once, with all the settings that we need.

Docker Compose is in some ways easier than running Docker, since all the tricky bits such as image names and port numbers are contained in a downloadable config file. The settings are stored in a structured text file that is meant to be easily read by humans (*YAML* format).

We have prepared a Docker Compose file that details how Docker can download and run both Business Central and KIE Server images. If you're looking for more detailed information, it is based on the instructions from the KIE team at `https://quay.io/repository/kiegroup/ kie-server-showcase`. Let's work through it:

1. Download the `docker-compose.yaml` file from the book's GitHub site at `https:// github.com/PacktPublishing/AI-and-Business-Rules-for-Excel- Power-Users`. Opening it in any text editor will allow you to view it, as shown in *Figure 10.24*:

```
version: '3'

services:
  business-central:
    image: quay.io/kiegroup/business-central-workbench-showcase:7.73.0.Final
    ports:
      - "8080:8080"
      - "8001:8001"
  kie-server:
    image: quay.io/kiegroup/kie-server-showcase:7.73.0.Final
    ports:
      - "8180:8080"
      - "8007:8001"
    environment:
      KIE_SERVER_ID: sample-server
      KIE_SERVER_LOCATION: http://0.0.0.0:8180/kie-server/services/rest/server
      KIE_SERVER_CONTROLLER: http://0.0.0.0:8080/business-central/rest/controller
      KIE_MAVEN_REPO: http://0.0.0.0:8080/business-central/maven2
    depends_on:
      - business-central
```

Figure 10.24 – The Docker Compose file to run Business Central and the KIE Server

2. If we have a quick read, there are some settings that are familiar (the Business Central image and port number) and some that are new (to download and run the KIE Server).

3. Since we have two images, each isolated in their own container, they use a pretend network (with the address 0.0.0.0) to communicate with each other. Your network admin may suggest changing this (for example, to the IP address of your computer) but for most people, the default used here will work fine.

4. If you haven't already, save this file in a location that you will remember. Make sure you give the file this exact name, all lowercase: docker-compose.yml.

5. To check that Windows has not modified the filename, open Windows File Explorer, making sure you can see file extensions (open **Options** and uncheck the checkbox beside **hide extensions for known file types**). This allows you to check that the spelling is exactly as in the previous step.

6. Right-click in the whitespace below the filename and select the option to **Open in Terminal**.

What if I don't have the Open in Terminal option?

Like before, we can still open the system terminal using *Windows + R* , typing cmd, then pressing **Ok**. We can then use the cd (**change directory**) command to move to where we saved our file.

In the following example, you would have to type cd C:\Users\paulf\OneDrive\Downloads – but watch out, the names on your computer will be different.

7. Check that we are in the right place (and have the right filename) by typing the `dir` command in the console, followed by *Enter*. You should see something close to *Figure 10.25*:

```
C:\Users\paulf\OneDrive\Downloads>dir
 Volume in drive C is OS
 Directory of C:\Users\paulf\OneDrive\Downloads

12/06/2022  16:00             1,268 docker-compose.yml
               1 File(s)          1,268 bytes
               2 Dir(s)  31,727,378,432 bytes free

C:\Users\paulf\OneDrive\Downloads>
```

Figure 10.25 – Making sure our Terminal is open in the right place

8. Make sure the spelling of our `.yml` file is exactly the same, all lowercase: `docker-compose.yml`.

9. Now that we are sure that we are in the right directory, type the following command to run, using the settings in this Docker Compose file: `docker-compose up` (and press *Enter*).

10. You may get a message asking you to log in first. If you get this, type `docker login`, then give your username and password when requested. Repeat *step 9* once you have logged in.

11. Like when we ran our previous images, Docker checks for a local copy and will then fetch the KIE Server image if needed. This could take a couple of minutes to download for the first time. You'll see the progress messages in the console as it does so.

12. You may get a message that the names of the image conflict with the name of an image already on your computer. If this happens, open Docker Desktop, delete the previous copies of the image and container, then try `docker-compose up` again.

13. When the number of messages in the console has slowed down, it's worth opening Docker Desktop to check everything has started correctly. You should see the screen shown in *Figure 10.26*:

Figure 10.26 – Docker Desktop showing both images we started with Docker Compose

14. Check that both containers are running correctly – in *Figure 10.26*, both are green (running). We can see Business Central running like before and our new KIE Server image running alongside it.

> **Docker Compose only needed once**
>
> One of the quirks of Docker is that Docker Compose is only needed the first time to download and run the images– after that, we can start and start the containers in Docker Desktop, just like in our previous examples. Since running two Docker containers is quite *heavy*, you may choose to stop one while you are working with the other to speed things up. Don't forget to start the container when you need it again!

15. To prove we have the KIE Server up and running, open `http://127.0.0.1:8180/ kie-server/services/rest/server`.

16. You may need to log in using the username/password `krisv`/`krisv`, and you'll be greeted with a summary of the KIE Server's capabilities, as shown in *Figure 10.27*:

```
-<response type="SUCCESS" msg="Kie Server info">
  -<kie-server-info>
     <capabilities>KieServer</capabilities>
     <capabilities>BRM</capabilities>
     <capabilities>BPM</capabilities>
     <capabilities>CaseMgmt</capabilities>
     <capabilities>BPM-UI</capabilities>
     <capabilities>BRP</capabilities>
     <capabilities>DMN</capabilities>
     <capabilities>Swagger</capabilities>
    -<location>
        http://192.168.68.114:8180/kie-server/services/rest/server
     </location>
     <mode>DEVELOPMENT</mode>
     <name>sample-server</name>
     <id>sample-server</id>
     <version>7.73.0.Final</version>
  </kie-server-info>
</response>
```

Figure 10.27 – Full KIE Server running

It's obvious from this summary the full KIE Server has many more capabilities than KIE Sandbox. We wanted to show you the server, so you know there is a fully featured platform to deploy onto, as you begin to build more advanced decision models for your business. For more information on the full range of options the KIE Server gives you (including how to deploy models from Business Central onto this server), take a look at the KIE documentation.

In the same spirit of explaining how easy it is to do deployments, let's take a quick look at how we could use Docker to deploy the KIE Server onto Microsoft Azure Cloud.

Can we deploy the KIE Server onto Azure or other cloud providers?

If we had the choice of one cloud service provider to host the KIE Server, it would be Red Hat OpenShift. This is because it has integrations (such as the one between KIE Sandbox and the OpenShift sandbox) that make decision model deployment much easier.

And if you do migrate to a paid service tier, the Red Hat OpenShift provides a managed service so that you need to deploy only the models, and not the entire decision service tier. This is much more cost-effective.

However, it is likely that your organization has already chosen a single cloud service provider for strategic reasons. Happily, we can leverage the power of Docker containers to deploy onto all the other major cloud providers (including Google Cloud Platform and Amazon Web Services). The steps we give in this section focus on Azure since your organization probably has a subscription with Microsoft for the Office 365 platform.

The instructions use the Docker command line since we want to show you how quickly we can do a deployment to Azure in just four steps. Since most people who are new to Azure will prefer a web-based interface, similar options are available via the Azure portal at `https://azure.microsoft.com` with free credits and tutorials to get started. We explore the Azure portal in more detail in *Chapter 11*.

> **You may already have deployed on Azure**
>
> If you've followed the instructions in *Appendix B*, you may already have deployed rules in Azure – using GitHub Codespaces and VS Code online automatically create an Azure container for you. That container was optimized for the development and writing of rules and is not suitable for day-to-day business use.

Docker tools are highly integrated with Azure. If you have an Azure account and an **Azure Container Instance** (**ACI**) set up to host the Docker containers online, the following four steps will allow you to deploy your containers into the Azure cloud:

1. Open Command Prompt on our laptop like in our previous examples.

2. Sign in to Azure using `docker login azure`.

3. Create an online container to host our image using `docker context create aci myacicontext`.

4. Run the container in Azure using the `docker --context myacicontext run -p 80:80 hello-world` command.

You'll notice that in our set of instructions, we deployed a **hello-world** image and not any of the KIE Server or Business Central images we used earlier in the chapter. This is because it's a bit like handing you the keys to a Formula 1 racing car – you know how to drive Azure, but please pause for a minute before you race off.

We want you to think before you carry out any deployment of the KIE Server in the cloud. In particular, familiarize yourself with the Azure security features, understand the billing and budget implications, and select an appropriate Docker image to deploy. The images we use in this chapter are optimized for ease of use rather than security, so please consult the KIE documentation to understand which of the other images best meet your needs.

Deploying the KIE Server is similar to the four steps we list, except we deploy a *kie-server* image instead of *hello-world*. Now that we understand that we can deploy KIE Server to the cloud, it's a good time to remind ourselves of all the deployment options we have covered in this book.

Roundup of decision model deployment options

Back in *Chapter 2*, we promised you four main ways to run our decision models. Now that we've completed deploying our rules into Docker-based servers, let's take a look at those options again. Our options for deploying our rules include the following:

- *Running KIE Sandbox with the web-based rules editor*: We have used this solution for most of this book, starting with *Chapter 3* and *Chapter 4*, as it is so easy to get started.

- *Running containers on your laptop or another computer (server) that you have access to*: We covered these methods in detail in this chapter and *Appendix C*, with containers giving us a wide range of deployment options.

- *Running an image in the cloud (hosted by Microsoft or IBM/Red Hat)*: We introduced this approach in *Chapter 5*, where we deployed our rules into OpenShift. We expanded this approach in *Chapter 9* and *Appendix B* to deploy into Codespaces and VS Code online on Azure. And this chapter introduced more cloud-based options using containers.

- We still have the final method to *set up the technology stack ourselves*: While we won't cover this, perhaps you have a bit more confidence to consider exploring this option than when you started this book. We suggest the KIE documentation as the next step.

Summary

This chapter gave you another option to access the Scenario Simulation tool, this time using Business Central. Since our method for running Business Central relied on Docker, we took advantage of container technology to explore many different ways of deploying KIE Server images, from locally on our laptop through to scaling a deployment into the cloud. That gives us the confidence that we have many more options to edit and deploy our Business Rules within our organization as the use of decision models grows.

We will return to Business Central in *Chapter 12*, where we use it as a platform to demonstrate some advanced rule editing techniques. Docker will prove useful in the next chapter, as we use it to host Docker images for machine learning. And we'll return to Azure, using Machine Learning Studio as a tool to train our models.

This book set out to focus on rules-based decision models within AI. But we would be remiss if we didn't touch on the other main area of AI – machine learning. In the next chapter, we will learn how to combine the best of both AI approaches, using the tools that KIE gives us.

11

Rules-Based AI and Machine Learning AI – Combining the Best of Both

When we introduced rules as the book's main approach to **artificial intelligence** (**AI**) back in *Chapter 1*, we mentioned **machine learning** (**ML**) as a complementary technique. We've spent the 10 chapters since then focusing on business rules and integrating them with Excel. So, it's about time that we returned to the ML side of AI—with a focus on how to combine the two approaches to AI to get the most effective use of AI in your business.

Taking a graphical approach, we'll explore the thinking behind ML based on sample data from our online chocolate shop. We'll introduce notebooks, Python, and **Azure Machine Learning** (**Azure ML**) and apply these tools to train a simple ML model. We'll integrate this trained model into a rules-based decision model to improve the recommendation sample we first met in *Chapter 4*. Finally, since this is only one chapter and very much opening the door for further learning, we'll signpost other technical solutions and options on your ML journey. Specifically, we will explore the following topics:

- Business rules as preparation for machine learning
- Graphical introduction to machine learning
- Training models in Azure ML
- Deploying the two kinds of AI together (machine learning and rules)
- Running our integrated model

To start, we'll take our first look at machine learning, and see how a rules-based approach to AI helps get your organization ready to use it.

Technical requirements

All the tools and techniques that we will use in this chapter are available in the cloud, so no new software needs to be installed on your laptop. While Azure is a highly sophisticated offering, it is fully online, and we guide you step by step through setting up your graphical machine learning notebook.

Two items that you have met in previous chapters are worth reminding you about:

- At the end of the chapter, we will combine our machine learning AI with a rules-based AI using KIE Sandbox. Having the KIE Extended Services running (which we set up in *Chapter 3*) may help.

- As usual, all the samples for this chapter are on the GitHub site at `https://github.com/PacktPublishing/AI-and-Business-Rules-for-Excel-Power-Users`.

Business rules as preparation for Machine Learning

In *Chapter 1*, we suggested combining the two AI approaches (rules and ML) to build a self-driving car. The ML approach is great for fuzzier requirements (to identify whether it is a dog or a child standing in the road). Rules are better for requirements we can state clearly and that must always be implemented (for example, swerve the car to avoid a child but do not swerve for an animal as it risks a more serious accident).

Your organization should be able to follow a similar approach—there are rules that can be clearly written by a human expert (for example, buyers must have a 20% deposit for their home loan). And there are experiences that are harder to express—a senior bank official might have a feeling that a loan application is fraudulent and need further investigation, but might struggle to explain exactly why. In our business, we are likely to need both rules and Machine learning approaches to mimic both these sets of knowledge.

Which approach to start with? Unless you are Google, Amazon, or Meta (Facebook), your organization is not going to have the millions (or even hundreds or millions) of examples needed to train cutting-edge ML models. Even a bank may only see thousands of loan applications in a year. But most businesses will have an expert who knows the rules around those applications—which makes a rules-based approach the obvious place to start.

But it's not just a lack of data that holds organizations back from adopting machine learning. Later in this chapter, we'll train an ML model in one simple step. So, why aren't more organizations using them? To be blunt, it's the time and the steps needed to gather and prepare the data and then afterward make use of the model's recommendation that is the issue.

Organizations will not dedicate teams to gathering and preparing data unless they know it will be valuable. But organizations don't know which data is valuable until they actually train the models.

Remember that ML projects are more like farming (you prepare the ground, then hope you get the harvest) than building (which is what corporate IT departments are very good at).

In short, rules allow you to demonstrate the value of AI while putting the teams in place to gather the data needed to move to machine learning. You'll see later in the chapter this is the approach we will take with our online chocolate shop. But before we get to that point, it's worth a quick graphical introduction to machine learning.

Graphical introduction to Machine Learning

Don't be scared of math—it's just numbers. And since every number can be plotted on a graph, we can think of machine learning as patterns and pictures and teaching the computer to recognize those pictures.

While that approach is simplistic, the truth is that nobody is smart enough to carry out all the math needed for machine learning. Even if you fully understood the theory behind it, it is impossible for the human brain to think in the many trillions (yes—trillions) of dimensions of data points used in some ML projects. And even if we got that far, the sheer volume of calculations needed would take longer than a human lifetime to work through.

Happily, the *machine* in machine learning means there are tools available to help us. There are prebuilt toolkits (libraries) available that we'll use to train our models. And while it does help to understand the strengths of each toolkit, you can get a long way with the following approach:

1. Gather and prepare our data, then split it into training and test sets.
2. Understand the different algorithms at a high level, and choose three or four most likely to give us results (even if we are still not entirely sure which).
3. Train a recommendation model against the data.
4. Using the test set of data, see how well the model performs.
5. Pick the model that works best and deploy it for day-to-day use.

There are even tools from Microsoft and other vendors to help automate the process of selecting and testing the best models. While this chapter is only an introduction, the toolkits we use allow you to experiment and find the best approach for your data. Let's start by working through our own data— from the online chocolate shop we met in previous examples.

Looking at the sales data from our online chocolate shop

Let's say that we implemented the rules-based recommendation engine for our chocolate shop that we walked through in previous chapters, and the recommendations have been so good that our sales have exceeded our expectations. We now have hundreds of thousands of customers, and when we run a report on our sales to see which products are most popular in different countries, we get a table like the one shown in *Figure 11.1* (showing only the first 11 rows of many):

Order	Country	Customer Age	Country-Region Code	Qty Silk Tray	Qty Lumpy Bar	Qty Peanut	Qty
1	South Africa	64	396	80	31		552
2	Netherlands	44	214	55			166
3	South Africa	63	400	79			237
4	New Zealand	56	228	70			210
5	South Africa	72	398	91			548
6	United States	80	139	100			300
7	Japan	87	300	109			110
8	Ireland	59	411	74			444
9	South Africa	64	402	81		55	244
10	United States	68	122	86			260
11	Japan	62	329	78			468

Figure 11.1 – Some of the sample data we will be using in this chapter

This information is really valuable—before, our decisions were made as best guesses using the information we found on *Wikipedia*. Now, we know what people actually want. And as we investigate, there are bound to be a few surprises.

> **Beware of HIPPOs**
>
> Be careful when sharing this information—most companies have **highly paid people's opinions (HIPPOs)**, which may or may not turn out to be true yet are often difficult to change.

You'll notice that we've already started processing this data. We've calculated customer age based on the date of birth, and we've assigned a country-region code (in our example, regions around 100 are in the US, and regions around 400 are in South Africa). We've also separated out our sales by product line into different columns. These changes are useful because ML models need numbers as input, but also (as we'll see shortly) they make it easier to graph our data.

If you want, you can download a copy of the data we are using to generate the graphs from the GitHub page. The graphs are in `11_ML_learning.xlsx`, and there is also a CSV equivalent (a text version separated by commas) that is easier for our toolkits to use.

> **Health warning on the sample data**
>
> It's no surprise that examples in this chapter use made-up data, a simple dataset of about 100 lines, designed to make our examples clearer. Real-life data would be much bigger and much noisier with fewer clear patterns, but also contain a lot more information about each customer.
>
> In short, please don't open a web shop based on this information or analysis. Instead, use it as inspiration to explore your own information in more detail.

Using a sample graph, let's draw a simple scatter plot in Excel, like the one shown in *Figure 11.2*. We've filtered the data a bit, to show the sales of just two product lines. We can identify two clear clusters—Americans (remember they have region codes around 100 in our data) tend to make large orders of Peanut Candy bars. And South Africans (region codes around 400) tend to make smaller orders of Lumpy Raisin and Nut bars.

In a very small nod to reality, we have one sale of Peanut Candy bar in South Africa—maybe it's somebody who has moved from New York to Johannesburg to study. That won't make difference to our analysis, but sometimes you may need to remove outliers such as this from the data:

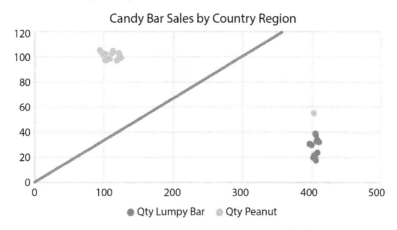

Figure 11.2 – Our sales data graphed as a scatter plot

You'll notice that in *Figure 11.2*, we've drawn a line across the chart to separate the two clusters. Given our simple chart, any order above the line is likely to be Peanut Candy, and anything below the line is likely to be a Lumpy chocolate bar. So, for new customers, we can make a recommendation based on their country code and order quantity based on this simple model.

This line can be drawn using the formula $x=3y$. Don't worry about the formula itself—remember that this is made-up data. What is important is that we can draw a line to separate those two groups. Once we learn what the formula is, we can use it to make predictions for new customers depending on which side of the line they fall on. That's what ML is—learning where to draw the line.

So far, our clusters have been easy to identify, but we had filtered our information down to two products. If we add Silk Tray sales to our graph, the situation is a lot more chaotic, as depicted in *Figure 11.3*:

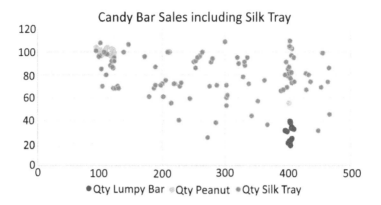

Figure 11.3 – Sales data plot including Silk Tray data

Don't look too hard to find a pattern in *Figure 11.3*—we're not going to be able to draw a line to separate the groups. The data, especially for US sales (the top left of graph), looks very chaotic.

However, if we introduce another feature (or dimension) to our graph, things look a lot clearer. In *Figure 11.4*, you'll see that we added more information (customer age) to move our graph from 2D to 3D.

Other tools to draw graphs

Excel is great but doesn't have an easy way to draw 3D scatter plots (or even 4D, if you allow for the colors we use on the next graph). We'll introduce the Python notebooks we used to draw this graph in the next section. You'll be able to modify and rotate the graph views to examine the data.

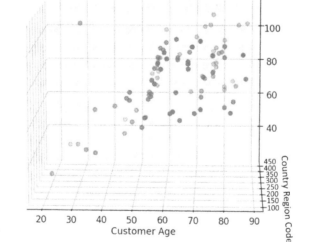

Figure 11.4 – Silk Tray data on a 3D scatter plot

We've filtered to Silk Tray sales only and rotated our view of the graph. It now is clear that customer age is a strong prediction factor—there is a trend line from bottom left to top right showing that older customers are more likely to buy Silk Tray.

This example shows three key things about ML:

- Choosing the right chart reveals a lot, in the same way that choosing the right algorithm will make the patterns in our data a lot clearer.

- Less information can sometimes mean more clarity—filtering our data can help us see the underlying patterns.

- More features (or dimensions) often make it easier to distinguish groups.

Most people can move from thinking in 2 to 3 dimensions but would struggle to visualize 4 dimensions, or even 40. Happily, we can get most of the work done using a computer, which is just as well as some models (such as GPT-4) effectively have 1.4 trillion dimensions to work with.

In *Figure 11.5*, we've added back our other products and tried to group them based on customer age, customer location, and order size:

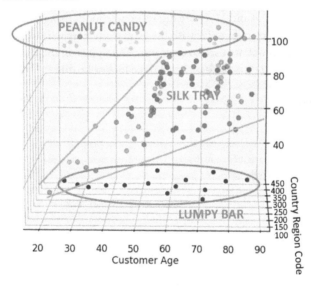

Figure 11.5 – 3D scatter plot with possible customer groupings

Using this chart, if we know customer age, customer region code, and order size, we can predict what the main part of the order is going to be:

- Peanut Candy—if the order is a high quantity

- Lumpy Bar—if the order is from South Africa

- Silk Tray—for older customers in all countries but is also a safe guess if we're unsure of what to recommend

These lines are clear on the graph, but how would we describe them as a mathematical formula that a computer could use to make predictions? Thankfully, there are toolkits to help the machine learn the formula. We'll play with these toolkits, using interactive Python notebooks.

> **Which to use – machine learning or business rules?**
>
> Our samples are simple enough that you could also implement them as business rules—after all, we've just described the recommendation model using three bullet points. In the next chapter, we'll meet the *decision tree* algorithm that allows us to discover the business rules hidden in our data.
>
> Not every dataset will suit this approach. Real-life data will be a lot more complicated and lend itself more to Machine learning.

Introduction to notebooks and Python

The graphs we drew in *Figures 11.4* and *11.5* were drawn in notebooks using Python scripts. It's worth taking a look at the notebooks to get familiar with the format since we'll be using notebooks later to train our ML models. The notebook we used to draw our 3D graph is on the Packt Publishing sample GitHub site. The start of the `c11_scatter.ipynb` file looks like this:

```
144 lines (144 sloc)    147 KB                                        ...
```

A notebook looks like a web page, but the code in the 'cells' below. In the right environment the code in the 'cells' below can be excecuted.

- If you are viewing this on GitHub, you need to download the file and open in VSCode, Azure ML Studio or another Notebook hosting service like myBinder.org. Opening the GitHub project in a Codespace should also work.

We've left the output inline so even if you can't run it, you can see what the output would be like.

```
In [14]:    pip install matplotlib

Requirement already satisfied: matplotlib in /home/
codespace/.local/lib/python3.10/site-packages (3.6.
```

Figure 11.6 – Python notebook to generate a 3D scatter chart

If you take a look at the notebook in *Figure 11.6*, you'll see that it is a mixture of the following:

- Text, which explains what the notebook does.
- Cell(s), in light gray. These are a bit like Excel cells—you can enter a formula in them and they will evaluate or execute. In this case, `pip install matplotlib` tells the notebook that we want to use Matplotlib for drawing charts.
- Output—the monospaced text after the cell starting with `Requirement already satisfied`. In *Figure 11.6*, we've left in the output that shows that we already have Matplotlib.

If you're viewing this example on GitHub, you won't have the **Execute** ▷ button needed to run the example. If you've already used GitHub Codespaces (see *Appendix B*), you'll know that we can easily fix this:

1. Go to the home page of the project on GitHub and click on the green **Code** button.
2. Click on the **Codespaces** tab that appears, then click + to create a new codespace, and then **Open in … Browser**.
3. The VS Code online editor will appear. Wait a few seconds for it to complete loading.
4. In this case, open the notebook (the `11_scatter.ipydb` file). The notebook will open, looking almost exactly the same as in *Figure 11.6*.
5. The difference is when we select the code cell, we have options to execute it within the notebook web page, as shown in *Figure 11.7*:

Figure 11.7 – The Execute Cell button in the notebook

Notebooks are a standard concept and a bedrock of ML. So, while it's easy to use them in VS Code online (Codespaces or in VS Code locally on your laptop), there are many other options. You may see them referred to as **Jupyter** notebooks (that can be run online, or in the browser at `mybinder.org`). There is also Google Colab if you prefer that platform, or a Jupyter Docker image if you want to host them locally.

Finally, Microsoft's Azure ML can host our notebooks. That's the option we'll use later in this chapter to train our models since it also offers us a lot of extra ML tools.

> **What is Python and why use it in the notebooks?**
>
> If you opened the notebook, you would see that it uses a scripting language called **Python**.
>
> This is a good choice—not only is Python easily understandable by Excel power users but it also has perhaps the widest range of toolkits and ML libraries available to help you. As a bonus, you're likely to find yourself using Python in other situations.
>
> The Python examples in this book are easily understandable. But if you are interested in learning more, Packt Publishing has many good books: `https://subscription.packtpub.com/search?query=python`.

Before we start using notebooks and Python to train our ML models, we need to take a quick look at the various classifiers available to use in our models.

Naïve Bayes and other classifiers

We've made some very simple statements in this chapter: all math is a graph; drawing a line can separate clusters on that graph; ML is about finding where to draw the line.

The reason we can make those high-level statements is that a lot of work has already gone into the ML algorithms, and those algorithms are available for us to download and use in Python (for example, using the `sklearn` package). And we can swap between algorithms in that package to find out what works best, without understanding the full detail of the math behind it.

Of course, understanding some of the math will help you get further faster, which is why I would encourage you to read the following article, which explains the key algorithms in a graphical, no-code way: `https://www.freecodecamp.org/news/a-no-code-intro-to-the-9-most-important-machine-learning-algorithms-today/`.

While this article explains the different approaches, a good default approach is the **naïve Bayes** algorithm. It's naïve in that it assumes there is no link between the various features or dimensions in your data, which is often not true. But it does provide a good starting point as it gives reasonable (but not outstanding) results on many datasets. Just to prove the math is understandable, google **naïve Bayes Excel implementation** to find a demonstration that it can be calculated in a spreadsheet. We'll stick with the Python version as it is much faster.

Simple classifiers versus neural networks

We'll refer to the ML algorithms we use in this chapter as simple classifiers. They are effective, simple to use, and fast. Typically, these types of classifiers can get to work after one pass through the training data. For many problems, these simple classifiers will get good results.

For more complicated problems, we may use neural networks. We touch on those in *Chapter 12* as neural networks are responsible for much of the buzz around AI in recent years. Neural networks need to be *trained* over multiple passes through the training data and are much more configurable (both the structure of the network and the initial weightings used).

We take a practical approach in this book, and toolkits such as `sklearn`, PMML, and KIE make it easy to switch between the approaches once you understand how each works.

Training models in Azure Machine Learning

Since our aim in this chapter is to give a broad introduction, we're going to train our first naïve Bayes model using Azure ML to give you a gateway into the other tools and techniques offered by Microsoft. Azure ML is not strictly required—the Python notebook will happily run in VS Code online using the method we introduced earlier in the chapter. If you're following this approach, skip to the *Step-by-step training of the ML model* section. But since Azure gives additional ML tools aimed at Excel power users, it is worth following the instructions in the next section to get up and running in Azure ML (formerly known as ML Studio).

Setting up Azure Machine Learning

To get started, if your organization doesn't already have an account, sign up for the free trial at `https://azure.microsoft.com/en-us/products/machine-learning/`. Microsoft typically offers $200 of credits, with many services free for the first year.

We won't detail the account creation process (including verification via phone number) as it is typical of many online services. We'll assume that you've created an account, have signed in, and are seeing the Azure home screen for the first time, as in *Figure 11.8*:

Azure services

Figure 11.8 – Microsoft Azure home screen

Before we start with ML, it's a good habit to get familiar with the **Cost Management** screen. While you're not spending any money during the trial period, there's no harm in monitoring your usage and setting budget alerts—for example, to let you know if you have left an expensive machine instance running when it is no longer needed.

There are many other services offered by Azure, but the service we are interested in is **Azure Machine Learning**. If it doesn't appear on the home screen, you can search for it in the box in the top middle of the screen. Clicking on it will make the home screen for this service appear, as in *Figure 11.9*:

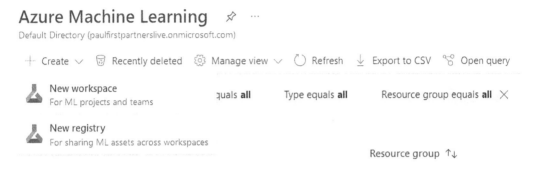

Figure 11.9 – Azure Machine Learning page

As expected, we have no projects set up. So, from the menu on the top left, click on **Create**, then select **New workspace**.

A wizard to create a new ML workspace will appear. There are several steps to this wizard, but we'll only show the most important of them in *Figure 11.10*:

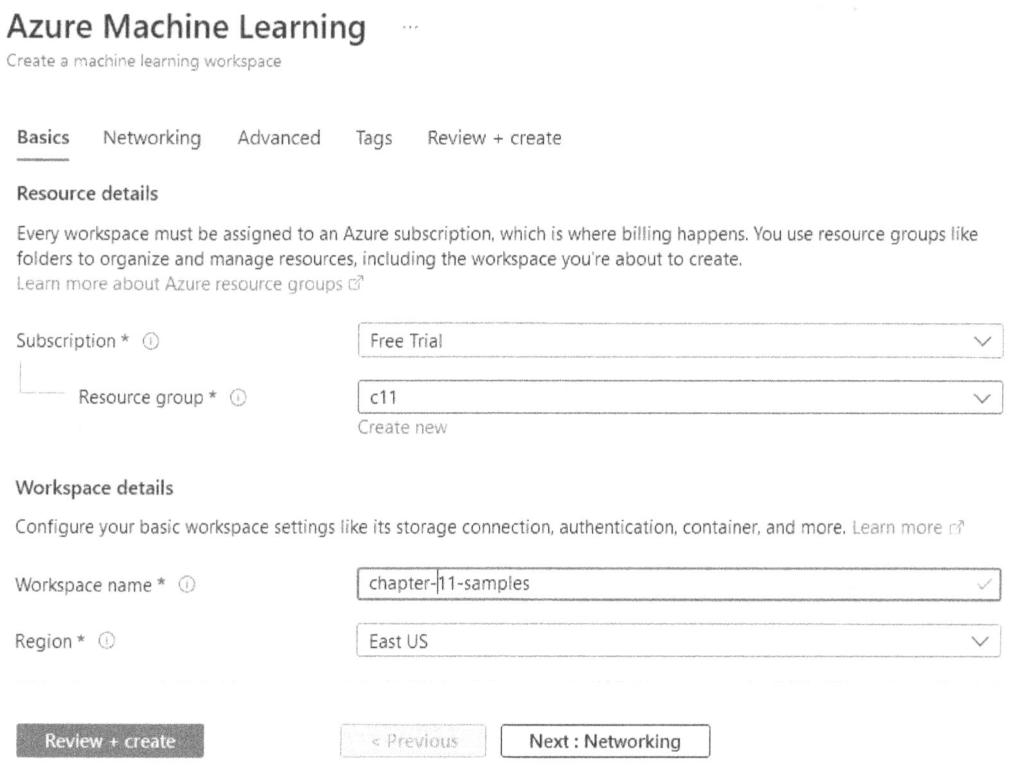

Azure Machine Learning ...
Create a machine learning workspace

Basics   Networking   Advanced   Tags   Review + create

Resource details

Every workspace must be assigned to an Azure subscription, which is where billing happens. You use resource groups like folders to organize and manage resources, including the workspace you're about to create.
Learn more about Azure resource groups ☐

Subscription * ⓘ | Free Trial   ⌄ |

└─   Resource group * ⓘ | c11   ⌄ |
                                     Create new

Workspace details

Configure your basic workspace settings like its storage connection, authentication, container, and more. Learn more ☐

Workspace name * ⓘ | chapter-11-samples   ✓ |

Region * ⓘ | East US   ⌄ |

[Review + create]   [< Previous]   [Next : Networking]

Figure 11.10 – Creating a new Azure Machine Learning workspace

Most of the values on this screen are prepopulated by Azure. The important values are **Subscription** (it should default to **Free Trial**), **Resource group** (Azure will create several items to support the project—think of the resource group as a folder to keep them in), and **Workspace name** (or the name of your project).

While there are other screens, we suggest you take the defaults for those. So, it's OK to click the **Review + create** button, and then click **Create** on the confirmation screen that appears.

You may have to wait a while with a **Deployment in progress** message before you get a **Deployment complete** message. Click on the **Go to Resource** option to see our newly created workspace. In this workspace, there will be a **Launch Machine Learning Studio** option. After clicking on that, you should see a screen like the one shown in *Figure 11.11*:

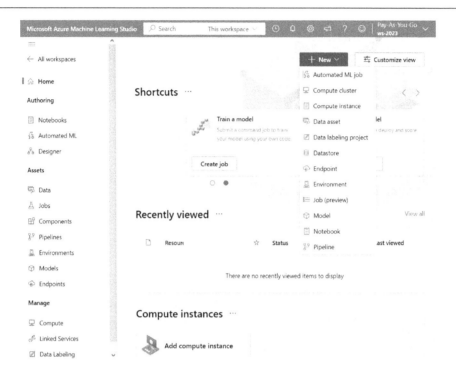

Figure 11.11 – Microsoft Azure Machine Learning Studio

You can glimpse the power of Azure, and Azure ML from the previous screen, in the options on the screen in *Figure 11.11* (both the main area and the navigation bar on the left-hand side). We encourage you to explore more, but since our focus is on running a notebook, click on the **Start now** option underneath the **Notebooks** icon. Your screen should look like the one shown in *Figure 11.12*:

Figure 11.12 – Notebooks in Microsoft Azure ML Studio

In this screenshot, you'll notice that we've already downloaded the sample data and sample notebook files from the book's GitHub site (`11_ML_Learning.csv` and `11-naieve_bayes.ipynb`). We uploaded them to Azure by clicking the + icon just above the folders, and then said **Yes** in the **Trust and Overwrite** popup that appeared.

Unlike in Codespaces, Azure ML doesn't automatically provision a compute instance for us—the engine that will run our scripts. To do this, click on the **Compute** icon on the bottom left of the screen (it looks like a computer), then select the + **New** button on the screen that appears. You'll see a **Create compute instance** wizard, as in *Figure 11.13*:

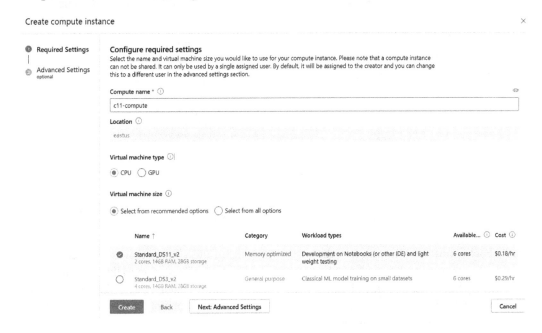

Figure 11.13 – Creating an Azure compute instance

You'll notice that we've picked the smallest (and cheapest) compute image, as our sample models are small and very easy to train. But you have the option to select more powerful instances for heavier workloads using larger datasets. This is another advantage of using Azure compared to training large datasets on your laptop.

One very important note to manage your Azure cloud compute expenditure: Click on **Next: Advanced Settings**. On that screen, set the options to automatically turn off your compute instance after a set period of time.

When we click on **Create**, and then open our notebook, Azure should automatically link the notebook to the compute instance we just created.

Step-by-step training of the Machine Learning model

Whether we have our sample notebook (`11-naive_bayes.ipynb`) open in Azure ML or in another viewer, you should see a screen similar to the one shown in *Figure 11.14*:

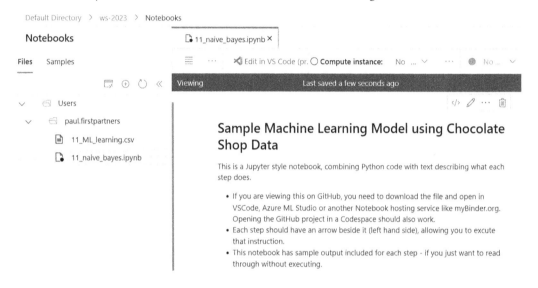

Figure 11.14 – Our ML notebook hosted in Azure

The notebook format for ML (with text, executable cells, output, and a button that executes each cell) is exactly the same as the 3D graph notebook we saw earlier. So, we'll focus on walking through the notebook step by step, and assume that you're pressing the **Execute** ▷ button each time to run each step in the notebook. If you're impatient, there is also an option at the top of the notebook to run all the steps at once—you'll still see the output of each step.

The notebook format means that each step is very well documented, so we'll walk through at a high level what is going on:

1. The first cell makes sure we have access to the ML toolkits we need to run our notebook. When you run this step for the first time, you'll have to wait for a couple of minutes as Python downloads the required libraries. It will be faster from the second time onward:

    ```
    pip install numpy matplotlib seaborn scikit-learn nyoka
    sklearn2pmml
    ```

2.   The next cell tells Python which of the supporting libraries and toolkits we want to use in our script. While this step appears redundant, it is helpful on larger scripts to know which supporting toolkits we are using when the names are similar:

```
# Standard tools for manipulating numeric data
import random
import seaborn as sns; sns.set()
import numpy as np
import pandas as pd
# For Generating our Graph later.
import matplotlib.pyplot as plt

#Import Gaussian Naive Bayes model
import sklearn
from sklearn.naive_bayes import GaussianNB

# For exporting our model later
from sklearn2pmml import sklearn2pmml
from sklearn2pmml.pipeline import PMMLPipeline
```

3.   Now, the real work of our notebook begins. The next cell contains Pandas (a supporting library for working with tabular data) to load our sample dataset:

```
# Load the information
sales_data = pd.read_csv("11_ML_learning.csv")
# print it so we can see a sample of the data we are
working with
print (sales_data)
```

4. *Figure 11.15* shows a sample of this data:

```
     Order Number          Country  Customer Age  Country-Region Code
0               9      South Africa            64                  402
1              14     United States            68                  103
2              84     United States            70                  118
3              16     United States            80                  108
4              21     United States            77                  101
..            ...              ...           ...                  ...
94             93                UK            56                  198
95             94         Sri Lanka            77                  260
96             97         Sri Lanka            73                  253
97             98       New Zealand            58                  230
98             99                UK            69                  190

    Qty Silk Tray  Qty Lumpy Bar  Qty Peanut   Qty   Main Product
0             NaN            NaN        55.0   244   Peanut Candy
1             NaN            NaN        97.0   268   Peanut Candy
2             NaN            NaN        97.0   451   Peanut Candy
3             NaN            NaN        98.0   500   Peanut Candy
4             NaN            NaN        98.0   389   Peanut Candy
..            ...            ...         ...   ...            ...
94           71.0            NaN         NaN   142      Silk Tray
95           97.0            NaN         NaN   292      Silk Tray
96           92.0            NaN         NaN   370      Silk Tray
97           73.0            NaN         NaN   220      Silk Tray
98           87.0            NaN         NaN   522      Silk Tray

[99 rows x 9 columns]
```

Figure 11.15 – The sample data loaded in Python

5. In the next cell, *features* and *labels* identify the columns (features) we use to make our prediction, and the output (labels) we expect in each case. This helps train our prediction model.

    To keep our example simple, we are only training on two features. In reality, you could use 10s or even 100s of features for training, and experiment to find which give the clearest predictions:

```
features = sales_data[['Customer Age' ,'Country-Region
Code']]
features.columns=["Customer_Age","Country_Code"]
label = sales_data["Main Product"]
```

6. Our notebook is missing a common step—splitting our data into 80% of data for training and keeping back 20% of lines to test how effective our training was. We'll do that inspection visually in a later step since our sample data step is so small (100 lines). Either way, we can experiment with different algorithms and see which works the best.

7. The next cell sets the algorithm we want to use as GaussianNB in this step:

```
model = PMMLPipeline([( "classifier", GaussianNB(),)])
```

> **Trying out other learning algorithms**
>
> This is the line we edit to switch to a different approach. Consult the `sklearn` documentation for details, but they are designed to be easily switchable. Test each one to see which works best for you.
>
> Most of the time, you will replace `GaussianNB` with the name of another algorithm. We do that in *Chapter 12* to demonstrate **decision trees**.

8.   The cell also trains our model in one simple line:

```
model.fit(features, label)
```

> **Is that it? Training a model in one line**
>
> You may be surprised that training our model takes only one simple line. Most of the work in training an ML model is in gathering and preparing the data beforehand.

9.   The cell containing `for loop in range(1000):` makes 1,000 predictions based on random data and captures the results for us to easily graph in the next step. We won't highlight this code sample, since it's quite long. The key line is this:

```
predicted= str(model.predict([[age,country_code]]))
```

This line calls our model to make the prediction (and convert the prediction into text).

10.   The cell starting `%matplotlib inline` generates a chart like the one shown in *Figure 11.16* to visualize this set of predictions:

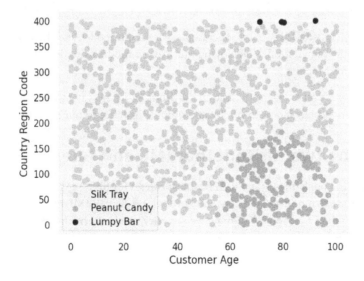

Figure 11.16 – A plot of the predictions made by naïve Bayes

Our graph should show three key types of predictions:

- The default recommendation, in green covering much of the graph, is that customers should buy our Silk Tray chocolate box

- On the bottom right (older customers based around region 100—the US), we recommend they buy Peanut Candy bars

- In a small area in the top right (older customers based in South Africa), the model should recommend they buy a Lumpy Raisin chocolate bar

If you reopen the dataset we originally used (in the CSV file), you'll see that these predictions are consistent with our training data. Note that we are graphing our predictions and *not* the original training data—run this notebook several times to see how our predictions change slightly each time.

> **Not a great prediction? Rubbish in, rubbish out**
>
> Since some people view ML as a magical black box, it's worth reminding ourselves that the quality of the model is only as good as the training data used.
>
> In this case, we need to be wary of **overfitting** since the sample data size is so small—the model works very well with customers who are exactly like the small batch we used in training. But the model has no experience to deal with anything outside of this and will easily get confused.

Since the next section is to combine ML and rules-based AI, our final step in the notebook is to export our newly trained model using the following line of code:

```
sklearn2pmml(model, "11_chocolate_recommendations.pmml")
```

This is a common pattern with ML—in one operation we train our model, and then in a separate step, we deploy and use our trained model. Deploying our trained model using PMML and KIE is what we will cover in our next section.

Quick reminder – even if you are using the free credits from Azure, now is a good time to click on the **Compute** tab in Azure portal, and to turn off your compute instance to minimize your bills.

Deploying the two AIs together (ML and rules)

ML is great, but this is a book mainly about AI business rules. Our first step to combine the two is to open and edit our PMML model in Azure, as in *Figure 11.17*. This PMML model was generated in the last step of our Python notebook. You may need to click on the **Refresh** button in Azure ML to see this newly generated model:

Figure 11.17 – PMML generated by the ML script

As you can see, **PMML** is an XML format that is largely human-readable. It also has the advantage of being an industry standard, so even though `sklearn` and a Python notebook generated the model, we are able to import and execute the model in KIE. In general, the interoperability works smoothly—but a bit like assembling a cabinet from Ikea, sometimes a few gentle knocks from a mallet are needed to get everything into place.

In our case, there are two edits needed to the PMML file so that Kogito can work with it:

- On the second line, edit the version number (4_4) to the one that Kogito supports. At the time of writing, this is 4_2. This version number is listed twice on the line—edit both so that it reads `<PMML xmlns="http://www.dmg.org/PMML-4_2" xmlns:data="http://jpmml.org/jpmml-model/InlineTable" version="4.2">`.

- Find the line starting `<NaiveBayesModel` and edit it so that it begins with `<NaiveBayesModel  modelName="chocolateRecommendation"`, keeping the rest of the line unchanged. This tells Kogito the name of the model, which it will display in the **Decision Model and Notation** (**DMN**) editor.

- Export the edited file from Azure ML Studio and save a copy on your laptop.

An edited version of the file is on the book's GitHub site as `11_chocolate_recommendations.pmml`.

A decision service combining rules and ML

Let's start by showing you the decision model that we're going to build, combining the best of rules and ML in one decision service, as shown in *Figure 11.18*:

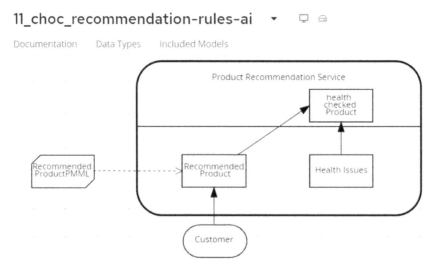

Figure 11.18 – A decision service combining AI rules and Machine Learning

You may recognize this as being based on the product recommendation service that we built in *Chapter 4*. There are two key differences that we will look at in more detail shortly:

- We import a **RecommendedProductPMML** external model, using exactly the same technique for importing models that we used in *Chapter 9*. This model is the PMML model that we just trained using Azure ML.

- We've updated the **RecommendedProduct** node so that it makes its recommendations based on the external ML model (previously, we used a decision table).

What hasn't changed is the two-step nature of our decision-making. We first recommend a product, and then we do a second rules-based check to make sure we're not recommending a product that might cause health issues (for example, a peanut allergy).

> **Rules and ML working together is a key concept**
>
> I got very excited when I first saw rules and ML working together in this way—it very clearly combines the best of both types of AI.
>
> We can learn customer preferences using machine learning but we can still guarantee important rules (such as health checks) using business rules. And having them all in one model makes it clear what is actually going to be executed in our decision service.

Key points in importing ML models to decision models

This model, as shown in *Figure 11.18*, is available to download as `11_choc_recommendation-rules-ai.dmn` and can easily be imported into KIE Sandbox. If you are looking to build your own decision model, perhaps importing an updated PMML file, there are some steps worth highlighting:

1. ML models (PMML files) can be uploaded to KIE Sandbox in the same way as any decision model. Once uploaded, the model will look similar to the one shown in *Figure 11.19*:

Figure 11.19 – Recommendation service in the KIE Sandbox

2. Both types of models need to be saved into the same folder for the imports to work—in this case, we call the folder `c11`, as can be seen in the top right of *Figure 11.19*.

3. In our decision (DMN) model, we need to reference our newly imported ML file. In KIE Sandbox, go to the **Included Models** tab, click on the + icon to add a new model, then pick the model we just imported from the dropdown. Give it an easy-to-remember name such as CR. These steps are the same as we carried out in *Chapter 9*, and your screen should now look like this:

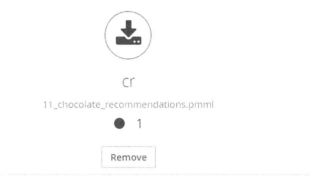

Figure 11.20 – Referring to the ML model in our decision model

4.   In our decision model, we dragged a new business model knowledge node—it's the node on the very left of *Figure 11.18*. We edit it as in *Figure 11.21*:

RecommendedProductPMML *(Function)*

P	RecommendedProductPMML *(string)*	
	(Country_Code, Customer_Age)	
	1	document *(string)*	"cr"
	2	model *(string)*	"chocolateRecommendation"

Figure 11.21 – The Business Model Knowledge node

There are several edits, including a name change, that we've made to the node. We set the type to **PMML**, hence the **P** in the top left of the screenshot. This prompts KIE Sandbox to ask us which document and model we want to refer to—cr and chocolateRecommendation values have been selected by dropdowns that will appear.

We've also edited the name and type of the parameters (Country_Code and Customer_Age)—the KIE sandbox has an editor to help guide you, but make sure that both match what is in the PMML model.

5.   The actual call to the ML model is done via a decision node, an **Invocation** node. In the decision model we previously saw in *Figure 11.18*, it is called **Recommended Product**. Opening it in the KIE Sandbox editor should show you something like this:

Recommended Product *(Invocation)*

#	Recommended Product *(number)*	
	RecommendedProductPMML	
1	Country_Code *(number)*	=fn_convert_country_to_code(Customer.Country of Residence)
2	Customer_Age *(number)*	=fu_convert_dob_to_age(Customer.Date of Birth)

Figure 11.22 – The Invocation node

Like when we were calling other external models in *Chapter 9*, the RecommendProductPMML name needs to match the name of the Business Model Knowledge node, and the names and types of the parameters need to be exactly the same. Note that we use a function to convert the data of birth and country into the numeric values that our ML model expects.

6.   We don't change the health check node—this is still a simple rule using a literal expression, but it could easily be a decision table or other type of DMN node. We show it again in *Figure 11.23* as it is a key part of proving that ML and business rules work well together:

health checked Product *(Literal expression)*

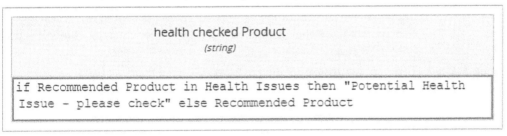

```
if Recommended Product in Health Issues then "Potential Health
Issue - please check" else Recommended Product
```

Figure 11.23 – The unchanged health check business rule

If we were to run this decision service and pass in a large order from a customer living in the US, it is highly likely that the ML model would recommend a Peanut Candy bar. If our customer has a known allergy, our second business rule would fire, triggering a **Potential Health Issue – please check** message as a recommendation from the decision service.

Running our integrated model

As you've seen, KIE Sandbox supports editing decision models with both ML and rule-based elements. Up until now, we've taken for granted the ability to *edit* these combined models using KIE Sandbox.

The ability to *execute* combined rules and ML model features is already present in the other KIE decision model tools—for example, the VS Code plugin you may have used in *Appendix B*. While it is on the roadmap to be added to the KIE Sandbox Extended Services, it has not yet (at the time of writing) been implemented.

While we have already proven the main point of this chapter (an introduction to ML), showing the power of the two approaches working together, this is a practical book. I really want to leave you with tools for running these combined ML and rules models. So, *Table 11.1* shows the choices you have right now as an Excel power user to execute these combined models:

Option to run combined ML and rules models	Advantage	Disadvantage
KIE Sandbox (and Extended Services)	The easiest option when implemented.	On the roadmap—date to be confirmed.
The VS Code plugin	Kogito provides working examples of PMML within DMN decision services. More in *Chapter 12*.	Slightly more technical, although no more so than using the test scenarios we covered in *Chapter 9*.
Business Central	Examples are given in Drools' documentation. Running Business Central is covered in *Chapter 10*.	Business Central works best if you have enterprise support with some knowledge of Java.
Integrate ML and rules models using Power Automate	The most accessible solution to Excel power users—we will cover this in *Chapter 12*.	Need to bring several easy-to-use pieces together using Python.

Table 11.1 – Options to execute our combined rules and ML models

As we'll see in *Chapter 12* when running the full PMML samples that come with Kogito, the capability to execute combined rules and ML models is already available. The challenge is to make it easily usable by Excel power users—so, in the next chapter, we also suggest an easy-to-use method based on what we know already in Power Automate and Python. Before we look at that, let's do a summary of what we have learned in this chapter.

Summary

The topics we covered in this chapter were the idea that ML is as simple as drawing a line on a graph, with the learning piece being teaching the machine to find where that line should go. We walked through a simple learning model based on naïve Bayes, and in the notebook that implemented the model, we highlighted where we could drop in other algorithms. We ran that notebook on Azure ML and generated a graph to test whether our predictions were in line with what we expected.

Exporting our trained model as a PMML file, we included it in a rules-based decision model. We updated our previous chocolate bar recommendation service using this technique and showed that it was very feasible to build a model combining the best of each type of AI. Finally, we discussed our options as Excel power users for executing these combined models.

This theme of introducing advanced topics to explore further continues in our next and final chapter. That extends several topics we glimpsed at in this chapter—including neural networks, explainable AI, and deploying combined ML and rule-based models in an enterprise situation.

Further reading

This chapter was written to give you the confidence and the desire to know more about machine learning. We introduced several key topics that your interests may lead you toward, from learning more about Azure and Azure ML to taking a deeper dive into Python notebooks and the different algorithms implemented in them. All of these topics have Packt Publishing books available on them.

At this point, it is also worth (re)viewing the Kogito and Drools documentation with a focus on the AI tools and integration, since much of the information there will now make a lot more sense to you, as well as giving practical steps on how to deploy combined rules and ML decision services.

One non-Packt Publishing book that I highly recommend is *Mathematics for Machine Learning*. It's available as a free/open book from `https://mml-book.github.io/`. While it is very clearly written and accessible, it is still a math book. So, while it is a fascinating read and will enhance your knowledge of ML, it is not essential to get value from the techniques we introduced in this chapter.

12

What Next? A Look inside Neural Networks, Enterprise Projects, Advanced Rules, and the Rule Engine

Since this is the final chapter of the book, we're going to use it to extend some tools and concepts we met in the first 11 chapters. We also want to answer the question *what's next?*, so we'll focus on areas that you can explore after you finish this book. We'll cover these areas in the following order:

- We will start by evolving the notebook we used in the previous chapter, demonstrating **decision trees** as another classification algorithm.

- Decision trees give us more **explainability**. We will explore this in more detail and show how they can be converted into the business rules and decision tables we first met in *Chapter 4*.

- **Neural networks** are among the most complex classifiers that you're likely to encounter. We will give you a high-level introduction via Excel, then show how you can generate them in Python.

- Neural networks are powerful but not very transparent in how they generate results. We will introduce **Trusty AI** as part of the KIE toolset to explain decisions.

- Another key feature of KIE is its ability to execute **combined ML and AI models**. We will show you how to execute them using the sample models that come with KIE.

- KIE's samples are comprehensive, but some readers may want an alternative method. We suggest using the tools we met in *Chapter 8*, combining **ML and rules models in a Power Automate flow.**

- Another type of **enterprise solution** is based on Java. We will introduce Red Piranha as a template to build on, leveraging its ability to read entire Excel spreadsheets.

- Red Piranha can also execute rules in the more **advanced DRL rule format**. We will look at this format and find that (under the covers) we've been using rules all along.

- Finally, since the DRL rule format helps clarify how rule engines actually work. We will peek inside the engine at the **RETE and PHREAK** algorithms that make it work so fast.

With so many topics, we'll take a slightly different approach in this chapter. We still aim to give you working examples, but they are often in the linked documentation rather than fully worked through step by step. We'll cover the topics in a way that suits you as an Excel power user, and for the most difficult topic (where we delve into a sample Kogito project) we'll provide a more simple alternative. We start with a continuation of *Chapter 11*, using the notebook we met there but with another machine learning algorithm.

Technical requirements

This chapter builds on tools we've seen before, rather than introducing any new ones – so if you worked through the book up until this point, there will be no new software to install.

The most detailed example (*Running the KIE machine learning examples using Java and VS Code*) should still be accessible to Excel power users. And we immediately follow it with an alternative, simpler proposal that some readers will prefer.

The samples referred to in the chapter are all available from the book's GitHub site here: `https://github.com/PacktPublishing/AI-and-Business-Rules-for-Excel-Power-Users`.

Another machine learning method – decision trees

In *Chapter 11*, we trained a machine learning model using Naïve Bayes. At the time, we mentioned that we only needed to change one line to swap in other machine learning methods. If you take a look at the `12_tree.ipynb` notebook on the book's GitHub page, you'll see we've done exactly that. The line we create our classifier in the notebook now reads as follows:

```
model = PMMLPipeline([( "classifier", DecisionTreeClassifier(),)])
```

Running the notebook in Azure or another notebook hosting option is the same as in the previous chapter, so we won't repeat ourselves. More importantly, when you run the notebook, you get a prediction graph, as shown in *Figure 12.1*:

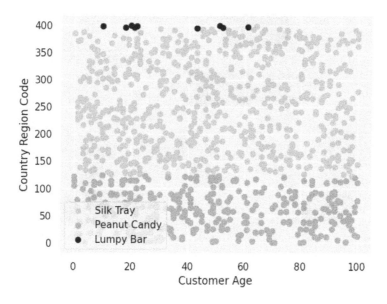

Figure 12.1 – Predictions from the decision tree model

Compare this result to *Figure 11.16* in the previous chapter. While the predictions are broadly similar, they are not as fine grained. This model is recommending Silk Tray, Peanut Candy, or Lumpy Bars more or less based on country, with little account being taken of the customer's age.

> **Reminder – try out different machine learning algorithms**
>
> We mentioned in the previous chapter that you should try three or four of the most likely algorithms and test their performance against your data. In this example, we did a graphical examination to see how well the predictions are performing.
>
> In reality, we'd use scikit-learn to split our data into training and test samples and generate a **confusion matrix** to compare hard numbers on how well each algorithm performed.

Don't let this put you off using decision trees on your own data. Since ours was such a small sample (100 customers) and only trained on 2 inputs, it's an unrealistic test that favors Naïve Bayes. But we also added an additional line at the end of the notebook, which asks the notebook to display the decision tree that it has generated, as shown in *Figure 12.2*:

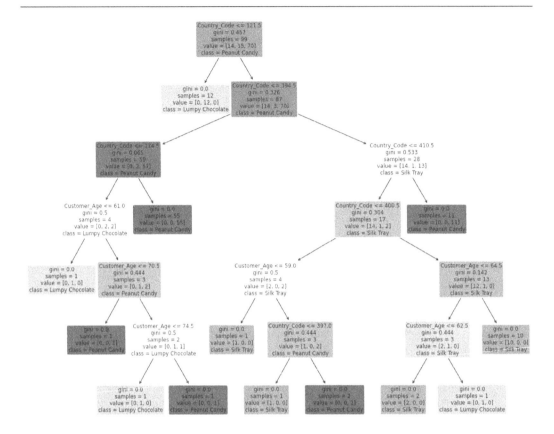

Figure 12.2 – Decision tree generated by the algorithm

We won't walk through the entire tree, but the tree diagram does explain how the model makes its prediction. You can see the values it is using for **Country_Code** and **Customer_Age**, and branches down the tree depending on the value passed into the model. Sometimes it can come to a quick decision (for example, the box in the top left is an early recommendation for Lumpy Bars), sometimes it needs to work through several levels (for example, when recommending Silk Tray in the box at the bottom right).

You'll notice that there are several different paths to making the same product recommendation, which means decision trees can make quite nuanced predictions. But let's remember two key points:

- Decision trees are human-readable. We haven't gone into too much detail, but you already have a high-level understanding of what is happening.

- Decision trees are auto-generated. All of the values used in *Figure 12.2* were discovered by the machine learning where and how it should branch in order to fit the tree to the available data.

You might be tempted to dive in and start tweaking the weights to see whether you can make the model predict better results. But rather than tweaking this model, let's show you a better way of doing this using a tool that you met in *Chapter 4*.

Decision trees and decision tables

Back in *Chapter 4*, we met decision tables as the key format for capturing business rules. If we take a look at the tree in *Figure 12.2*, we can imagine how we could write these rules. Since our tree has 25 nodes, we're likely to have 25+ nodes – we're only showing the first 3 here:

U	Customer Age	Country Code	Recommended Product
1	>20	<100	Peanut Candy
2	>50	>=100 and <400	Silk Tray
3	>50	>=400	Lumpy Bar
...			

Table 12.1 – Decision table generated from the decision tree

Remember that the first two columns (**Customer Age** and **Country Code**) are our inputs and the final column is the product we recommend.

You'll also notice that we've set the Table HIT Policy to **U** or **unique**. Decision trees branch until they come to a single, final, recommendation node. So, a decision table equivalent of a tree can only ever match one line or rule against a value. The KIE sandbox is smart enough to inspect the table and warn you if the rules **overlap** (if two rules would be triggered by the same value), but only if you set the HIT policy to unique.

Even better, KIE gives you a tool (**kie-dmn-ruleset2dmn**) to automatically translate between the decision tree and table. The KIE documentation and blog cover how to use that tool in detail if you want to investigate further.

More importantly, what we have learned in this section is as follows:

- Machine learning doesn't always have to be a black box – there are algorithms such as decision trees that can explain how a decision is made. This algorithm can effectively auto-discover the business rules in our data.

- Whether we translate the tree into rules manually or via the rules2dmn tool, we can move our algorithm into a human-readable decision table format where we can edit as needed.

We'll come back in the section after the next to look at explainability in AI, and why it is so important. But right now, we have a dilemma – we might be forced to choose an algorithm (decision trees) that performs worse than an alternative (in this case, Naïve Bayes), purely because it can explain what it is doing.

Let's make that dilemma worse by introducing neural networks in the next section. They are even more powerful, but it's even less clear how they make decisions.

> **Spoiler alert – we solve this problem in the section after next**
>
> In the *Ethics and explainability in decision making – how KIE helps* section, we solve this dilemma of how to choose the most powerful algorithm and still get it to explain how it makes its decision. You didn't really think we'd introduce a serious problem without giving you a solution?

Neural networks in machine learning

This is not a book about neural networks. But since the tools we've introduced (KIE and Python notebooks) also allow you to work more effectively with neural networks, it's worth having a simple introduction to them.

To see the problem neural networks can help solve, imagine we took our sales graph (*Figure 11.4* from *Chapter 11*) and added the sales data for our chocolate crunch bars. We might end up with a graph such as *Figure 12.3*:

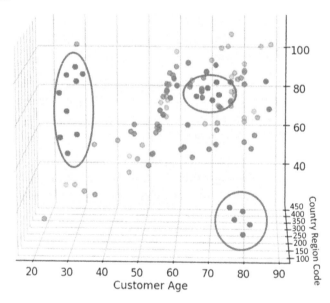

Figure 12.3 – More complicated sales data

This graph is more difficult to describe – while we've highlighted our Chocolate Crunch sales with red circles, the group in the top right is mixed in with Silk Tray orders. There is no single sentence we can use to describe the pattern and there is no extra feature (or dimension) that we can use to clarify this situation. It is for processing complex patterns like this that neural networks work best.

> **Reality check – don't give up on simple classifiers too easily**
>
> To clarify that last statement, since we need to keep our examples simple, for this dataset simple classifiers such as **support vector machines** or **k-nearest neighbors** would probably still give you good enough results. I encourage you to try these classifiers first on your own data.
>
> However, at some stage, you're going to encounter a dataset that is too complicated for these algorithms, which is where the power of neural networks is useful.

A neural network implemented in Excel

Neural networks are a big deal, and you've almost certainly heard of them already. You may be surprised that we can implement one in Excel, as shown in *Figure 12.4*. The actual Excel file is available on the book's GitHub site as `12_Neural_Network.xlsx`:

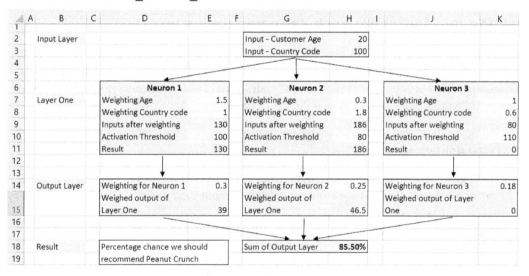

Figure 12.4 – A neural network in Excel

You should be able to easily understand the concept as you can work through it in Excel:

- Normally, all we care about are the **inputs** at the top of sheet in green (**Customer Age** and **Country Code**) and the recommendation **output** at the end of the sheet (also in green). The output is the percentage chance that our customer will buy a Peanut Crunch bar.

- To calculate our output, we pass the inputs through three neurons each with the same pattern. We have different weightings that we can set within each neuron (the light gray box).

- Those weighting values allow us to modify how much importance we put on each input, which we use to calculate our **Inputs after weighting** field.

- We then have our Activation T**hreshold**. In this example, the activation function is all or nothing. If the input after weighting is higher than the threshold, we pass it on. If not, we pass on zero. Other (more subtle and complicated) activation functions could be used.

- Our **Output Layer** applies a weighting to the values coming out of the neuron in the previous layer. This weighting (in gray) can also be adjusted.

- Finally, our **Result** is the sum of the three neurons in the output layer. This output represents the percentage chance that this customer will buy a Peanut Crunch bar.

This type of network is a **feedforward perceptron**. Despite the impressive name, we can see from the Excel file that it's just a bunch of simple calculations. And in the sheet, there are values we can tweak to build toward the result that we want. So, what makes such a network effective? It's due to how we train the network. We'll explain how training works in the next section.

Training our neural network – can you do better?

If you've downloaded and tried out the Excel file, you'll see that our model is pretty effective at predicting Peanut Crunch bar sales to US customers. But it's not so good at recommending products for customers based in South Africa. For country codes around 400, it generates nonsensical values such as a 357% probability the customer will make a purchase.

If you were given the challenge of tweaking the inputs in gray to help these customers *without changing the networks structure*, what would you do?

1. You'd gather a set of training data (South African region codes across all ranges) in most cases saying we should predict a low chance of buying a Peanut Crunch bar.

2. With this end goal in mind, you'd tweak the sheet values (in gray) to produce a result closer to what we want (**backpropagation**).

3. You would test the changes with a range of values (from both US and South African values) and see how far the entire model is away from the ideal result.

4. If our changes were an improvement, we continue making changes in the same direction (**gradient descent**); otherwise, we discard the last lot of changes and try another direction.

5. We repeat this training for a set number of iterations, or until we're no longer getting any noticeable improvement in our model's results.

If you've followed those instructions to tweak the spreadsheet, congratulations; you've trained your first neural network. If you held off the exercise because it was too tedious, or you guessed that the machine could do the work for us – also congratulations. You've already seen most of the tools that you will need.

You already have tools to train neural networks

Part of the reason that we introduced neural networks but won't cover executing them in detail is that you already have all the tools you need to explore further:

- We used Python scripts for machine learning, within notebooks, in this and the previous chapter.

- Those notebooks had machine learning samples based on the scikit-learn toolkit. And we wrote the notebooks so we could drop in different classifiers (such as decision trees).

- The scikit-learn library gives us a way of training and using a neural network. Its power makes it slightly trickier to use, but the neural network classifier is almost a drop-in replacement for the more simple classifiers we've used so far. Find out more at `https://scikit-learn.org/stable/modules/neural_networks_supervised.html`.

- Like our previous machine learning examples, we can execute our trained neural network in Python, or export our notebooks to PMML for hosting in KIE as part of our decision models.

The Packt books on machine learning we recommended in the previous chapter also cover neural networks. They're a good place to start since you're probably looking for gentle introduction rather than immediate deep-dive, but the internet has many other tutorials that use both approaches.

I encourage you to explore these tools in more detail, especially as they are now very accessible to you. Remember, the tools are easy to use but hard to use well, so don't be discouraged if not every machine learning experiment gives you the results that expected.

Neural networks – more powerful but less explainable

Our simple network only had one layer with three neurons, plus the input/output layer. Real-life neural networks will often have many more layers, many more neurons per layer, and different activation functions. The skill in machine learning is structuring the network to obtain the best training results.

> **Azure Machine Learning can help you design your network**
>
> Ironically, Microsoft is applying machine learning to the task of designing neural networks. It won't replace an experienced machine learning expert, but it might help you as you start exploring the area. Look for the **AutoML** tools within the Azure portal.

Regardless of how we design our network, we've just made the explainability situation worse. Even with a network as simple as the one in *Figure 12.4*, could you tell a customer how you made that decision? Thankfully, we'll look at the solution KIE proposes in the next section.

Ethics and explainability in decision making – how KIE helps

We touched on ethics in *Chapter 5* when we talked about the importance of being respectful of customer data. While it made good business sense, our approach was also driven by the European GDPR legislation, which has a worldwide impact even if you don't live in the region.

The EU is proposing similar legislation for AI that is expected to have an equally wide impact. Like the GDPR, its focus is on things that also make good business sense. And since you're reading a book on business rules and KIE, you're better prepared than most people for when it comes into operation. There are many reasons, but we'll focus on two – why AI rules are explainable by default, and how KIE shines a light to explain more on the decisions made by neural networks.

Business rules are explainable by default

One of the things that attracted us to the business rule approach to AI is that rules are explainable by default. That (internally) allows our business experts to review and confirm that our rules-based business models are running as they should. This means that if there is a customer request under the EU's new AI Act to explain why they were denied a home loan, the rules can be audited and the reason for the decision shared. It is important to note that the entire decision model need not be exposed, only the portion that directly contributed to the decision.

There is no technical reason why we couldn't write an unethical rule denying a home loan offer to somebody with an Irish-sounding name such as Murphy. But the fact that such a rule would be highly visible and reviewable across all levels of an organization means it would be quickly highlighted and deleted. And if not, it's unlikely that you would want to work for a company that maintains clearly discriminatory rules.

But what about more subtle discrimination that we may not even realize is happening?

Explainability in machine learning

One (in)famous case of machine learning being biased was a sentencing guidance system used by the US courts. Since it was a neural network trained on biased data where people from poorer area codes had previously received harsher sentences, it inadvertently started discriminating against people from the ethnic groups that were more likely to live in those areas. At no point was there a rule (or training data) stating that any particular group should receive harsher treatment – but the effect was the same.

Since the trained decision model was a black box, it was impossible to audit the decisions. And the fact that it operated at the group level (on average, a longer sentence was given out to certain groups) meant that the effect was subtle and not immediately obvious for any given individual. It shouldn't take a new law for you to want to avoid a similar situation in your own business, so what practical steps can you take?

One solution is to use decision trees as the basis for our machine learning system. As we saw earlier, we can convert decision trees into business rules and benefit from all the transparency and auditability that they provide. But like the earlier example, decision trees may not always give you the best predictions, and you may find yourself sacrificing accuracy for explainability.

It is to address black-box situations that the KIE team is building out a set of **TrustyAI** tools. The KIE blog has technical details, and the videos on the KIE YouTube channel are very clear. There are three main techniques that the tools use to illuminate what were previously black-box prediction models:

- **LIME** illustrates the relative importance of each feature (or type of data) to the result. If you think of *Figure 11.16* in the previous chapter (a plot of the predictions made by Naïve Bayes), it was possible to describe that graph as a series of shapes. While most prediction models will be more complex, LIME overcomes this by focusing on the local area around our prediction point. Generating this clear picture using LIME goes some way to being able to check it for bias.

- **Counterfactuals** enable us to clarify the model by asking what the smallest changes are that we would need to make to the input values to get the result we want. Doing this systematically across the model can help us detect bias.

- **Shapley Additive Explanations (SHAP)** aims to explain how much each input contributed to the final decision. It does so by getting an average decision and then generating hybrid data points (with additional data) around it.

While this is a high-level introduction to TrustyAI technique, this section does validate the choice of KIE as a host for your AI models. KIE is already a good choice for future-proofing your AI as the business rules are inherently transparent. And when you move to combining rules and machine learning in your models, KIE gives you tools to maintain transparency and explainability for your business.

Speaking of combining rules and machine learning models, we combined both types of AI in the KIE Sandbox editor in the previous chapter. Let's look now at how to execute those combined models.

Executing combined rules and machine learning models

At the end of *Chapter 11*, we set out four different ways to execute combined business rules and machine learning models in KIE. There are good reasons for wanting to explore the different options, so we'll cover three of them in the following order:

1. We'll first explore the method that comes with the KIE samples, since these official examples are the most robust. Having some technical knowledge makes this method easier.

2. As a side note, we look at an approach using Business Central. It might be easier for a smaller group of people. While Business Central is a user-friendly tool, it works better for users who can draw on technical and enterprise support.

3. Finally, we propose a method suitable for people who are looking for the most practical solution. Combining Power Automate and Python is the method most accessible now to Excel power users.

Of course, if the fourth method (the execution of combined models within KIE Sandbox) is available by the time you are reading this, I highly recommend it as the one to use. For the moment, let's start with the samples that come with KIE.

Running the KIE machine learning samples using Java and VS Code

KIE provides samples to demonstrate how to execute combined machine learning and rules-based decision models. It's the same decision model format that we encountered in *Chapter 11* using KIE Sandbox, but some of the supporting tools were originally aimed at a non-business user audience.

This section assumes you walked through instructions in *Appendix B* – setting up VS Code online. A determined Excel power user (with or without a colleague supporting them) should have no problem following these steps. From working through *Appendix B*, you'll already be familiar with the following:

- Starting Codespaces (VS Code online) by clicking on the *green button* on the GitHub page.

- Within the VS Code online editor, making sure we have DMN Editor installed. This means we can edit our Decision Models, just like we would within KIE Sandbox.

- Using the Terminal (the text area) with the VS Code editor to start scripts to run our tests.

Note that the GitHub site for this section is different from the previous example in this chapter, and the folder we use in this example is different from the one we used in *Appendix B*. But otherwise, many of the steps are the same:

1. Go to the main *Kogito* examples GitHub page: `https://github.com/kiegroup/kogito-examples`.

2. Make sure you are logged into GitHub, and then open the project in Codespaces. Go to the `kogito-examples` folder and click the green **Code** button when it appears.

3. When the VS Code editor opens, ensure you have the DMN plugin installed so you can view and edit the decision models. Remember that this copy of Codespaces is a fresh instance, so you'll need to go through those (simple) plugin setup step again – see *Appendix B*.

4. We want to view the model in the main VS Code Editor. Press *Ctrl + P* to search all the files in the project and start typing `KiePMMLRegression.dmn`. Your screen should look similar to *Figure 12.5*, showing the decision model open in the VS Code editor.

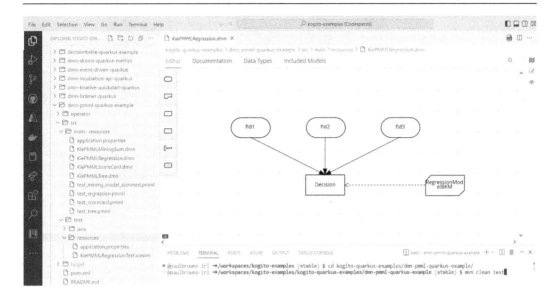

Figure 12.5 – Combined machine learning and decision model

5. Note that there are several other models in this folder, but we've chosen `KiePMMLRegression.dmn` as it's the closest example to the model we trained in *Chapter 11*. The decision service has three input fields and then calls the embedded machine learning model to a prediction based on it.

> **Differences between VS Code and KIE Sandbox**
>
> Running a decision model in VS Code is different from KIE Sandbox. For example, there is no **Run... as Form** button to try out the model. Instead, we can either write Java code to call our model (which we will show one example of using the Red Piranha project later in this chapter) or we can use the scenario testing tool that we met in *Chapter 9* and *Appendix B*.

6. Scenario testing is the easier option, especially since there is a scenario already set up in the `KiePMMLRegressionTest.scesim` file. You can either navigate through the folder structure on the left-hand side (`test/resources/`), or you can press *Ctrl + P* and start typing the filename to quickly jump to the file. The scenario test is pretty straightforward – the first three columns in light blue are input values, and the fourth column is a prediction of the value that we expect. That's shown in *Figure 12.6*:

Scenario description	GIVEN			EXPECT
	fld1	fld2	fld3	Decision
	value	value	value	value
First Case	3.0	2.0	"y"	52.5
Second Case	3.0	2.0	"x"	46.5
Third Case	4.0	3.0	"y"	89.5
Forth Case	4.0	3.0	"x"	83.5

Figure 12.6 – Sample scenario test

7. *Figure 12.7* gives an extract of the machine learning model, saved in PMML, that Kogito will run as part of the test. Like with the other classifiers, the PMML can be very compact, with much of the file detailing the input and output fields.

```
<RegressionModel algorithmName="linearRegression" functionName="regression"
  <MiningSchema>
    <MiningField name="fld1"/>
    <MiningField name="fld2"/>
    <MiningField name="fld3"/>
    <MiningField name="fld4" usageType="predicted"/>
  </MiningSchema>
  <Output>
    <OutputField name="result" targetField="fld4" />
  </Output>
  <RegressionTable intercept="0.5">
    <NumericPredictor coefficient="5" exponent="2" name="fld1"/>
    <NumericPredictor coefficient="2" exponent="1" name="fld2"/>
    <CategoricalPredictor coefficient="-3" name="fld3" value="x"/>
    <CategoricalPredictor coefficient="3" name="fld3" value="y"/>
  </RegressionTable>
```

Figure 12.7 – Extract of a PMML regression model

8. In the terminal, we need to navigate to the specific example that demonstrates the machine learning and decision model combined. The quickest way to do this is to type cd kogito-quarkus-examples/dmn-quarkus-example/ in the terminal – the large textbox area on the bottom right of the screen. You can just about see this in *Figure 12.5*.

9. Before running the tests, check we're in the correct folder. Type ls in the terminal and check that we see the pom.xml build file as part of the list of files returned.

10. Running our combined decision model is just like the scenario tests we demonstrated in *Appendix B*. Type mvn clean test to execute the scenario tests that are already in this model.

11. Like our previous example, the first time this is run, a lot of the supporting libraries will be downloaded into the image. You will get an update as each of the tests runs and passes (which is what we'd expect).

12. You will get a summary of the multiple tests that ran, and details (in the **Surefire** reports files, which will be saved into a newly created `Target` folder).

As expected, there was nothing dramatic. Kogito executed our combined model using the parameters in the test, and the output matched what we expected for each line of our scenario.

No surprises here

The KIE team runs these tests automatically before releasing the code, so it would have been a surprise if any of the tests had failed.

However, there have been a couple of instances where Codespaces upgrades to the latest version of Maven before the KIE team does. This shouldn't, but occasionally does, cause a Maven build error. If you're unlucky enough to encounter this problem, your options are as follows:

- To wait. The teams will resolve the issue once they move to the latest version of Maven. Normally, this is quite fast – days rather than weeks.

- To set up VS Code on your laptop. While this is easy to do, and we give hints in *Appendix B* on how to do this, you will probably need technical support.

- To change the version of Maven used by Codespaces. Typically, you will want a slightly older version than the one currently installed. Instructions are at `https://maven.apache.org/install.html`, but again we suggest support from a more technical colleague.

What next from here – exploring other models and building your own

Now that we're more comfortable in a slightly more technical rule-editing environment, you may want to read the following article, which gives more details on the example we just ran: `https://blog.kie.org/2021/01/how-to-use-a-pmml-file-in-dmn-editor-vscode.html`.

You may also wish to explore the test project further. There are other decision models and unit tests in this folder that are worth exploring. Finally, it's worth taking a machine learning model that you've trained yourself and following the example to get KIE and Kogito to execute it yourself.

We promised two easier ways of executing the models that might suit other readers that don't want to use VS Code. Let's touch quickly on Business Central, which is very similar to the example we just ran.

Executing machine learning and rule models in Business Central

In *Chapter 9*, we saw that Business Central had many capabilities that we didn't have time to explore. One of these is the ability to edit and execute combined machine learning and rule models. We won't provide a detailed run through since the approach (based on the scenario simulation testing tool, and decision model editor, is so similar to what we covered in the previous section using VS Code).

If it is an area you are interested in, or maybe you want useful information to help you execute models better in VS Code, the following points may help you explore more:

- Red Hat has two good articles on PMML models in Business Central, starting at `https://developers.redhat.com/blog/2021/01/14/knowledge-meets-machine-learning-for-smarter-decisions-part-1#artificial_intelligence__machine_learning__and_data_science`

- The KIE team has a great video covering a similar topic on YouTube – search `[KIELive#42] The Intelligent Decisions journey with DMN and PMML`

- The Pragmatic AI section of the Drools documentation includes a detailed walkthrough of a sophisticated home loan example using Business Central as the editor: `https://docs.drools.org/8.29.0.Final/drools-docs/docs-website/drools/pragmatic-ai/index.html`

The Business Central and VS Code online approaches have a lot in common. It's worth presenting a completely different alternative that is more workflow-focused, which many people will find the easiest.

Alternative – integrating rules and ML in a Power Automate flow

Our alternative approach to combining rules and machine decision services is very simple and is based on the Power Automate tool that we introduced in *Chapter 8*. *Figure 12.8* shows the flow we have in mind:

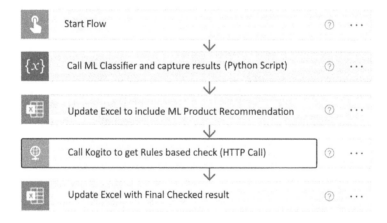

Figure 12.8 – A Power Automate flow integrating machine learning and rules

This flow could be implemented in either Power Automate Online or Power Automate Desktop. Either way, the flow is very simple in concept and has only five steps:

1. We start our flow in the normal way – this flow has a manual trigger, but it could easily be an online form submission.

2. In the second step, we call our machine learning model (and only the machine learning model) from Power Automate.

> **Don't worry – we'll cover how to do this shortly**
>
> *Step 2* is the only step we haven't shown you yet – it's pretty simple, as you'll see in the next section.

3. We update Excel with the results of the machine learning model.

4. We make a separate call to our rules-based decision service using any one of the techniques we covered in *Chapters 6, 7*, and *8*. We make sure to pass in all the information, including the results we gathered earlier from the machine learning model.

5. We update Excel with the result of the final decision service call.

If we used this approach for our chocolate bar recommendation service, *step 2* might recommend Peanut Crunch bars to US customers, while *step 4* does a rules-based health check to stop us from causing harm to anybody with allergies.

Many Excel power users find this Power Automate approach easier than using VS Code – not only are the tools within their control but also doing things as simple, separate steps is easier to understand and test. Since we know how to implement the other steps, let's focus on how to call the machine learning model from Power Automate.

Calling the machine learning model from Power Automate

There are many possible ways to call the machine learning model from a Power Automate action. We've used Python so much in this and the previous chapter, and Power Automate has good options for working with Python, so we'll use that method. We're going to keep our Python script simple even though there are many ways we could extend it. When you view the script on the book's GitHub site at `12_use_existing_pmml_model.py`, it will look like *Figure 12.9*:

```
12 lines (8 sloc)    389 Bytes

1    ## Simple script to demonstate running our pretrained model, stored as pmml, in python

2

3    from pypmml import Model

4

5    #Import our previously trained model
6    model = Model.fromFile('11_chocolate_recommendations.pmml')

7

8    ## call the model - note the format on how we pass in the parameters needed
9    result = model.predict({'Customer_Age': 50, 'Country_Code': 100})

10

11   ## print the result
12   print(result)
```

Figure 12.9 – Python script to call a pre-trained machine learning model

This Python script to run our pre-trained model has four simple steps:

1. We import the `pypmml` toolkit because we'll need it to open our pre-trained model.

2. The next step opens the machine learning model we trained in the previous chapter.

3. The step to get the prediction from our model is similar to the one we used in the previous chapter (although PMML expects input numbers in simple JSON format instead).

4. We print the result. For the value we passed in *step 3*, it will produce a message of `'probability(Peanut Candy)': 0.15329348021087122, 'probability(Lumpy Bar)': 0.0}`.

There are so many different ways to extend and use this script. How you do this will depend on the Power Automate flow that you want to use it in. For example, you may want to pass in a value to a Python function, or you may want the script to open and read its inputs from an Excel file. Likewise, you might want to return a simple value, or instead open an Excel sheet and update that. All are easy to do using Python and its supporting toolkits – and a good summary of all the toolkits for working with Python and Excel is available at `https://www.python-excel.org/`.

Testing this script in VS Code online

If you wanted, you could also run this Python script in VS Code online. The steps are like the previous VS Code examples. Just remember in the terminal that we may need to type `pip install pypmml` to make sure we have installed the supporting toolkits. To run the script, type `python 12_use_existing_pmml_model.py`.

This section has given you multiple options for running decision models with machine learning and/or rules. Since the most likely longer-term deployment of your models is as part of a wider enterprise system, we wanted to show you Red Piranha as a template enterprise project for your rules.

Red Piranha as a template enterprise project

The main focus of this book is to show you as an Excel power user how to leverage the power of a business rules engine. That gives you a workable solution, but it is likely that your decision models will sooner or later be deployed as part of a larger enterprise system. That's a good thing! Remember the full enterprise system diagram we saw back in *Chapter 2*? Your decision models won't need to change, but now they will have a more robust infrastructure around them.

As an Excel power user or business rules author, you don't need to know the full detail of how to do this. But since you're investing your time in this area, it is very reassuring to see how it can be done. The section will show you a working example of such an enterprise system using the Red Piranha project.

Before we start, we have two other reasons for introducing the Red Piranha project:

- Red Piranha shows you another way of integrating Excel data with KIE. Previously, we passed selected cells. Red Piranha allows us to load entire Excel sheets into the rule engine.

- Red Piranha is based on Spring Boot, a widely used Java framework. So, it's a useful starting point for you if you wanted to explore the Java world.

Red Piranha allows to you specify an input Excel file, then state which rules file or decision model to apply to it, and finally say which output Excel file you want to use (so your original file never gets overwritten). It's a more robust approach since it works on **named ranges** within the Excel file – it's harder for edits to make the Excel file break.

The Red Piranha project grew out of the examples in the previous book by the author (*JBoss Drools Business Rules*) and subsequent work. But please view it as a *proof of concept* – a useful way to demonstrate the concepts of a full production system before building the actual system. We'll shortly take a detailed look inside the Red Piranha project. But first, let's use the Docker skills we acquired in *Chapter 10* to quickly download and run it.

Running the Red Piranha Docker image

Make sure we have Docker Desktop or the background service running using the instructions in *Chapter 10*. Not only does Red Piranha package the KIE/Drools rule engine with examples to make it easier to use with Excel, it also provides an easy-to-use Docker image. Let's get that Docker image up and running:

1. Open Command Prompt by pressing *Windows Key + R*, then type cmd.

2. In the console, type `docker run -it -p 7000:7000 --mount type=bind,source=c:\some-shared-folder,target=/some-shared-folder paulbrowne/redpiranha:latest`. Then, press *Enter* to execute the command (only at the end).

    Be careful – everything should be lowercase. Note that there are two dashes in front of `mount`, and note the direction of the `/` slashes.

> **Why this detailed command?**
>
> The basic syntax to run Docker and get the latest Red Piranha image is simple. The `-p 7000:7000` flag means we can communicate with the web server *within* the container on that port. Similarly, the `–mount` flag means Windows Explorer can see the files shared by the container to this folder.
>
> Depending on how your laptop is set up, you may get an **Access Denied** message. You may need to create `C:\some-shared-folder` if it doesn't exist. You may also need to right-click on the folder and select **Properties** and then **Sharing** to allow full sharing with *everyone*.

3. There will be several messages as Docker pulls the layers needed to run Red Piranha. When this is complete, you should see text like the following:

```
  .   ____          _            __ _ _
 /\\ / ___'_ __ _ _(_)_ __  __ _ \ \ \ \
( ( )\___ | '_ | '_| | '_ \/ _` | \ \ \ \
 \\/  ___)| |_)| | | | | || (_| |  ) ) ) )
  '  |____| .__|_| |_|_| |_\__, | / / / /
 |_|=============|___/=/_/_/_/
 :: Spring Boot ::                (v2.6.2)


2022-05-27 20:47:59.429  INFO 1 --- [           main]
net.firstpartners.Application            : Starting
Application v2.0.1-SNAPSHOT using Java 17.0.3 on
8de964479f93 with PID 1 (/workspace/BOOT-INF/classes
started by cnb in /workspace)
2022-
2022-05-27 20:48:02.974  INFO 1 --- [           main]
net.firstpartners.Application: Started Application in
3.965 seconds (JVM running for 4.529)
net.firstpartners.core.Config@5856dbe4[
   sampleBaseDirAlternate=src/main/resources/examples/
   sampleBaseDirDefault=/workspace/BOOT-INF/classes/
```

```
examples/
    showFullRuleEngineLogs=false
]
```

Once you see the application started message, the image is ready to use. We mentioned that Red Piranha has a mini-web server, so why don't we take a look at the web pages it has available?

1. Open a web browser on your laptop and go to `http://localhost:7000/`.

2. Your web browser will connect to the Docker image using the access (on port `7000`) that we specified earlier. You should see a page similar to *Figure 12.10*:

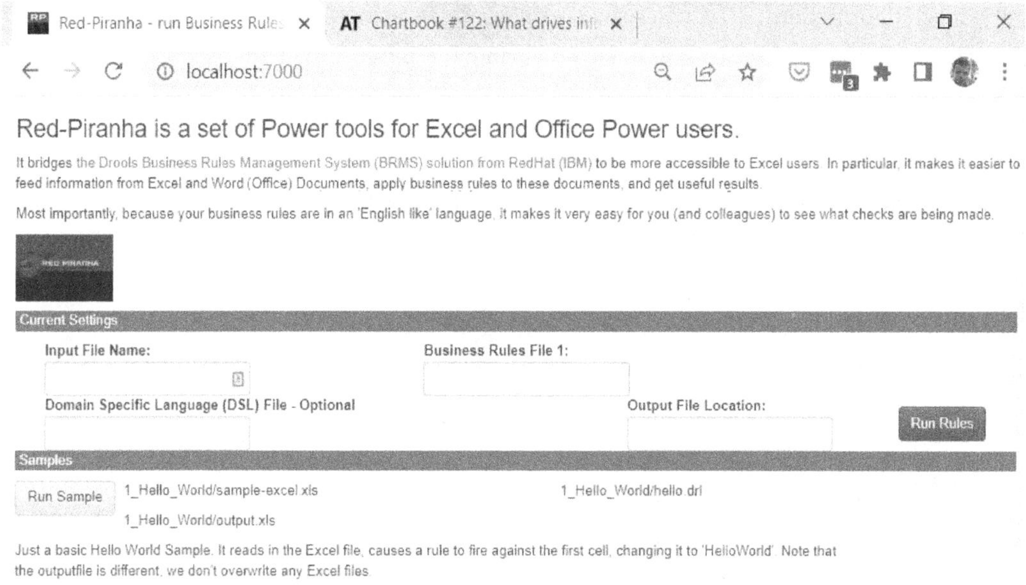

Figure 12.10 – Red Piranha ready to run the business rules samples

3. First, we going to run the Hello World sample. If you read down the page, you should see a heading, **Samples**, and just below that, a button, **Run Sample**. That sets the Excel input, rules, and output files for this example.

4. Click on the **Run Sample** button to tell Red Piranha/KIE to apply rules to the Excel file.

5. Once the sample has run, you should see a **Rules Complete** message and, further down the screen, you'll see `Hello World`.

Congratulations – you've just run your first business rule using Red Piranha. In the rules, we want to highlight three important things:

- Near the top of screen, Red Piranha lists the Excel file it read (input) information from, the file with the Business Rules it supplied to the Drools rule engine, and the Excel file it wrote the output information to.

- Further down the screen, we should see information about all the information being read in from Excel, messages as the rules fire, and what is about to be output into another Excel file. Much of this is clickable, so it's worth spending a few moments to explore it now.

> **Too much information?**
>
> Since Red Piranha maps all of the data available in Excel into a format KIE can use, a lot of information can be displayed. It uses **named ranges** in Excel to decide which data to extract and convert.

We'll explore the exact conversion format soon, but the data format being used within Red Piranha is similar to the custom data type we set up in the KIE sandbox in *Chapter 4*. *Figure 12.11* shows (some) of the information it has converted from Excel during the conversion process.

Figure 12.11 – Information that Red Piranha has read from Excel

All of this information is also printed to the console, if you prefer to view it there.

You'll notice that there are several other examples listed on the screen. It's worth exploring them as well. But you're probably keener to run your own examples within Red Piranha.

> **Different versions of Red Piranha**
>
> Red Piranha is under active development, so it likely that what you seen on screen will differ slightly from the screenshots shown here. There will always be a stable Docker image, and a stable `main` (default) branch.

Running your own files in Red Piranha

While the samples are interesting, you probably want to run your own files through Red Piranha. Given that the web page (in *Figure 12.10*) has instructions on how to select your own files (an Excel input file, a rules file, or an output file), this is easy. There are also detailed notes on the Red Piranha GitHub page. But I'm highlighting four key points to save you time:

- Docker runs Red Piranha in a container isolated from your laptop. That is great for security but means you need to think about how you make files from your laptop available to Red Piranha. Fortunately, our command to start the Docker container used the –mount flag to link a folder on your computer, `c:\some-shared-folder`, to a folder within the Docker container, `\some-shared-folder`.

- Once we have these folders mounted, an Excel file containing our input data can be saved in the `c:\some-shared-folder\someinput.xlsx` folder. We can then tell Red Piranha (running within Docker) to read from that file by putting `\some-shared-folder\someinput.xlsx` in the **Input File Name** box that we saw in *Figure 12.10*.

- Red Piranha converts Excel files (or the named ranges within Excel files) into a set of custom **Cell** objects. The details in *Figure 12.11* show this conversion in progress, which is useful when writing rules to match against the data contained in these **Cell** objects.

- While Red Piranha supports decision models, most of the examples use the more advanced **DRL** format. We'll explore this format later in the chapter, as it is very useful to know.

While Docker makes it easy to use Red Piranha, it is almost as easy to use Codespaces and VS Code online to customize the project to do exactly what you want. It is open source after all, so let's try that out.

A look inside the Red Piranha project using Codespaces and VS Code

Even if you don't intend to dive into Java development using Red Piranha as a launching point, it is useful to take a look at the code. That way you can see more of the layout of the custom data model (Cells) and edit the sample DRL (rules) files.

Running Red Piranha in Codespace is almost exactly the same as running the Kogito examples earlier in the chapter:

1. Open the Project on GitHub: `https://github.com/firstpartners-net/red-piranha`.

2. Click on the green <>**Code** button in the menu that appears, then click on the + button to create a Codespace on the default main branch.

3. After a couple of moments, while Codespaces starts, the VS Code online editor will appear in the browser.

4. In the terminal, type `cd code` to go to the correct directory. Then, to start Red Piranha using Spring and Maven, type `mvn spring-boot:run`.

5. The project will start up (downloading libraries as needed) and show a message with the Spring logo and the directories it is using.

6. Eventually, VS Code will display a message, like in *Figure 12.12*, showing that the application is on.

Figure 12.12 – Red Piranha running in the cloud in VS Code online

7. Clicking on **Open in Browser** will open a version of Red Piranha hosted in the cloud. That screen should be exactly the same as in *Figure 12.10*.

Congratulations! You have just built and run your first enterprise Java project in the cloud. To encourage you to explore Java (and the Red Piranha source code) in more detail, we are going to suggest some useful starting points:

*   Red Piranha is a standard Spring Boot project. There is plenty of information on this framework at `https://spring.io/projects/spring-boot`.

*   If you edit the Red Piranha code (for example, to update a rule or to add a feature that you need), Spring should detect the change automatically. But if it doesn't, you can stop the project (using *Ctrl + C* in the VS Code terminal), and start again from *step 4*.

*   A key file you should look at in the project is `Cell.java`, since it defines the structure of the data that is available to your rules. When the data is being extracted from Excel, it is converted into a series of Cell objects. The concept of objects is similar to the custom data type you created in the KIE sandbox in *Chapter 4*.

*   Unless you're a Java developer, you're unlikely to need to change much of the project structure. But since The Spring Framework maps a lot of the web requests to `RedController.java`, that makes it a good place to start if you're interested.

- Mainly, you'll want to edit the rules files. *Figure 12.11* shows the DRL rules file for the second Red Piranha example open in the editor:

```
EXPLORER: RED-PIRANHA...              log-then-modify-rules.drl  ×

> .github                     code > src > main > resources > examples > 2_chocolate-factory > 2_chocolate-factory > log-then-modify-rules.drl
∨ code                         1    package examples;
  ∨ src                        2
    ∨ main                     3    import net.firstpartners.core.log.IStatusUpdate;
      > java                   4
      ∨ resources              5    import net.firstpartners.data.Cell;
        ∨ examples             6    import net.firstpartners.data.Range;
          > 1_hello_world      7
          ∨ 2_chocolate-factory / 2_chocolate...   8    global IStatusUpdate log;
              chocolate-data.xls   9
              log-then-modify-rules.drl  10    rule "example 2 log then modify cell values"
          > 3_simple_dmn       11
            examples.json      12        when
      > META-INF               13            $cell : Cell(modified==false)
      > static                 14
      > templates              15        then
        application.properties 16
        logback.xml            17            //Note: use the 'modify' block instead
  > test                       18            //want to give the rule engine a chance to react to these changes
  > target                     19            $cell.setModified(true);
    mvnw                       20
    mvnw.cmd                   21            //Logging message
                               22            log.addUIInfoMessage("initial cell value:"+$cell);
                               23
                               24    end
```

Figure 12.13 – DRL rules file for the second Red Piranha example in VS Code

This rule file is in the DRL format, which KIE also supports. Since DRL is a more advanced rules format, let's go through this rule format in detail in the next section.

Advanced DRL rules in VS Code and Business Central

When we first introduced business rules in *Chapter 1*, we used a slightly formal when .... then format – when something is true, then do this action. The rule in our Red Piranha example in *Figure 12.11* follows this format exactly:

- **When** a Cell object is marked as unmodified
- **Then** update the status flag to modified/print a message to the console

So, the basic format is simple and very human-readable. There is a lot of power available when writing individual rules this way, and DRL files can be mixed and matched with the decision models that we've been using for most of this book.

Each line in a decision table is equivalent to one DRL rule

We described decision tables as having columns equivalent to when (conditions) and columns that activate when matched (then, on the right-hand side of a decision table). So, you can think of each line of a decision table as being equivalent to one rule in a DRL file.

While *Figure 12.11* shows the DRL format as part of a Java project hosted in VS Code, it's good to know that **Business Central** also supports the DRL rules format. You may remember that it was one of the (many) options we saw when creating a file in Business Central in *Chapter 10*, *Figure 10.17*.

So, why do we describe the DRL format as more powerful that the Decision Table format?

- For each rule, we have a lot of options in the data model we use. We use a **Cell** object here, but it could be any other Java file that describes a data structure.

- We are not bounded by the strict table structure of decision tables; we can tailor rules to highly specific needs on a case-by-case basis.

- We can set attributes on the rule such as **salience**, which suggests to the rule engine which rules we want to fire first.

- We have the option of using a **domain-specific language** (**DSL**), which allows us to simplify our rules even further and write the rules in a format similar to English (or Spanish or any other human language) .

- In our actions (the `then` part), we can trigger any action that can be implemented in Java. In fact, the format follows a very Java-like syntax that many developers are more familiar with.

Individual DRL rules versus decision tables

Given how powerful they are, why does the book focus on decision tables instead of DRL rules for much of the book?

The reality is that individual rules in a DRL format are very powerful. But you are likely to have hundreds (if not thousands) of similar business rules in your project. The repetitive format and structure of decision tables make them much easier to use and maintain in most real-life situations.

There is comprehensive DRL documentation on the Drools site if you think the DRL would enhance your project. The video *Understanding DRL (Drools Rule Language)* on the KIE Live channel also has a great hour-long introduction to walk you through the format.

We mentioned that each line in a decision table was the equivalent of a single DRL rule. Let's take a look at how that works, as it helps explain why rule engines are so fast.

Why are rule engines and decision models so fast?

From experience, several times, I've seen business users propose using a rule engine to the IT development team. The IT folks mistakenly think they've learned about them on their college course (hint, they may use the term **state machine**) before attempting to build one themselves. Several months later, they have a half-working solution, good enough to solve the immediate problem, but cut off from all the mainstream tooling as KIE continues to evolve and improve.

It is for that reason that we have given you (and colleagues) a glimpse within the rule engine and show the sophistication that almost 20 years of continual development gives you. Let's summarize why we should use KIE instead of a home-grown solution:

- Developers – you want to use KIE as the cutting-edge AI tool from Red Hat and IBM. That looks far better on your CV than building your own.

- Business users – you want to get the benefit of almost 20 years of development and have a ready pool of technical people to support the project. And you get all the authoring tools, training, and support that comes from IBM, Red Hat, and the wider community.

There are many areas where the many years of KIE development will outclass a home-grown solution (for example, you're not going to get a home-built version with the clarity of KIE Sandbox). But we'll focus on the **RETE-PHREAK** algorithm because that also explains why rules engines are fast – faster than Excel, and faster than custom code.

The RETE and PHREAK approach to running rules (fast)

The initial RETE algorithm came from Dr Charles Forgy (written in papers between 1974 and 1979) and underlines the theory underpinning rule engines such as KIE and Drools. The PHREAK algorithm is a fundamental rewrite by the Drools team, taking advantage of 40 years of technology updates since then. Details of both papers are easily found online and well worth a read, but the key point is that all this thinking is pre-baked into Drools; we don't have to build it ourselves.

Remember that almost all the elements of our decision models (including decision tables) can be translated into something similar to rules in a when...then format – perhaps with additional attributes of which rules should be grouped together. Of course, this is an oversimplification. The Drools documentation has full details of what is actually going on in **working memory** – the space within Drools where all this evaluation is being carried out. But here is a summary:

1. Firstly, our rules (including decision models) are loaded into working memory. The left-hand side (when) of a rule is evaluated. If one or more rules have all or part of a when part in common, we don't need to evaluate it twice – we can link this part of the rules. This means we can build our rules into a network, not unlike *Figure 12.12*.

2. Note that in this network, Drools has also done some analysis on the right-hand side (the then part of the rule). This is because when a rule is fired, it may trigger changes in the then part that bring other rules into play.

3. While we build this network as the very first step, it is possible to dynamically change it during rule execution, but we'll ignore this ability to keep things simple.

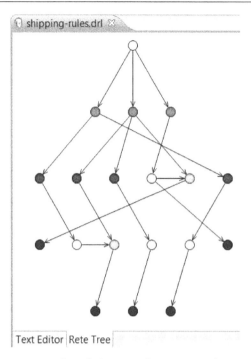

Figure 12.14 – Sample Rete tree from our simple project

4. Next, we load the facts into working memory. Facts can be as simple as the customer data that we passed into our decision model in earlier examples in KIE Sandbox.

5. The presence of facts in the working memory activates certain rules (the when part of the rule is now true). Unlike traditional code, if there is more than one rule available to fire (the **Agenda**), the rule engine decides which to fire (and in which order) using **conflict resolution**.

6. It is possible that a rule change executing a then condition causes a change in facts in working memory so that a rule once on the agenda is no longer lined up to fire. But other when parts of rules may match, so they will be added to the agenda instead.

7. The process of evaluating rules against new/updated facts is known as **truth maintenance**. There are also measures within the rule engine to avoid **circular rules** (where a rule updates a fact, which sooner or later causes the same rule to fire again).

The fact is that a home-grown solution won't have network analysis nor robustness that has been tested by hundreds of thousands of users. And building a RETE network means that only a small set of rules needs to be evaluated with every change – this is different from traditional solutions where all possible solutions need to be evaluated, perhaps multiple times. So the speed advantage of rule engines increases the more business rules you have.

As a final word, this was only one small area out of many that the Drools team has worked on to optimize the engine. And hopefully, it helps confirm your choice of Drools rules and KIE decision services to evolve past the problems you previously faced in Excel.

Summary

This chapter set out to build on the previous 11 – extending some of the ideas that we met earlier in the book and giving you signposts for where to go next.

In this chapter, we swapped out the previous machine learning algorithm for decision trees and saw how this allowed us to explain what is going on within our decision model. Lack of explainability became an issue when we introduced neural networks as more powerful classifiers, but we solved the problem using cutting-edge TrustyAI tools.

We introduced three ways to deploy combined machine learning and rules-based AI models at a high level via Business Central, and in more depth using KIE and Kogito samples, and again using Python and Power Automate workflows. We introduced another method using Red Piranha as a template enterprise solution to build on, including its ability to read entire Excel spreadsheets and apply rules to them.

We looked at the more advanced DRL rule format and saw that it gave us additional options for writing rules in VS Code and Business Central. At the end of this chapter, we used this knowledge to explore the RETE and PHREAK algorithms to understand why rule engines are so robust and so fast.

What we've learned in this book

We started this book in a slightly dark place – we were avid users of Excel, but unsure of how to solve the problems we were encountering. *Chapter 1* of this book brought some light; we learned that we were not alone in having these problems and there were rule-based AI tools that might help solve them. *Chapter 2* went further, looking at the range of available engines and choosing KIE and Drools as the best available option to work with in Excel.

We got very practical in *Chapters 3* and *4* – writing our first decision models and executing them online in KIE Sandbox, before exploring more of the power of the editor, backed up the KIE Services execution tool. We then shared our work in *Chapter 5*, allowing colleagues to view our rules in the OpenShift cloud and collaborate with us in editing the rules via GitHub.

Chapter 6, *7*, and *8* allowed us to use our newly learned decision modeling powers within Excel using a range of options, from Power Query to Visual Basic and from Script Lab to Office Scripts, and finally within Microsoft Power Automate. In *Chapter 9*, we learned more about FEEL expressions, but also learned the need to test our models (and found the automated tools to do so).

The final quarter of the book was more heavyweight as we evolved toward more enterprise solutions; *Chapter 10* introduced Docker as a tool to scale our solution into the cloud while giving us more editing and testing options using Business Central. *Chapter 11* introduced the other type of AI, machine learning, and showed how we could combine machine learning and rules models together to get very powerful and consistent decision-making. This final chapter brought a lot of these topics together and suggested the next steps on topics ranging from neural networks to enterprise Java projects and articulating why KIE is the right choice to work alongside Excel in your business.

Back in *Chapter 1*, I made a promise to help solve some of the Excel problems you face in your business. I hope you agree that the tools you have learned about in the book will result in a more robust, faster, and more intelligent working environment for you and your colleagues. But nothing will change unless you make it change, so I wish you luck as you apply what you have learned on your own.

As you explore, I encourage you to share what you have learned. I hope to meet you online as you share your experiences with the Excel, AI, decision models, and business rules communities.

Appendix A
Introduction to Visual Basic for Applications

Chapter 7 showed you how to call your decision service using **Visual Basic for Applications** (**VBA**). Since not every reader has used VBA before, we include this appendix to get you started.

Introduction to macros and VBA

When launched in 1993 (yes, 1993), VBA was revolutionary. Earlier versions of Excel and other spreadsheets had **Macros, which** offered little more than a replay of user keystrokes. VBA provided the ability to record user actions as a programming language (similar to the popular **Basic** language of the day) and then allowed users to modify that in the code editor. It gave an easy path for Excel power users (like you!) to learn to solve problems while leaving the door open to upgrade to more scalable enterprise solutions.

These days, VBA is not switched on by default in Excel, so you'll need to enable it so you can see what it looks like. We'll start by enabling the **Developer** tab on the Excel ribbon:

1. In the **Excel Options** menu, select the **File** options, then **Customize Ribbon**. You'll see a dialog similar to *Figure AA.1*:

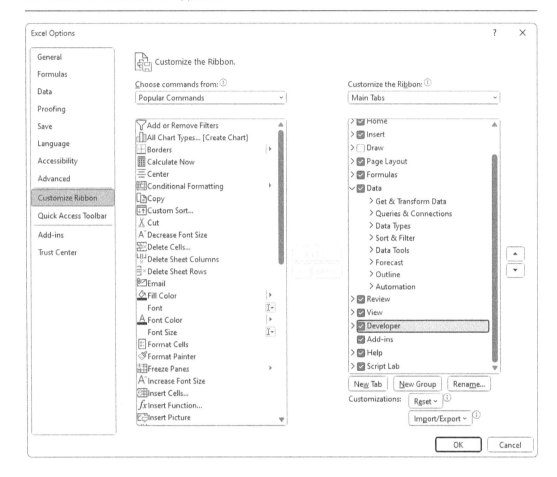

Figure AA.1 – Enabling the Developer ribbon in Excel

2. Within this dialog, on the top right, select **Main Tabs** under **Customize the Ribbon**.

3. In the box below, make sure the **Developer** toolbar option is selected.

4. Click **OK**, the dialog will close, and the **Developer** tab will now appear on the toolbar.

The **Developer** toolbar gives several useful options that are worth exploring in your own time. Perhaps the most useful for us now is the **Record Macro** feature. Let's work through this to record our steps, view and then modify the generated code, and then play back the steps:

1. On the **Developer** toolbar, click **Record Macro**. A dialog similar to *Figure AA.2* appears:

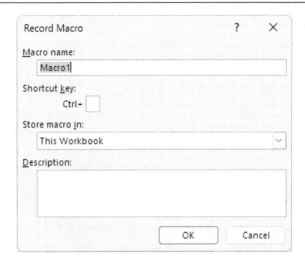

Figure AA.2 – The Record Macro dialog in Excel

2. For our simple example, we're happy with the default **Macro name** option (**Macro1**) and storing the macro in the current workbook. So, click on the **OK** button.

3. Now that we're recording our actions, let's modify one cell – it doesn't really matter which. Enter some text and change the background color to yellow – as shown in *Figure AA.3*:

Figure AA.3 – Some sample updates that we recorded

4. On the **Developer** menu, click on the **Stop Recording** button.

5. We want to view the code that VBA for Excel has captured for us. On the **Developer** toolbar, click on **Macros**, and select **Macro 1 | Edit**. The **Macro editor** screen shows what you have recorded, as shown in *Figure AA.4*:

```
Book1 - Module1 (Code)

(General)                                      Macro1

    Sub Macro1()
    '
    ' Macro1 Macro

        Range("D4").Select
        ActiveCell.FormulaR1C1 = "This is a test"
        Range("D4").Select
        With Selection.Interior
            .Pattern = xlSolid
            .Color = 65535
        End With
    End Sub
```

Figure AA.4 – Our actions automatically recorded as VBA code

Understanding VBA code, especially if it is manipulating onscreen objects, is not too difficult – so it should be fairly obvious what is happening within the code for this simple example.

While the recording is impressive, what is even more powerful is being able to modify the VBA code and execute the updated script. So, let's do that now:

1. Within **Macro Editor**, change the cell (range) in the code – we'll update it from **D4** to **A4**.

2. Click on the green run arrow on the top toolbar to execute the updated code. You'll see a result similar to *Figure AA.5*:

Figure AA.5 – Running our updated macro

Congratulations – you're now a VBA programmer! Seriously, if this is a path you feel you need to take, there are plenty of resources available on the internet. Some good starting points are listed here:

*   From Packt – *The Starter book on Excel Programming for VBA* available at https://www.packtpub.com/product/excel-programming-with-vba-starter/9781849688444

*   From Microsoft – *A series of guides to get you started with Visual Basic for Applications within Office* available at https://learn.microsoft.com/en-us/office/vba/library-reference/concepts/getting-started-with-vba-in-office

Appendix B
Testing Using VSCode, Azure, and GitHub Codespaces

While using VSCode goes beyond the scope of this book, it should still be accessible to many readers. It has been made even easier by the release by Microsoft of **GitHub Codespaces** – an online version of the **VSCode** editor. Because it runs fully in the **Azure** cloud and can be accessed via your browser, it doesn't require any installation of software on your laptop.

If you've read *Chapter 9*, you may have come to this appendix to learn how to use VSCode (online) to run the Scenario Simulation tool. We'll cover all the steps needed to set that up, as well as an alternative method that you might prefer since it also allows you to run the KIE samples showcasing scenario testing.

This appendix also provides an introduction to VSCode. VSCode opens up a range of other possibilities if you are interested in exploring not only decision models but also data science, machine learning, and programming languages such as Python, JavaScript, Java, and C#. We won't cover the specific plugins needed for that – but since we give instructions on how to install the DMN plugin, you'll have a very good basis to take the next steps in those other areas. While this book isn't aimed at developers, the steps in the chapter are also the ones you need to get started with more powerful developer tools.

Like the other appendices, we assume a willingness to explore more technical topics. While step-by-step instructions have been provided that are accessible to Excel power users, we don't go into a lot of detail on how to fix all possible problems. For that, we encourage you to get support from more technical colleagues as needed. If you do get stuck, there is another avenue to run the Scenario Simulation tool using Business Central, which we covered in *Chapter 10*.

Finally, if you prefer to run VSCode on your laptop (rather than online in the cloud), we have some notes on how you can do this at the end of the appendix. Many of the steps will be the same.

Getting started with VSCode and Codespaces

A key first step is to make sure you have a GitHub account created and you are logged in to the site using a web browser. You should have already done this if you worked your way through *Chapter 5*. Once logged in, open the repository containing your decision models – *Figure AB.1* shows the repository with the models we used in *Chapter 9*.

> **VSCode.Dev or Codespaces?**
>
> In KIE Sandbox, you'll see an option to open the project in **VSCode.Dev**. This is *not* what you're looking for. It will open a Visual Studio editor and allow you to modify the decision model. But you will still need to find the **Connect to Codespaces** button in this editor to provision the Azure cloud, which does the heavy lifting or running/testing rules.
>
> For most people, it's quicker to open **Codespaces** via GitHub using the instructions that follow.

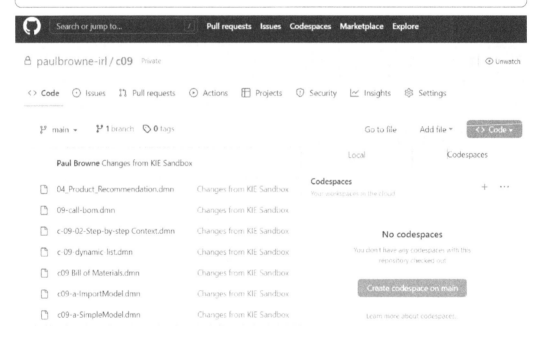

Figure AB.1 – Starting Codespaces from GitHub

Microsoft has now rolled out Codespaces (free and paid options) to most GitHub accounts. To start setting up Codespaces to run these files, follow these steps:

1. With the repository open as in *Figure AB.1*, there should be a large green **Code** button on the top right-hand side. Clicking the button gives us the option to create a Codespace on the main branch (which is what we want most of the time).

Cloud machine settings

It's worth returning to this Codespaces menu as shown in *Figure AB.1* once the virtual machine is set up.

The **...** symbol in the Codespaces menu gives you options to manage the virtual machines that Codespaces runs on Azure. They allow you to stop your machine when not in use, which is important as we only get so many hours of use in the free tier.

This **...** menu also allows us to increase the virtual memory size from the standard 4 GB to 8 GB. If you keep getting a **killed** message when running commands in later steps, increasing the memory size like this should help resolve it.

2. After clicking the green button, you should see a message that Codespaces is being set up for a couple of seconds. Then, the VSCode editor will appear in your web browser with a list of files from your repository ready to edit, as in *Figure AB.2*.

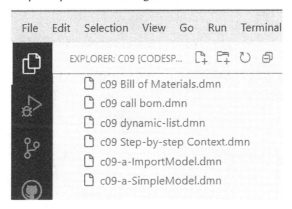

Figure AB.2 – VSCode in Codespaces with the list of decision models to edit

3. Click on one of these decision model files. VSCode will detect that it has an extension available to edit .dmn files and offer to find an extension for you as in *Figure AB.3*.

Figure AB.3 – VSCode suggesting an extension is available to edit your decision model

> **Disposable virtual machines**
>
> Be aware that virtual machines are more disposable than real ones – your files are safe when you push them to GitHub (a similar process to what you've done in KIE Sandbox). While Codespaces can be stopped and restarted, sometimes you'll get a fresh instance. In those cases, you'll be prompted to reinstall the extensions again.

4. VSCode should suggest DMN Editor from Red Hat (which may migrate in the future to IBM), as in *Figure AB.4*. Make sure you install the official version (marked with a blue tick):

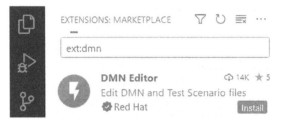

Figure AB.4 – Selecting DMN Editor from the Marketplace

5. After a couple of seconds, the extension will install, the screen will refresh, and you should be able to see the decision model in VSCode (see *Figure AB.5*) exactly like you're used to in KIE Sandbox.

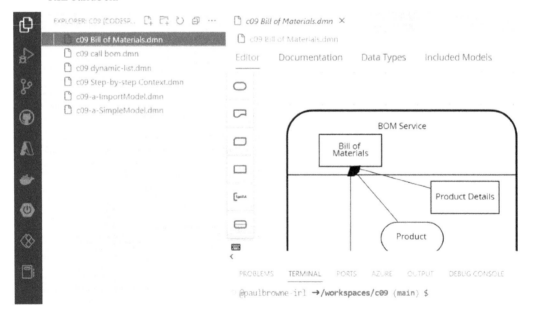

Figure AB.5 – Editing a decision model in KIE Sandbox

It's worth taking a tour of the VSCode screen in your browser. We'll assume that you already took the tour of the VSCode screen from *Chapter 9* but it's worth confirming that everything looks familiar.

We encourage you to make edits to the decision model, explore the source control tab (the icon third down from the top left), and push and pull items to and from GitHub (make sure you hit the sync button and check that they appear on the GitHub web page). While the mechanism is the same as in the KIE Sandbox editor, you have some more options (such as adding a commit message).

If your files get out of sync (for example, if somebody has edited them in KIE Sandbox at the same time), there are options in VSCode to help you resolve these conflicts. A good starting point to learn more is at `https://vscode.github.com/`. In this appendix, we'll continue on to setting up scenario testing within VSCode.

Setting up scenario testing in VSCode

Now that we're a little bit more familiar with the VSCode environment, let's use it to set up the KIE Scenario Simulation and testing tools. Since VSCode is an advanced text editor focused on development, the test tools are designed to be run automatically as part of the build process.

What is a build tool?

A build tool is needed to transform text source files into a running project. The steps the build tool can take include downloading supporting libraries, compiling the text into runnable code, packaging the project into a deployable file, and running any specified tests. Since KIE and Kogito is a Java-based project, Maven is the standard build tool.

As a build tool, Maven can also automate many of the setup steps for us. The steps we suggest in this section are based on the following article from the KIE team: `https://blog.kie.org/2021/04/how-to-use-test-scenario-editor-to-test-your-dmn-asset-in-vscode.html`. Because this article provides a clear sample, the following instructions use a slightly older version of KIE to match it. The benefits of the additional documentation are worth it if you are using the scenario testing tool for the first time.

However, since KIE is evolving rapidly, it is important that we also give you instructions on how to use the latest versions. With that in mind, consider the following:

- The *alternative method* listed in the next section can be run using the very latest version of the KIE Project source – at the price of delving slightly deeper into the project.

- If you're intending to set up a Kogito project for development purposes, you are better off following the official instructions here: `https://docs.kogito.kie.org/latest/html_single/#proc-kogito-creating-project_kogito-creating-running`.

Remember, if you're copy-pasting any of the following code samples to set up scenario testing, make sure that all the text is on one line:

1. In VSCode, go to the terminal (the text box at the bottom right of the screen). Type the following command, all on one line, and press the *Enter* key:

    ```
    mvn archetype:generate -DarchetypeGroupId=org.
    kie.kogito -DarchetypeArtifactId=kogito-quarkus-
    archetype -DgroupId=org.acme -DartifactId=sample-kogito
    -DarchetypeVersion=1.10.0.Final -Dversion=1.0.0-SNAPSHOT
    ```

    This command tells the Maven build tool (`mvn`) to generate a test project (`archetype:generate`) using a template from `org.kie.kogito`, specifically the `quarkus`-based example. It generates samples under the `org.acme` folder. The generated project is called `sample-kogito`, with a version number of `1.0-SNAPSHOT`.

2. Maven will automatically download the necessary supporting libraries. If you haven't increased the memory size of the virtual machine (as we suggested previously), it is likely this step will fail with a **killed** message. Should you get an error like this, it is OK to repeat exactly the same `build` command once you've adjusted the memory size.

3. You may be asked to confirm halfway through the build process (press *Y* when prompted). After several seconds, the build process should complete, and you should get a success message as in *Figure AB.6*.

```
[INFO] Parameter: groupId, Value: org.acme
[INFO] Parameter: artifactId, Value: sample-kogito
[INFO] Parameter: version, Value: 1.0.0-SNAPSHOT
[INFO] Project created from Archetype in dir: /workspaces/c09/sample-kogito
[INFO] ------------------------------------------------------------------------
[INFO] BUILD SUCCESS
[INFO] ------------------------------------------------------------------------
[INFO] Total time:  10.309 s
[INFO] Finished at: 2022-12-10T23:16:14Z
[INFO] ------------------------------------------------------------------------
```

Figure AB.6 – Maven project build success

4. Maven will have created a lot of new folders under the sample Kogito – if you expand them, it will look like *Figure AB.7*:

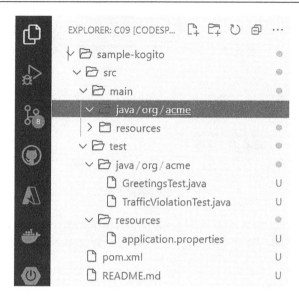

Figure AB.7 – The folders generated by Maven for our Kogito example

5. The pom.xml file is the recipe book used by Maven to understand the kind of project we want to build. Open it in the VSCode editor. We're going to modify it to tell Maven we want to include the Kogito scenario testing tool.

6. In pom.xml, look for the </dependencies> line. Replace it with the following line, so that there is still only one </dependencies> tag in the project:

```
<dependency> <groupId>org.kie.kogito</groupId>
<artifactId>kogito-scenario-simulation</artifactId>
<scope>test</scope> </dependency> </dependencies>
```

7. Press *Ctrl + S* to save this file.

8. In the terminal, move into the newly created folder by typing cd sample-kogito.

9. Since the sample already includes some tests, it is possible to run them using mvn clean test. These two commands will look like *Figure AB.8* in your terminal:

Figure AB.8 – Changing directory and running tests

10. Maven will automatically download the testing libraries needed and run the tests. Your `build success` method now includes the number of tests run and their status, as in *Figure AB.9*.

```
[INFO] Tests run: 2, Failures: 0, Errors: 0, Skipped: 0
[INFO]
[INFO] ------------------------------------------------
[INFO] BUILD SUCCESS
[INFO] ------------------------------------------------
[INFO] Total time:  01:42 min
[INFO] Finished at: 2022-12-13T20:45:46Z
[INFO] ------------------------------------------------
```

Figure AB.9 – Successful test run

11. If you need more information on the success or failure of each test, look in the newly created `target` folder. A subfolder within that, `surefire-reports`, will contain details of each test.

While it's great to have tests running in our project, we still don't have Scenario Simulation tests running yet. Let's fix that now.

Running scenario testing in VSCode

Setting up the scenario testing to be included in these automatic tests requires some final small steps:

1. Our decision models (`dmn` files) are currently in the root folder of the project. To be included in our Maven testing, they need to be in the `sample-kogito/src/main/resources` folder. Drag and drop the files across to this location.

> **Moving the decision model files is important**
>
> If you don't move the decision files, most of the following steps will appear to work, but the actual tests won't run correctly.

2. To let the automatic tests know that they should run Scenario Simulation, create the `KogitoScenarioJunitActivatorTest.java` file in the `sample-kogito src/test/testscenario` folder.

3. Open this new file in the editor and put the following contents in – this will automatically pick up and run any *scesim* (Scenario Simulation) tests:

```
package testscenario;

@org.junit.runner.RunWith(org.kogito.scenariosimulation.
runner.KogitoJunitActivator.class)

public class KogitoScenarioJunitActivatorTest {}
```

4. We'll create our `test1.Scesim` file in the `sample-kogito src/test/resources` directory.

5. When we open this file for the first time, we'll see a dialog as in *Figure AB.10*:

Create Test Scenario

Source type

○ RULE ⓘ

◉ DMN

Choose a valid DMN asset from the list

| c09 Bill of Materials.dmn   ^ |

Figure AB.10 – Creating a test scenario

6. Choose **DMN**, then select our **Bill of Materials** model from the dropdown, and click on the **Create** button. The main scenario simulator editor will open. We've populated it using similar values to the ones we used in *Chapter 9* – as shown in *Figure AB.11*:

		GIVEN		EXPECT	
#	Scenario description	Product	Qty	Bill of Materials	Product Details
		value	value	value	value
1	Silk Tray	"Silk Tray"	125	18750	150
2	Crunch	"Crunch"	10	100	10
3	Crunch	"Crunch"	-10	0	0

Figure AB.11 – Our test scenario

7. Now, when we run our scenarios using `mvn clean test`, the scenarios will get included in the automatic tests:

```
[INFO] Tests run: 6, Failures: 1, Errors: 0, Skipped: 0
[INFO]
[INFO] ------------------------------------------------
--

[INFO] BUILD FAILURE
[INFO] ------------------------------------------------
--
```

You'll notice that in this case, we have a build failure – the scenario testing tool has correctly highlighted that our Bill of Materials decision model doesn't handle negative values very well. We can see more details on this in the Surefire models and logs to help us investigate and fix the model.

Test-first approach – test failures are a good thing

We wanted to highlight that the instructions in this part of the Appendix are setup deliberately to fail. That it because we took a **test-first** approach – we wrote our tests modeling the expected behaviour, before we had implemented that behaviour in the decision model (for example, to handle negative numbers).

Think of the tests as enforcing the business contract we have with users. Our tests give us a safety net in highlighting that our model is not behaving as expected, which reminds us of the edits we still need to do, but also alerts us should we accidentally break anything in the future. Since this is an appendix, we leave it to the reader to make the necessary updates to model, and rerun the scenario tests to ensure they pass. We will move on to demonstrating an alternation method of running the scenario simulation tool.

Alternative method – starting with Kogito scenario samples

The step-by-step instructions from the previous section are very clear and help us understand the files we need to edit to carry out testing.

As an alternative method, many people prefer to take an existing project and then add their own scenarios to it. Because the Kogito samples are part of the overnight KIE build, the samples should be in an always-working condition. This method allows you to add your decision models and test scenarios to a project that you know is set up correctly.

It is good to have worked through the previous set of instructions. As we'll soon see, there are a lot of files in the Kogito samples. It helps if we know which ones we want to look out for. The steps are as follows:

1. Open the Kogito sample project that demonstrates scenarios on GitHub at `https://github.com/kiegroup/kogito-examples/tree/stable/kogito-quarkus-examples/dmn-quarkus-example`.

2. Make sure you are logged in to GitHub, and then open this project in Codespaces. If you are not on the main page of the project, you will need to navigate to the top folder, `kogito-examples`, before the green **Code** button option appears.

3. Once you have opened the `kogito-examples` project in Codespaces, we need to navigate to the specific example we were just looking at. In the terminal, type `cd kogito-quarkus-examples/dmn-quarkus-example/`.

4. We know we're in the correct folder if we type `ls` in the console and we see the `pom.xml` build file.

5. Like the previous example, type mvn clean test to execute the scenario tests that are already in this model – these samples are the Scenario tests for Traffic Violation decision model, which is pretty clear to understand since we talked about it in detail in *Chapter 10*.

6. Like our previous example, you will get a summary (in the terminal) and details (in the Surefire reports) of the scenario test progress – for the Kogito examples, we'd expect all the tests to pass at this point.

Now that we have a project set up to run scenario tests, we can add the decision model (Bill of Materials) and test scenario to the same project locations as described in the previous example. VSCode online supports dragging and dropping files from your laptop to add them to the project.

You do not need to edit pom.xml, nor add the Java test file, as these steps are already contained in the project.

At some point, you will probably end up modifying the Kogito samples as the basis for your own project. We encourage you to do this, as while it's outside the scope of the book, it is a step toward the way that Java developers interact with decision models and business rules.

Running VSCode on your laptop

As we've just seen, running VSCode in the Azure cloud and Codespaces is very convenient. While there is some setup, a lot of the tools are preconfigured for you. But sometimes, the tools don't have the latest update, which might cause KIE to throw an error if it expects a different version.

For whatever reason, running VSCode on your laptop is very achievable – but you will need to make sure the following software tools are installed on your laptop before you work through the preceding steps:

*   VSCode from Microsoft
*   Java (**Java Development Kit (JDK)**)
*   Maven, the build tool from Apache

We haven't covered the installation of these tools on a laptop since they are not needed for the cloud version, and they are freely available with full install instructions on the respective websites.

Appendix C
Troubleshooting Docker

While this is a book mainly about KIE and not Docker, we did want to give enough detail to get things up and running. The topics in *Chapter 10* and this appendix are straightforward but are at the edge of what we would reasonably expect an Excel power user to know. Using Docker gives us a gateway to running Business Central and deploying it into the cloud – both areas that will take a team, not just an individual, to build. So don't be afraid to ask colleagues for help!

In an ideal scenario, you will not need to read this appendix, since it contains suggestions on how to fix things if something goes wrong in starting Docker. We have written these instructions with an Excel power user in mind – so if you are an experienced Docker developer, you may wish to go directly to the Docker guides to start your troubleshooting.

There are three main sections in this appendix:

- Preparing your laptop to use Docker
- Troubleshooting error messages when you try to run Docker
- More help on Docker

Like in the other appendices, we will move faster than the main chapters of the book, and we assume a willingness to search on your own for additional information as needed. We can't cover every possible error but we will try to address most of the common ones.

As a final suggestion to get images working – remember that tools such as *Podman* provide a drop-in replacement for Docker. While we haven't cover them in this book, it might be an alternative if all other attempts have failed.

Preparing your laptop for Docker

There are also some simple steps you may need to take to prepare your computer before installing Docker:

- Behind the scenes, Docker will use one of two sophisticated technologies to run containers: Hyper-V or WSL.

- Hyper-V is a very clever technology that allows software running in containers (such as Docker) to run almost as fast as native applications. It's a combination of hardware and **operating system** (**OS**) support.

- **Windows Subsystem for Linux** (**WSL**) allows you to run the full power of the Linux OS (and enterprise solutions that run on it) on your Windows laptop. If this sounds similar to what Docker gives you, you'd be correct. Both technologies use many of the same components, even if they are optimized for different things.

- The approach Docker chooses will depend on the specification of your laptop. To keep things simple, the following instructions walk through how to switch between both.

Switching between Hyper-V and WSL

To turn on Hyper-V and WSL on your laptop, do the following:

1. Click on the ⊞ Windows key icon.
2. In the menu that appears, click on the ⚙ settings icon to open settings.
3. Right-click on the *Windows* button and select **Apps and Features**.
4. Select **Programs and Features** on the right, under **Related settings**.
5. Select **Turn Windows features on or off**.
6. Check whether **Hyper-V**, **Virtual Machine Platform**, and **Windows Subsystem for Linux** are enabled (as shown in the screenshot); if not, check them and click **OK**.

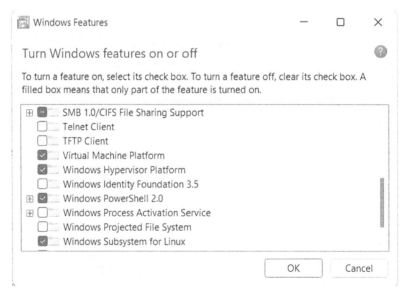

Figure AC.1 – Turning on Hyper-V and WSL on your laptop

7.   When the installation has been completed, you may be asked to restart your laptop.

8.   After your laptop has restarted, go back into **Settings** and ensure that these options are still selected.

If you prefer, the official Microsoft guide to turning on Hyper-V is available at `https://docs.microsoft.com/en-us/virtualization/hyper-v-on-windows/quick-start/enable-hyper-v`.

Troubleshooting Docker – some obvious things

Most people will not need this section of the book. But if you do need it, then you will be reassured that you're not the only person to meet these common issues:

- Check that your laptop meets the technical requirements (the type of laptop and version of Windows) for running Docker. These are listed at `https://docs.docker.com/desktop/windows/install/`. Docker will give you a clear error message if it doesn't.

- When installing software, you may have seen a popup similar to the following screenshot. It means that your computer is under the control of your IT team. This is mainly a good thing (as it stops malicious software), but it does mean you need their support to install Docker:

Figure AC.2 – An admin permission dialog

- Windows Defender sometimes blocks network and internet access – we want to allow it as we need to be able to connect and run our samples.

- Following a similar approach, check whether you have a connection to the internet (open a web browser) – connections can drop and cause strange errors.

- If you have something break halfway through an install (for example, the connection dropping or you hit the wrong button), it can be worth uninstalling Docker and starting the install process again.

- Only half a joke, but have you tried turning your laptop off and on again? For some parts of the following instructions (for example, after switching on Hyper-V and WSL), restarting your laptop is required.

- After installing Docker, it can sometimes take a couple of moments to start up. Check whether you have any container running or something worth pausing, and try the instructions again.

- Remember we cover four different ways to run the samples in this book. You may run into an issue (such as your laptop is 32-bit and cannot support Docker or Hyper-V), for which there is no way around.

Troubleshooting Hyper-V and WSL

If switching on Hyper-V and WSL worked for you – then feel free to skip this section. If not, you probably got an error message indicating whether the issue was related to Windows or hardware. Remember that you only need one of these to work to be able to run Docker.

Windows-related error messages

Your version of Windows may not have support for Hyper-V. For example, it is not available in *Windows 10 Home*. You do have the option of taking advantage of the free upgrade to Windows 11 (including the insider preview), which appears to be more generous in allowing this feature. More information about updating to Windows 11 can be found here: `https://www.microsoft.com/en-gb/windows/windows-11`.

It may be that you are *stuck* with Windows 10 Home and unwilling to pay for an upgrade to Windows 10 Pro. There are still workarounds if your hardware supports it, but you will need technical knowledge that you may need to request a friend or colleague to support. For example, the workaround at the following link explains how to use **VMware** (an alternative virtualization technology) to run Docker: `https://www.freecodecamp.org/news/how-to-run-docker-on-windows-10-home-edition/`.

Hardware-related error messages

For hardware support, the good news is that most laptops sold in the last couple of years should support Hyper-V. And the better news is that strictly speaking, Docker doesn't require it to run. So even if you are unable to enable Hyper-V, it is still worth checking whether Docker can be installed – but pay extra attention to the error messages.

However, these hardware-related Hyper-V workarounds can become quite technical. We haven't linked to these workarounds since they require in-depth technical knowledge – but know that they can be found on Google in the rare case that you need them and you are feeling technically confident enough to work through them.

More help on Docker

If you need more help, it's worth looking at the Docker website (these links are for Windows, but there is equivalent detail for macOS and Linux): `https://docs.docker.com/desktop/windows/install/` and `https://docs.docker.com/desktop/windows/troubleshoot/`.

If you don't like the style of these guides, there are many other videos and *how-to* guides to walk you through the process:

- `https://www.systemconf.com/2020/07/05/docker-installation-on-windows-10`

- `https://www.geeksforgeeks.org/how-to-install-docker-on-macos/`

- `https://www.digitalocean.com/community/tutorials/how-to-install-and-use-docker-on-ubuntu-20-04`

There are also a lot of community forums to post questions and ask for help (both on Docker and third-party sites). And finally, if you don't have colleagues to help you, there are many Docker experts that you can pay for support – `Freelancer.com` is a site I've used in the past, but there are many others out there.

Index

www.packtpub.com

Subscribe to our online digital library for full access to over 7,000 books and videos, as well as industry leading tools to help you plan your personal development and advance your career. For more information, please visit our website.

Why subscribe?

- Spend less time learning and more time coding with practical eBooks and Videos from over 4,000 industry professionals

- Improve your learning with Skill Plans built especially for you

- Get a free eBook or video every month

- Fully searchable for easy access to vital information

- Copy and paste, print, and bookmark content

Did you know that Packt offers eBook versions of every book published, with PDF and ePub files available? You can upgrade to the eBook version at packtpub.com and as a print book customer, you are entitled to a discount on the eBook copy. Get in touch with us at customercare@packtpub.com for more details.

At www.packtpub.com, you can also read a collection of free technical articles, sign up for a range of free newsletters, and receive exclusive discounts and offers on Packt books and eBooks.

Other Books You May Enjoy

If you enjoyed this book, you may be interested in these other books by Packt:

Exploring Microsoft Excel's Hidden Treasures

David Ringstrom

ISBN: 978-1-80324-394-8

- Explore hidden and overlooked features that will save your time
- Implement disaster prevention and recovery techniques
- Improve spreadsheet accessibility for all users
- Bolster data integrity and spreadsheet resilience
- Craft code-free custom worksheet functions with LAMBDA
- Create code-free report automation with Power Query
- Integrate spreadsheet automation techniques with ease

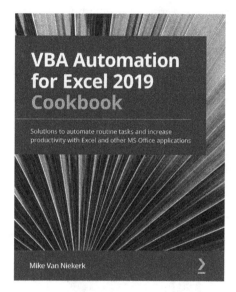

VBA Automation for Excel 2019 Cookbook

Mike Van Niekerk

ISBN: 978-1-78961-003-1

- Understand the VBA programming language's role in the context of the MS Office suite
- Discover various aspects of VBA programming such as its terminology, syntax, procedures, functions, and forms
- Investigate the elements, features, and characteristics of the VBA Editor to write and edit custom scripts
- Automate Excel sheets with the help of ranges
- Explore error handling and debugging techniques to catch bugs in your programs
- Create and use custom dialog boxes to collect data from users
- Customize and extend Office apps such as Excel, PowerPoint, and Word

Packt is searching for authors like you

If you're interested in becoming an author for Packt, please visit `authors.packtpub.com` and apply today. We have worked with thousands of developers and tech professionals, just like you, to help them share their insight with the global tech community. You can make a general application, apply for a specific hot topic that we are recruiting an author for, or submit your own idea.

Share Your Thoughts

Now you've finished *AI and Business Rule Engines for Excel Power Users*, we'd love to hear your thoughts! Scan the QR code below to go straight to the Amazon review page for this book and share your feedback or leave a review on the site that you purchased it from.

`https://packt.link/r/180461954X`

Your review is important to us and the tech community and will help us make sure we're delivering excellent quality content.

Download a free PDF copy of this book

Thanks for purchasing this book!

Do you like to read on the go but are unable to carry your print books everywhere? Is your eBook purchase not compatible with the device of your choice?

Don't worry, now with every Packt book you get a DRM-free PDF version of that book at no cost.

Read anywhere, any place, on any device. Search, copy, and paste code from your favorite technical books directly into your application.

The perks don't stop there, you can get exclusive access to discounts, newsletters, and great free content in your inbox daily

Follow these simple steps to get the benefits:

1. Scan the QR code or visit the link below

https://packt.link/free-ebook/9781804619544

2. Submit your proof of purchase
3. That's it! We'll send your free PDF and other benefits to your email directly

www.ingramcontent.com/pod-product-compliance
Lightning Source LLC
Chambersburg PA
CBHW062045050326
40690CB00016B/2990